AN INTRODUCTION TO THE ROMAN WORLD

Peter D. Arnott

Peter D. Arnott was born in England in 1931
and educated at Ipswich School, the
University of Wales, and Exeter College,
Oxford. In 1958 he went to America where
he combined academic and creative work,
dividing his time between lecturing and
working as stage director, actor and
puppetmaster for his own Marionette Theatre.
He is the author of several books on classical
themes, and has written numerous scholarly
articles on literary criticism and theatre
history. He is now Professor of Drama and
Speech at Tufts University in America where
he lives permanently with his wife and
children.

Also by Peter D. Arnott aud available in Sphere Books

AN INTRODUCTION TO THE GREEK WORLD

AN INTRODUCTION TO
THE ROMAN WORLD

This book is affectionately dedicated to
Lois Larson, a fine teacher and
a good friend

An Introduction to the Roman World

PETER D. ARNOTT

SPHERE BOOKS LIMITED
30/32 Gray's Inn Road, London, WC1X 8JL

First published in Great Britain in 1970
by Macmillan & Co. Ltd.
© Peter D. Arnott, 1970
First Sphere Books edition 1972

TRADE
MARK

Printed in Great Britain by
Hazell Watson & Viney Ltd,
Aylesbury, Bucks

Contents

List of Illustrations

... trellised garden with water channel, Pompeii ...
... and peristyle, atrium and street door, Herculaneum
Hypocaust for central heating, Fishbourne, Sussex
The houses of the workers: bakery with oven and mills, Pompeii
    ...
... and barman's-eye view of the street, Herculaneum
Row of tenements, Ostia
Public utilities: town water cistern, Nîmes ...
... and public pleasure: Nîmes, amphitheatre
Building for grandeur: staircase leading to the Temple of Jupiter,
    Baalbek

Author's Preface

THIS book is offered as a companion volume to *An Introduction to the Greek World* (Macmillan, 1967). It is longer, and has a different shape: both things are made necessary by the subject matter. When one writes of Greece one is dealing, for the most part, with the activity of one city over a single century. But in the case of Rome, even within the conventional limits from the foundation to Alaric's conquest, one is concerned with a recorded history of almost twelve hundred years; with a diversity of peoples, each with its important part to play; and with an empire that covered the greater part of the known world. The study extends, in space, from the camel tracks of the Middle East to the inaccessible savages of Ireland, from the Teutoburgerwald to the sunbaked cities of Africa, and in time from the amorphousness of myth to men who foreshadowed the Renaissance. It deals, too, with a culture that was continually, and violently, reforming itself, adopting new leaders, new ideals and a new pattern of life. In the Greek book, I found it sufficient to give a brief chronological account at the beginning, and then discuss specific aspects of the Greek achievement within this framework. In the Roman, it has seemed desirable to interweave history and culture more closely, while still isolating certain phenomena for particular attention. I have tried to give an impressionistic picture of the Roman world in a montage of people, places and incidents that seem particularly interesting or relevant, glimpses of a busy people in a multiplicity of activities.

Any single book on this vast subject that is not merely a chronological catalogue must be selective to a degree where the author's prejudices demand explanation and apology. Some of mine are inherited. There is, for instance, comparatively little on military matters. Not that they are unimportant, but they tend to be over-done, particularly for those whose acquaintance with the ancient world is minimal – and it is for this sort of reader that the book is written. I was fortunate enough myself, once I had gone through the necessarily dismal early stages, to be taught Latin by a brilliant teacher who surmised – rightly – that, after two years devoted to the study of Caesar's campaigns for examination purposes, we would have the impression that the Romans did nothing else but sally forth against the Allobroges, or retire to winter quarters. He therefore put us through a course of reading that showed the Romans making speeches, furniture, love, voyages – anything but war. I have never ceased to be grateful for it, and hope that something of the spirit of N. T. Stonex remains in this book. It will be read, I know, by many whose knowledge of Roman history is limited to the *Gallic Wars*. For ridiculous and outmoded reasons, this still remains the beginning Latin textbook. In England, perhaps, there is some defence for it. Many schoolboys read their Caesar at the places where his legions marched. But the interest of the average American high-school student in such campaigns is, to say the least, perfunctory. He deserves to be told of other things, and I hope this book will help to tell him.

Another prejudice is more personal. It may seem that I have given far too much time to local colour, and to peripheral matter which is (to steal a line from Rutilius Namatianus, from whom I have taken my exodos) 'too frivolous for a sober tale'. There are reasons for this, apart from the garrulousness of the professional traveller. Firstly, as most of my work is now for the theatre, I have become accustomed to thinking in terms of the total *mise en scène*. As a photographer, I cultivate the appropriate moment, the sense of atmosphere. My own travels have been singularly blessed in this regard. I first saw Mycenae by lightning, Pompeii in a torrential storm, the amphitheatre at Nîmes when it was being set up for an ice show, a ridiculous and mechanically com-plex entertainment that the Romans would have loved. I have tried to communicate my personal enjoyment of such godsends to the reader. Secondly, of the two schools of archaeology – one believing that buildings should be restored, even if details must be guessed at, the other that ruins should be left bare – I belong very firmly to the first. Few people have the eye or learning, even with a guidebook, to make sense out of a jumble of shattered masonry. They need reconstructions, if the past is to make its impact on them, and it is, oddly enough, those who do not need such help who would most vociferously deny it to others. The same thing, I believe, holds true in the literary-historical framework. For the layman, a good historical novel does more than a museum catalogue. This book is not a novel. It tries to be factually accurate, and to give some idea of how we acquire our information, and what the gaps are; but it does also try, like a good zoo, to present the exhibits in their natural environment.

This leads me to another favourite hobby-horse; the conviction that, in classical studies, idolatry is a greater danger than indifference. I once gave a broadcast talk entitled 'The Greeks Were People, Too', in which I argued against the popular, if involuntary, habit of putting the ancients on a pedestal. This manifests itself in many ways. We see it in historical films, where the Rome of the Caesars is invariably presented as spotlessly clean, with houses of gleaming marble and streets where no horse, obviously, ever set hoof. We see it in translations, where professionals have only recently begun to use ordinary, readable, commonsense English and students and amateurs are still convinced that such ancient and illustrious works must be conveyed into an archaic and unnatural tongue. We see it in criticism. We are all romantics at heart. Like Tacitus, we prefer to think of the ancients as better than ourselves, and grow censorious when we detect a fault. We allow D. H. Lawrence to combine the spiritual and the sexual, but not Ausonius. We concede the necessity for political manœuvring to Hubert Humphrey, but not to Cicero. We know that Queen Elizabeth's speeches are not written by herself, but sneer at Nero for using similar assistance. I believe that if we are to show that the works of dead authors still endure we must apply mouth-to-mouth resuscitation. The breath of living men must be pumped into them. The authors must be shown as human, and, like the buildings, seen in their environment. And when our knowledge of the past is lacking it is surely legitimate to extrapolate from the present, for in many vital ways the Italian spirit is unchanged. One can come closer to Roman ways over *pasta* and Frascati in a back-street *trattoria* than in the reading-room of the British Museum.

I have tried in this book to talk about the works in such a context; to focus on literature that the armchair traveller may easily read, and monuments that the visitor may easily see; and to clothe them in the sight, smell and sound of actuality, as a reminder for those who know Italy, and some small compensation for those who do not. I have tried to introduce meaningful parallels to help those who, for instance, enjoy *A Funny Thing Happened on the Way to the Forum* but find it impossible or undignified to apply the same standards to Plautus. This book makes no claims to originality. It does hope to be interesting. For those who will complain that it is far too elementary, I can only say, apologetically, 'It was not written for you'.

I must acknowledge two particular debts of gratitude; to my friend, colleague and travelling companion Margaret Hall, whose pertinent observations have sharpened my own; and to my wife, Eva, who willingly accepts the compulsion of typing my manuscripts as the only living person who can read my handwriting.

Chapter One

The Founding of a City

HOWEVER one approaches Athens – by land, sea or air – it is impressive. The ancient citadel rears up like a beacon, austere by day, floodlit at night, welcoming and admonishing the traveller. Rome should properly be entered after dark. For a city with so gaudy a reputation (like a fair proportion of its history, a deliberately concocted myth) the streets fall quiet surprisingly early. The snarling, clogging traffic vanishes, the floodlights shine, and the past takes over. Modern Romans know, as their ancestors did, how to dramatize their public persona. For the airborne traveller landing among the glass and glitter of Fiumicino, the coach ride to the city terminal is a course in Roman history and a study in the continuity of the national character. The highway runs straight through flat fields, flanked by giant hoardings advertising the latest modern marvels; drabness vanishes, and the Romans, experienced theatrical producers, let you see only what they want you to see. At the Ostia Gate, now the Porta san Paolo, from which the modern *autostrada* follows the ancient road to the coast, the past assumes its right of seniority.

A pyramid swims in the light. It was built to entomb an official of minor importance when Rome was shifting from Republic to Empire and interest in things Egyptian was intense. The Romans of the Middle Ages, with an inherited preference for the impressive over the merely accurate, dubbed it the tomb of Romulus, their city's legendary founder. Petrarch believed the story; Boccaccio, the cynic, rejected it; and a later age gave the site a new cult-hero when Keats was buried nearby. Shelley, whose own remains were to rest in the same place, wrote the famous description in *Adonais*:

And grey walls moulder round, on which dull Time
Feeds, like slow fire upon a hoary brand;
And one keen pyramid with wedge sublime,
Pavilioning the dust of him who planned
This refuge for his memory, doth stand
Like flame transformed to marble. . . .

Floodlights now transform the marble into flame again; image has become reality. The grey walls are still there also, abutting onto the pyramid. They were erected three centuries later, part of the system created by the Emperor Aurelian to protect the capital. Military encroachments, from the Gothic invasions to the Allied bombing in the Second World War, have but flecked their surface. They still help to define the city, and in some districts whole families have burrowed into their imperishable monumentality to make their homes.

Round the corner are the Baths of Caracalla, opened in A.D. 216 for an emperor's pleasure, the grandiose bauble of an inflated economy. Sixteen hundred people could bathe here at the same time, under granite columns in pools carved of alabaster. Their bare feet trod the grandeur of mosaic floors, and elaborate ceilings vaulted over their heads. The building has now become, appropriately, an opera house. Modern concrete and tubular steel encroach upon the ancient fabric, looking strangely weak and scrawny against the brickwork. On summer evenings the triumphal procession from *Aida* may be staged here with suitable magnificence. The building was copied in 1910 by the American architect Charles Follen McKim when he designed New York's Pennsylvania Station; he appreciated its value as a monumental gateway to the Rome of the New World. It is a sad commentary on the durability of modern grandeur that Caracalla's monument still stands, while McKim's lasted little more than half a century.

Next, the Colosseum, one of that select group of buildings whose shape is known to everybody in the world, and whose name has become synonymous with 'extravagant showplace'; Rome's bloodthirsty Radio City Music Hall, where men battled for the amusement of fifty thousand spectators, and rare beasts were imported from the far corners of the empire to meet their deaths. Though used briefly for other purposes – by the noble family of the Frangipani as a castle, by Pope Clement IX as a storehouse for saltpetre – it has remained a showplace, of one sort or another, for a fair part of its life, and the shows have always retained something of their pagan overtones. At a bullfight given by noble Romans in the Colosseum in 1332, eighteen men were gored to death. At the accession of Pope Hadrian VI, a Greek sorcerer sacrificed a bull in the amphitheatre with the full panoply of ancient ritual. Christian propagandists represented it as a place of martyrdom, exaggerating the number of their faith who had died there in the persecutions, and the legends took hold. As if in appeasement, the citizens of Rome presented passion plays in the ruins in the fifteenth and sixteenth centuries; the adjacent, gutted palace of the Anibaldi served as dressing-rooms, and emphasis seems to have been on the bloodier episodes of the Christian story. Nevertheless the site remained peopled by ghosts and demons; Cellini recounts a celebrated conjuration there in 1534. In further appeasement, Benedict IV erected a Christian cross in the centre, later removed for excavations and subsequently renewed. The shape of the Colosseum, again not inappropriately, was adopted by the same Charles Follen McKim for Harvard Stadium.

We have been travelling backwards through time, seeing the later works first. Now we are close to the heart of things, the Roman Forum, the administrative and social centre of the city whose buildings overlay the site of the earliest settlement. Flanked by the ice-cream-cake extravagances of the Victor Emmanuel Monument, the triumphal arches and the speaker's platform, the shattered temples and broken colonnades have kept their dignity through centuries of seekers after the picturesque or – more dangerous – of marble. Once abandoned, the Forum became the *campo vaccino*, a grazing-place and cattle-market. The huge granite basin which now serves as a fountain in front of the Quirinal was once used as a water-trough. But the popes were concerned to restore the past. Paul III appointed one Manetti as commissioner

for monuments, with orders to clear and preserve, to forbid the
erection of new buildings and stop the disappearance of the old
into the lime-kilns. The results of these continuing excavations
are what we see today. On a summer night the Forum itself
becomes a theatre. *Son et lumière*, the modern magic, awakens
echoes of the past; the marching feet of triumphal processions are
heard again among the ruins, and the trumpets sound; spectators
sit where Romulus once stood, on the slopes of the Palatine. A
statue of Julius Caesar stands guard over the modern road. Every
year, on the Ides of March, a laurel wreath is laid at its feet.

Ancient attitudes, like the ancient buildings, remain. They can
be seen in a speech which might equally well have been delivered
by a Republican orator in the Forum we have just passed; by Cola
di Rienzo, the fourteenth-century fanatic and visionary who had
his brief moment of glory in attempting to restore the Rome of
the consuls; by any one of a series of popes.

> The speech which I have the honour and pleasure of addressing
> to you will be of Roman style, conforming in its conciseness to the
> antique Roman character of this ceremony. I shall exclude every
> rhetorical digression. My speech will contain praise for what you
> have already achieved, and a precise instruction for what remains to
> be done. . . .
> I remember, when . . . you conferred on me the supreme honour
> of admitting me among the citizens of Rome, I told you that the
> problems of the capital were divided into two groups; those dic-
> tated by imminent need, and those inspired by the idea of Roman
> grandeur. . . .

These words were, in fact, spoken by Mussolini in December
1925, before the assembled dignitaries of Rome. He goes on:

> You will continue liberating the trunk of the great oak of every-
> thing that is still blocking it; you will create space around the
> Augusteum, the Theatre of Marcellus, the Capitol, the Pantheon.
> All the stuff grown around these buildings during centuries of
> decadence must be brushed aside. In five years, by means of a great
> aperture, the vast building of the Pantheon must be visible from
> Piazza Colonna. Also the majestic temples of Christian Rome must
> be liberated from the profane and parasitical constructions around
> them.

Mussolini, like the ancients, believed in the glorification of the past, and in justification through public works. The excavations of the Republican temples in the Largo Argentina were due to him, as was, largely, the rediscovery of the ancient port of Ostia. It was he who raised the columns in Trajan's Forum, and restored the vaulting of the amphitheatre of Capua. He built new works on the grand scale. The Termini at which our coach ride ends was his, a monument hardly less impressive than those we have passed: a combination of tracks, restaurants and shopping-arcades, like the Forum a commercial necessity transformed into a showplace. When Mussolini built it he saw himself as cast in the mould of the Caesars. It was he, too, who built the Ostia road and the Via Imperio over which we have just travelled, the Foro Mussolini (now Italico) and the canal through the Pomptine Marshes. He inherited the genius for self-advertisement, and the grand gesture, that belonged to the emperors: he inherited also their penchant for folly on a monumental scale. At a critical point in the war he had a large part of the Italian army tied up in Rome, making a film about the ancient glories. It was a grandiose stupidity worthy of Caligula.

What we have seen, in the floodlights, has been a nation advertising itself. Modern technology merely emphasizes the ancient purpose. The Romans built to impress, and succeeded. The builders knew their stature in the world, and saw no reason to conceal the fact. Public works became national propaganda. What we see in Rome was repeated, to a greater or lesser degree, in whatever land the Romans touched. In Lebanon, a Roman colonnade crowns the hill overlooking Byblos, 'the oldest harbour in the world', from which the Phoenicians had once sailed to colonize the Mediterranean. An arch to the Emperor Hadrian affronts the Acropolis in Athens. The world's oldest civilizations, remoulded by the Romans, received the stamp of the conqueror in their buildings. At the other end of civilization, on the wild fringes of the world, the same monumental testimony exists. Hadrian's Wall, built to bar off the British province from barbaric hordes, still stands. Roman architects brought the Gallic tribes temples and municipal buildings, and ran aqueducts through Spain.

The solidity of Roman structures represented a stable world. The occupiers dressed their culture in foreign borrowings, as they dressed their buildings with marble. They were given, in their architecture as in their history, to periods of wild ostentation and freakish excess. But there was solid brick underneath, which still stands when the marble has crumbled away. Roman systems, ideals and institutions have remained embedded in the fabric of civilized society. Europe still uses roads first mapped out by the Romans. Prospective barristers still study Roman law as the foundation of their own systems. The Latin language has been taught for centuries after it vanished as a living tongue – not merely as the key to an impressive literature and to its own derivatives, but as an illustration of logic applied to language and of the human intellect at its most systematic and precise.

We have seen, too, in this short journey a testimony to the continuity of history, to the living past. In Greece, though topography and temperament have remained virtually unaltered, the classical past is often remote. In Italy, it is woven into the present. This has always been true. The buildings flanking our entry into Rome have a history of continuous re-use. All over Italy we may find the same. The piazza at Lucca preserves the outline of the amphitheatre which once stood there. The cathedral of Santa Maria Maggiore is adorned with columns pillaged from the amphitheatre of ancient Capua nearby. Pope Urban VIII removed the brazen tubes that supported the roof of the Pantheon, and turned them into cannon for Castel Sant' Angelo, which had itself begun as an imperial mausoleum. *Quod non fecerunt barbari, fecerunt Barberini*, said the critics: what the barbarians did not do, the Barberini did. In Benevento, a classical capital forms a wellhead in an eleventh-century monastery which has been turned into a museum of imperial antiquities. In Milan, the fungoid growth of the cathedral sprawls across the chaste lines of a fourth-century baptistery. The list is endless. In Greece it is often easier to see the past, for the country is poor, uncut by modern roads, unclogged by modern traffic. In Italy, once one has learned to penetrate the surface, the vitality of the past is often easier to sense.

The Romans themselves knew how to utilize the past. Expert mythmakers and skilled adaptors, they felt that the national front could best be erected on solid historical foundations. It did not matter if the stories were borrowed, only how they were used. An illustrious past was an asset. Greek cities and families liked to derive their ancestry from the gods, but the Romans, on the whole, minimized the role of the divine and preferred an estimable mortal genealogy. A good Roman liked to count the number of his ancestors. Their masks hung in his house, and were worn through the street and in the Forum on ceremonial occasions. But he also liked to moralize about the value of hard work and self-reliance. Here is the elder Seneca, a professor of rhetoric during the transition from Republic to Empire, the beginning of the lavish age; in a model speech composed for the instruction of his pupils, he evokes the Roman affectation of rugged simplicity.

If men could elect their own birthright, no one would be poor, no one would be of low station; each and every man would find a happy home. But given that such decisions are out of our hands, we must submit to the natural order of things, and accept whatever fortune is appointed us. And so we must be judged by what we make of ourselves. Where would you find Marius in the social register? Repeatedly elected consul, his most distinguished achievement was himself. If Pompey's reputation had depended on his ancestors, he would never have been called 'the Great'. Rome had Servius for her king; his humble name is his most outstanding virtue. And what of those men who came from the plough to grace the state with their frugal lives? Consider any man of rank you please, and you will find his origins were humble. But why cite individuals, when the whole city illustrates my point? . . . Our fellow-countrymen could have allowed their humble beginnings to lapse into obscurity. Far from it; they are proud to admit them. They believe that nothing is worth anything, that did not start from nothing.[1]

An illustrious city, by hindsight, requires an illustrious founder. The Christian mythographers of the Middle Ages, in attributing the foundation to Noah, were merely following an earlier pattern. Rome, like its citizens, was ambivalent in its attitudes towards the past. It recognized, in effect, two distinct foundation-stories, one designed to illustrate how sturdy self-reliance (assisted a little by divine favour) could triumph over humble beginnings, the other borrowing grandeur by association with a great city of the past. One story is basically Italian, the other largely Greek. The Roman historians, with characteristic organizational dexterity, wove them into a consistent whole and had the best of both worlds.

The ancient mind, liking to personalize, reasoned that a city called Rome must have been founded by someone of similar name. At least as early as the fifth century B.C. the establishment of the city was already being ascribed to a vague figure known in some sources as Romulus, in others as Rhomos. As the legend developed, the two forms of the name emerged as distinct individuals. At one point Rhomos is seen as Romulus's grandfather. Later, with a change of vowel and relationship, he becomes his twin brother, Remus.

According to the familiar story, their life began precariously. Two brothers, Numitor and Amulius, were rivals for the kingdom. Numitor was expelled, his sons killed and his daughter, Rhea Silvia, forced to become a Vestal Virgin so that no future male issue could threaten the usurper. Livy, the sober Augustan historian, relates how these designs were thwarted.

But in my opinion it was pre-ordained that this great city should be founded, and this mightiest of empires, second in dominion only to the gods, should come into being. The Vestal was ravished and bore twin sons. She cited Mars as the father of her illegitimate children, perhaps in all sincerity, perhaps in an effort to exculpate herself by making a deity responsible. But no power human or divine could protect mother or babes from the king's animosity. The priestess was thrown into prison in chains; the boys he ordered to be consigned to the river. . . .

According to versions of the story still current, the boys were exposed in a basket, which kept afloat until the water left it high and dry. A she-wolf, coming down from the surrounding hills to slake her thirst, was attracted by the infants' cries. She gave them her teats to suck, and was so tenderly disposed towards them that the king's herdsman found her licking them clean. Tradition gives him the name of Faustulus, and adds that he took them to his cabin for his wife Larentia to bring up.[2]

The boys grew to manhood, avenged their grandfather, and set out to found a city of their own. For the next episode we may look to the thumping verse of Ennius, one of the earliest Latin writers and himself of sturdy pioneer stock. Having selected a site, the brothers await a decisive omen:

> *Then, with surpassing care – for each desired*
> *To reign – they sought for omens from the birds.*
> *Remus, aloof, engrossed, scanned heaven for*
> *A bird of favour. Handsome Romulus*
> *Sought his winged quarry high on Aventine.*
> *Should Rome or Remora be the city's name?*
> *And which should rule? This question filled their hearts.*
>
> *Meanwhile the incandescent orb of heaven dipped*
> *In darkness, and a vivid beam shot forth.*
> *Then, in one moment, on the left flew down*
> *A bird, auspicious prophet, and the sun*
> *Rose gold again. Three times four birds descended*
> *From heaven to bless the places of good omen.*
> *So Romulus, by the auspices' assurance,*
> *Perceived the royal seat was his to hold.[3]*

The Aventine Hill, one of Rome's seven, now looks down on the site of the former Circus Maximus, and across to the ruinous warrens of the imperial palaces on the Palatine. For some time it lay outside the limits of the city proper, and retained its ceremonial associations as the site of some of the region's earliest temples. Ennius himself came to live there. It was on the Palatine that Romulus established his first settlement.

The brothers quarrelled. In some versions Romulus slew his twin because of a supposed slight to his authority. Cicero found this behaviour reprehensible; St Augustine compared it to the murder of Abel by Cain, the first city-builder in biblical tradition. The elegant jingles of Ovid, penned under the early Empire, mitigate the offence by attributing the murder to Romulus's lieutenant.

So Celer worked as Romulus instructed him to do.
'The task is yours,' the leader said; 'I leave it all to you.
Let no man cross the furrow where the shining ploughshare went.
For him who dares to jump our walls, death be the punishment.'
But Remus did not know of this, and started to deride.
'What sort of wall is this', he said, 'to keep folk safe inside?'
And without more hesitation Remus leaped across the wall.
Celer seized a spade and slew him, and the earth bled from his fall.
When Romulus was told of it, his heart within him broke,
But he never showed his anguish, and he never wept or spoke.
He thought it cowardly to let the others see him cry.
'Just so', he said, 'may any foe who jumps our ramparts die.'
But at his brother's funeral his tears came running fast;
He forgot his resolution, and displayed his love at last.
Kissing him upon the bier where he lay cold and still
He said, 'Farewell, dear brother mine. It was against my will.'
. . . And so was born a city – who would have believed it then? –
To attain renown and glory, and impose its will on men.[4]

The Romulus legend, as transmitted through generations of Romans, was little more than a convenient and agreeable fiction. Ancient critics were already pointing out that *lupa*, 'she-wolf', is also Latin slang for 'prostitute'; the romantic fable of the maternal animal may disguise a more sordid truth. Nevertheless, the story has interesting cross-cultural affinities, and its roots seem to lie in the earliest stratum of Italian religious thought. The mystique of identical twins invites comparison with a world-wide corpus of such stories, stretching from Europe to the South Pacific. The minor characters suggest more local religious affinities. Faustulus, the twins' foster-father, has been identified with Faunus, an early Latin fertility god, and his wife Larentia may also have been a deity. Thus the Romulus legend, like so many others, is argued to have originated from ancient religious practices and half-forgotten beliefs.

Plutarch, the Greek biographer, gives the children another

nurse in the form of a woodpecker, a bird we know to have been the centre of a local cult. The death of Remus, on the other hand, must be a later addition, a clear example of myth-tidying. A city could not conveniently have two founders, and Remus was expendable. In its closing stages the story shows obvious Greek retouching. Romulus wanders off into a mysterious storm and is translated to heaven under the name of Quirinus.

Historians disputed the date of this foundation. Varro, the contemporary and friend of Cicero, finally set it at 753 B.C., and from this date all subsequent Roman history was measured. Events were dated *ab urbe condita*, 'from the foundation of the city'. Some historians, even today, follow this pious but now inconvenient custom. Though individuals might dissent, the Romulus story became the official version and was remembered with pride. The Romans identified the sites of these legendary events and preserved a 'hut of Romulus' on the Palatine as Americans preserve Lincoln's log cabin. It is described by Dionysius of Halicarnassus, a Greek who taught in Rome under Augustus:

> Romulus and Remus led a pastoral life, and supported themselves by the sweat of their brows – in the mountains, for the most part, where they built themselves wattle cabins with thatched roofs. One of these, the 'hut of Romulus', was still standing on the Palatine in my own time. The government preserves it as a shrine, doing nothing to augment its primitive simplicity, but merely repairing the ravages of age and weather and restoring it as closely as possible to its original condition.[5]

We have other evidence of this reverential care; we know, for instance, that the hut was burned down in 38 B.C. and promptly restored. Besides the replica, the form of such primitive buildings was preserved in the Temple of Vesta, the hearth-goddess, the remains of which may still be seen in the Roman Forum, and which reproduces the shape of the primitive round hut. Archaeology has proved that such memories and reconstructions are based on fact. In 1907 Italian excavators uncovered the foundations of an Iron Age hut under the Palatine. Further work after the Second World War allowed the structure to be hypothetically reconstructed, to make it clear that, on this point at least, the Romulus legend touched history.

Nearby stood a cave, still pointed out by guides as the scene of the she-wolf's ministrations. This friendly beast particularly caught the public imagination, and became for Rome what the owl was for Athens. In the third century B.C. a play about Romulus was being performed in Rome when a wolf ran into the theatre, occasioning happy comment. At least, that was the story. A live she-wolf still prowls disconsolately in a cage by the steps leading up to the Capitol.

The Romans also believed that they had identified Romulus's burial place. Rediscovered by the archaeologist Boni in 1899, it is the oldest monument in the Forum, located in the north-east corner and protected today by an ugly corrugated iron roof. Descending some narrow, tricky steps one sees a slab of black volcanic stone (a copy: the original has been removed for safe keeping) bearing what seems to be a minatory inscription in archaic Latin. One interpretation would read it as follows:

> Whosoever violates this place, let him be forfeit to the powers of the underworld. Whosoever defiles this place with filth, it shall be lawful for the king to hold him for trial and take his goods from him. And whatsoever persons the king shall find passing on this road, let him bid the herald take their beasts by the reins and turn them aside forthwith, so that they may go about by the lawful way. And whosoever shall not turn from this road and go about by the lawful way, let him stand trial and his person be sold by auction.[6]

Is this, then, a taboo on a place of particular sanctity? The Romans thought so. Even in Cicero's time, it was held to mark the tomb of Romulus, and Festus, writing in the second century A.D., knew it as a place of ill omen. A physical location for the burial place does not tally with the legend of Romulus's disappearance into the storm, but the Romans were not likely to be worried by such discrepancies. The archaeological findings were inconclusive; excavators uncovered what may or may not have been a sepulchre, but, if so, we do not know whose. The mention of the 'king', if correctly interpreted, would date the monument in the earliest period of Roman history. Some scholars take a more cynical view, and argue that the inscription may have no more sanctity than the modern 'Do not allow your dog to foul the footpath.'

In the Middle Ages the Romulus story acquired even more picturesque accretions. We have seen how the Pyramid of Cestius came to be known as Romulus's tomb. The later traditions also identified the Temple of Romulus on the Sacred Way with the asylum he is said to have founded to attract fugitives and thus increase the population of his new city. The *Mirabilia Romae, Romae*, a medieval Baedeker dating from the twelfth or thirteenth century, tells how Romulus raised two temples in the gardens of one of his palaces. In one stood a golden statue, destined never to fall until a virgin was delivered of a child. By such means the Christian writers sought to put pagan grandeur in its place.

This, then, is the Romulus story, a curious compound of fiction, folk-memory, prehistory and sacred ritual that nevertheless provided the Romans with an acceptable image for their city. The name retained its associations of honour. Augustus saw himself as a second Romulus, a new founder. In the Forum stands a temple dedicated to a later Romulus, the young son of the Emperor Maxentius. By one of those ironies in which history shows itself as deft as art, Romulus was the name of Rome's last ruler as well as of its first; the deposition by invading Germans of Romulus Augustulus in A.D. 476 marked the end of Roman power in the West.

Another legend, competing with that of Romulus, sought a more prestigious origin for the city by tracing its foundation back to Troy, traditionally destroyed by the Greeks in 1185 B.C. Even after defeat Troy ranked high in the ancient world, and Rome was not alone in seeking to borrow its glory, claiming Aeneas, son of the murdered King Priam, as a founder. As with Romulus and Remus, the legend took some time to evolve into its canonical form. According to the *Iliad*, Aeneas belonged to a junior branch of the royal house, and inherited a grudge against Priam for depriving him of his rights; Homer makes it clear that he hoped to succeed to the throne. He appears throughout as a noble and valiant warrior, and the poem contains a prophecy that he will be the future leader of his people. In Book Twenty, Aeneas is engaged in combat with Achilles and in imminent danger of death. Poseidon announces to his fellow deities that he will go to his assistance:

> Come, let us go to him, and lead him from the way
> Of death; for Zeus will be angry if Achilles
> Should kill this man. He is fated to escape
> So that the race of Dardanus may not
> Be blasted without issue from the earth – for Zeus
> Of all his mortal children loved him best.
> His rancour has destroyed the house of Priam.
> But Aeneas and his progeny shall rule
> In might among the Trojans in the time to come.[7]

Homer makes no suggestion that Aeneas and his descendants will leave Troy to continue their rule elsewhere. This was part of the later tradition; and the continuity of the legend seems to derive from one of those etymological confusions that bedevil ancient history.

Aeneas had an immortal mother, the goddess of love, Aphrodite, known under one of her cult-names as Aineias, 'goddess of piety'. In another aspect, she was goddess of the safe voyage and protectress of sailors (a function usurped in Christian times by the Virgin Mary: as so often in the Aegean, only the names have altered) and her shrines were established on a number of the islands. Forgetting the original meaning of her cult-name, men fell into the easy error of associating it with the Homeric hero, believing that the shrines marked various stages in his journey from Troy to Italy. Serious Greek historians gave colour to the theory of a migration by reporting Trojan settlements in Africa, Sicily or Italy proper. A local tradition, used by Virgil, spoke of an asylum for Trojan expatriates in Sicily: there too the Elymians, believing themselves descended from the refugees, regularly observed the anniversary of Troy's fall as a day of mourning. Strabo, the imperial geographer, cites archaeological evidence: 'On the Siris there used to be a Trojan city named after the river . . . writers offer as proof of its Trojan settlement the wooden image of the Trojan Athena to be found on the site. Legend has it that the image closed its eyes when the suppliants were dragged away by the invading Greeks.'[8]

He goes on to refer to the images supposedly brought from Troy, and still to be seen in his time in Rome itself, in Luceria towards the east coast and in Larinium further south. Certainly the story of a Trojan foundation seems to have enjoyed official credence at Rome by about 230 B.C.; one Greek community used it to support their appeal for Roman favour, arguing that theirs was the only city that had refrained from sending arms against Troy.

It remained to combine the two traditions into one, a task to which the Roman poets and mythographers lent their imaginative support. To account for the chronological discrepancy between a Trojan founder who had landed, presumably, in the twelfth century B.C., and a native ancestor some four hundred years later, Aeneas and his descendants were supposed to have founded various cities in the neighbourhood, while to Romulus was left the honour of establishing the city itself. The early Latin poets elaborated the story, and Virgil transformed the saga of Aeneas into a national epic. The Trojan emigration became for Rome what the voyage of the *Mayflower* has been for the United States. There was magic in the ancient name. At the beginning of the Christian era, a citizen of Roman Troy still proudly traced his family tree back to Priam. In Italy itself the so-called *Trojugenae*, 'the Troy-born' took no less delight in their ancestry. As late as the fourth century A.D. Christian friends of St Jerome were still claiming Aeneas as their ancestor.

Once again, the story has elements that are not peculiar to Italy but belong to a wider cultural pattern. The city of Paris, in popular tradition, derived its name from the fateful Trojan prince. Britain had its own Trojan legend, running on remarkably similar lines to the Roman and exhibiting the same types of confusion.

In this version Brutus, grandson or great-grandson of Aeneas, sailed from Italy after murdering his father, collecting on his way the surviving descendants of the Trojans who were still living under Greek domination. After many battles and adventures in Africa, Spain and France he landed in Britain. There, having subdued giants, 'he conceived the desire to build a city. Seeking a place suitable for such a foundation he came to the river Thames, and found a place apt for his design. And so he founded a city in that place, and called it New Troy, which afterwards, by a corruption of the name, came to be called Trinovantum.'[9]

Thus London's legendary beginnings parallel those of Rome; the classical name Brutus was confused with the Old English *Bryt*, 'a Briton'. The story captured the imagination and inspired, as in Italy, a tradition of patriotic poetry. Wace's Norman-French *Roman de Brut* (1155) and Layamon's Middle English *Brut* (c. 1200) were the native counterparts of the *Aeneid*. John Milton, in the seventeenth century, could still write in all seriousness a history of Britain under Trojan rule.

So much for legend. What of the history? Archaeology in no way contradicts the possibility of a foreign settlement. Linguistic studies support the idea of a difference between the Romans and their near neighbours. Exploration of Italian prehistory has revealed the existence of two distinct cultures, separated by a line passing through the future site of Rome. To the south and east lived aboriginal inhabitants who buried their dead, and to the north and west, late-comers who cremated them. Excavations under the Roman Forum have uncovered a necropolis shared by both cultures, evidence of a peaceful coexistence between the tribes inhabiting the surrounding hills. One puzzle is why the site was not occupied earlier. It had the advantages that were customarily sought – hills that could be fortified, and a river wide enough for navigation but narrow enough, in its upper reaches, to be bridged. (It was not until much later, when vessels grew too large to use the Tiber, that Rome developed Ostia as a coastal port.) Closer examination suggests reasons why the site may have seemed initially unattractive. It was too well watered; the Roman Forum is built over an ancient marsh, as was the Pantheon that Agrippa built for Augustus. For years after the city was built, the lower regions were flooded annually, and a drain was one of the earliest construction projects. The region was also subject to volcanic activity. Profiles of extinct volcanoes appear in the Alban Hills, south of Rome; they produced the characteristic stone, *tufa*, *pozzolana*, *peperino*, that Appius Claudius used to pave the highway named after him, and which provided a favourite building material. Virgil includes a picturesque memory of these early dangers in the *Aeneid* when he describes the combat between Hercules and the monster Cacus. Hercules found his quarry in a cave protected by a huge rock:

> *He threw his strength against it, and his grip*
> *Unseated it. One thrust and off it went*
> *Downhill. Its fall made thunder ring in heaven.*
> *The rivers gaped, and in their fear ran backwards,*
> *And Cacus' pit lay open, where he held*
> *Grim court among the grey light underground –*
> *A vision as if Earth were rent asunder*
> *To open Hell, and lay bare to the sun*
> *The shadow-world where gods go gingerly,*
> *Casting a cruel light on the caverned ghosts . . . .*
> *The monster sought his only means of refuge,*
> *Smoke billowed from his jaws – I swear to you –*
> *To blind the hunter's eyes, and make his den*
> *As black as pitch. Night lay upon the cavern,*
> *And here and there a sullen tongue of flame.*[10]

We have here, surely, a dim memory of volcanic eruption transformed by time and imagination into a monster. Comparatively quiet during classical times, the shocks were felt again at later periods in Rome's history. The Colosseum owes its familiar fractured outline less to the ravages of time and vandals than to the earthquakes of the fifth and sixth centuries A.D. There were other disturbances in 847, 1231 and 1255. As a result, the whole outer arcade of the Colosseum has vanished; its rubble for some years formed a monumental quarry. Only the inner ring of the structure has survived. Such activity occurred regularly down the whole length of the Western seaboard, the most famous example being the eruption of Vesuvius that destroyed Pompeii in A.D. 79.

The settlers' early years were not easy. Rome grew up in an Italy already populated and was forced to compete with long-established and powerful cultures. Both its history and its national temperament were affected thereby. Of the two great powers of the Mediterranean world, it may be said that the Greeks defined themselves in relation to nature, the Romans in terms of the peoples around them. The Greek foundation-stories show cities coming spontaneously into being, asking and receiving help from none. Athens' first ruler is born from the soil; Thebes traces its descent from a dragon's teeth planted in the ground to produce a crop of warriors. But the legendary history of Rome, in both form and substance, demonstrates the city's dependence on its neighbours, and its cultural debt. Tradition recognized six kings after Romulus. The name of the first, Numa Pompilius, is Sabine; it was from this neighbouring tribe that the first Romans were said to have taken their wives by force. The celebrated rape represents a period of cultural fusion. For centuries afterwards, the Roman marriage ceremony contained ritual elements in which the bride went through a pretence of being taken by force. The names of the last three kings, Tarquinius Priscus, Servius Tullius and Tarquinius Superbus, are Etruscan. It was this people that provided the first strong external influence on Roman affairs.

The Etruscans lived to the north-west of Rome, dominating an area roughly equivalent to the modern Tuscany which recalls their name and reflects their personality in the harsh contradictions of its terrain. They called themselves Rasna or Rasenna; the Greeks knew them as Tyrsenoi or Tyrrhenoi, and the Romans as Tusci or Etrusci. Their origin was a mystery even to the ancients. Dionysius of Halicarnassus believed them to be of indigenous Italian stock, but four centuries earlier Herodotus, in a long and circumstantial account, had described them as migrating from the East:

In the reign of Atys son of Manes, the whole of Lydia suffered from a severe famine. For a while the people tightened their belts and bore it, but eventually, when there was no relief in sight, began to search for some way to alleviate their misery. They devised various expedients according to their dispositions, and this period saw the invention of dice, knucklebones and ball-games – every sort of amusement, in fact, except draughts, which the Lydians do not claim as theirs. This was the defence they evolved against starvation. One day out of two they would devote to gaming, to distract their minds from thoughts of food, and the next day put their games aside and eat. They hung on in this way for eighteen years. But their sufferings, far from ending, grew so much worse that the king was forced to divide the population into two parts and draw lots to decide which should stay and which should emigrate. He appointed himself as ruler of those who were to remain, and his son Tyrsenos as leader of the expatriates. Those who were selected to leave went to Smyrna, on the coast. Here they built ships, embarked with whatever effects they thought would be useful, and sailed away to make their living in a new country. Skirting a number of places that were already populated they finally settled in Umbria, where they still live today. They changed their names from Lydians to Tyrrhenians, after the prince who led the expedition.[11]

Herodotus's theory, shorn of its embellishments, is the one most in favour today. The Etruscan language, surviving mostly in short inscriptions, remains largely indecipherable, but philologists have been able to make certain judgements about it: first that it is probably not a member of the Indo-European group of languages to which Latin and the other Italian dialects belong; secondly, that it has some resemblance, in structure and alphabet, to languages once spoken in the eastern Aegean and Asia Minor itself. Archaeology supports this view by tracing similar types of artifacts along three principal routes from Asia Minor to Italy. Although there is no conclusive proof, these various hints help to substantiate the theory of an overseas migration.

The Etruscan settlements themselves give little help in establishing their origin. It is often argued that the coastal position of the more important cities demonstrates colonization by water. In this view the inland centres (for example the modern Orvieto, Perugia and Arezzo) were later, smaller offshoots. Others object that this coastal propinquity has been exaggerated; that the cities were, in fact, set back some way from the sea; and that the movement was from the centre out rather than from the coastland in. Some would go so far as to say that the Etruscans entered overland from the north, or, reviving Dionysius's theory, that they were an aboriginal population encroached upon and eventually dominated by newcomers. The origin of the Etruscans remains an intriguing and probably insoluble problem, the prime mystery of a culture which possesses many cryptic features.

The ancients knew of the Etruscans as a formidable power, and were sometimes led to exaggerate the amount of their influence. The Greeks knew them as pirates with a reputation for cruelty. Euripides, by an obvious association of ideas, speaks of the legendary monster Scylla as 'haunting the Tyrrhenian rocks'. This need not be construed as an outright condemnation. Piracy and merchant seafaring were largely synonymous in the early Mediterranean, and the Greeks engaged in trade with the Etruscans on a large scale. The Romans themselves, in spite of the unpleasantness associated with the Etruscan domination of their city and the odium thereafter attached to the name of king, looked back on them with fascinated respect. In Virgil's epic the Etruscan cities align themselves with Aeneas. Livy remarks that the power of Etruria 'had a reputation which extended the whole length of Italy, land and sea alike, from the Alps to the Straits of Messina',[12] and describes this power at its zenith:

> The dominion of the Etruscans prior to the rise of Rome covered a wide stretch of land and sea. The extent of their power on the upper and lower seas that frame the Italian peninsula is shown in their names: the Italians have called one the Tuscan, after the race as a whole, and the other the Hadriatic, after the Etruscan colony of Hadria (Tyrrhenian and Adriatic in Greek). They built twelve cities on the eastern coastal slope and a similar number on the western. Those on this side of the Apennines, by the lower sea, came first; they subsequently added another twelve across the mountains, sending out one colony for each original city and appropriating all the

territory between the Po and the Alps, except for the enclave held by the Veneti round the gulf.[13]

Roman scholars and antiquarians of the first century B.C., contemporaries of Cicero, traced back many of their customs, titles and traditions to the Etruscans. The Emperor Claudius, an amateur historian of note, identified Servius Tullius, the penultimate king of Rome, with the Etruscan hero Mastarna. Whether this was true or not the tradition is important, for Servius Tullius was a figure of renown in Roman eyes. The son of a slave woman, he was marked as a future king by a halo of fire playing round his head. (The same portent, in the Middle Ages, was said to have marked Pope Clement VII, another strengthener of Roman dominion born from humble origins.) To him were attributed a liberal constitution and the so-called 'Servian Wall', the early fortifications, a stretch of which can still be seen near Rome's Terminal Station. Scholarship has dismissed the constitution as a fiction and shown that Servius's contribution to the extant wall was limited to an earthwork; but the fact remains that, for the Romans, Etruscan power was inextricably intertwined with the development of their city into something greater than merely one more settlement among the patchwork of peoples inhabiting early Italy.

We can make some certain pronouncements about the Etruscans. They were strong, though less so than later tradition represented them. Their power expanded north at least as far as the Po Valley, and south to Naples; there were also important settlements across the Apennines on the Adriatic coast. At their strongest in the sixth and fifth centuries B.C., they controlled a long and important stretch of the seaboard. Evidence of this is that the Greeks, prolific colonizers, established no mainland settlement north of Cumae. Their only foothold was on the island of Corsica, a poor second best, and even this was eradicated by the Etruscans and their allies in the latter part of the sixth century. Etruscan trade reached far afield. Its products have been found throughout the Greek-dominated south, in France, Germany, Britain and even Scandinavia. Control of the sea-coast and the trade-routes was the Etruscan strength. Their weakness was a lack of political cohesion. Such unity as existed among the cities was limited to religious ties. When Rome from one side, and the invading Gauls from the other, began to exert their pressure, the cities fell individually. There seems to have been no attempt at national resistance.

A popular image has arisen of the Etruscans as a sinister people, preoccupied with thoughts of death. This is in part a bias born of limited knowledge, for we know more about their dying than their living. There are still parts of Tuscany, however, where the Etruscan world seems close. As we travel from Florence southwest towards the coast, the road narrows, coils and lifts itself with difficulty over the hills. At first lush and green, the vegetation becomes sparser and the colours more muted; the countryside assumes a stern air, and though far from unfruitful (the Etruscans grew their vines here, and it is Chianti country now) it is laid out in orderly patches of grey and brown, a palette for Braque crisscrossed by furrows and punctuated by tall trees. Landslides (*balze*) have sliced into the terrain. It was in such a serrated landscape that the painters of the Middle Ages liked to set their saints and anchorites, finding the splintered rock an apt background for the ascetic life.

The road continues to twist and climb through a series of small villages to Volterra. This was the Velathri of the Etruscans, standing high on the hill and commanding a magnificent view of the coastal plain. The Romans made it a municipality under the name of Volaterrae. In the Middle Ages it shrank, so that the Florentine walls embrace a narrower circuit than the Etruscan, and the modern town covers only a fraction of the ancient. But long stretches of the Etruscan walls still stand, built of huge, irregular blocks holding place by weight alone. They seem to be populated by ghosts now, men and boys white with the dust of alabaster that is worked here. But in the surrounding fields oxen still draw the ploughs and carts as they used to, and modern traffic squeezes with difficulty through an Etruscan gate. It bears the heads of three divinities, a faceless triad whose features have been abraded by time. Their date is uncertain, their presence disquieting. Are they the Roman Jupiter, Castor and Pollux? The trinity of Jupiter, Juno and Minerva which presided over the Capitol in Rome? Or are they relics of a more barbaric age, recalling the tradition of adorning a city wall with the severed heads of enemies?

Outside the limits of the modern town, near the Church of San Giusto, a landslide swallowed up, in 1710, part of the Etruscan walls. By way of compensation, it allowed the archaeologist access to a number of early burial spots. A wealth of prehistoric and Etruscan finds is now contained in the Giarnacci Museum. The Romans, when they assumed control, began to embellish after their own fashion. An elaborate Roman cistern may still be seen, and the theatre, dating from the end of the first century B.C., is one of the best examples of its kind. But Volterra still bears the Etruscan stamp, a rugged town, a warrior town, beside the monumental walls of which the Florentine constructions look puny by comparison.

The case of Volterra is typical: little material evidence of the Etruscan culture has survived apart from the tombs. Excavations have uncovered several important burial-grounds. There are fifth-century tombs at Orvieto, once Volsinii, destroyed by the Romans in 265 B.C. At Cerveteri, the ancient Caere, just off the main coastal road between Civitavecchia and Rome, there are three necropolises. It may be more appropriate, however, to use Tarquinii (now Tarquinia) as an example. This was the oldest of the Etruscan cities, founded according to ancient authority by Tarchon, son of the leader of the Lydian migration. It gave Rome its two least popular kings.

Tarquinia lies some sixty miles north-west of Rome. Like Volterra it is built on a hill, which used to be nearer the sea than it is now. The coastline, once the dreaded and malarious Maremma, has shifted outwards, and a lido stands where the Etruscan ships once dropped anchor, heavy with trade. The outline of the town is medieval, for the site has shifted too; the scanty remains of Tarquinii may be seen to the east, on a rocky hill. All that is of interest lies underground. The necropolis occupies a considerable stretch of land, at one corner abutting against and underlying a Christian cemetery. Although the Etruscan tombs were not discovered until 1824 it is tempting to believe that a dim folk-memory may have preserved the site as a place of burial, just as local tales kept the memory of Pompeii alive long after all visible traces of the city, and its very name, had disappeared.

The tombs vary in size and splendour, but until the period of the decline have the same basic structure and characteristic decoration. A long flight of stairs, steep and narrow, leads down to a vaulted rectangular chamber. It is decorated like a house, with the long roof-beam and the principal supports painted in place. Almost invariably a closed door, the symbolic gateway to the after-life, is painted on the far wall. Sometimes there are ante-chambers, to hold one body or two. In some cases one may still see how the tomb was first explored. A round hole remains in the ceiling where the first drilling was made. Through this a peri-scopic camera was lowered to show the excavators the nature of their find and record features which would not survive exposure to the air.

The sarcophagi have been removed to museums, but the painted walls, carefully restored, still stand out fresh and vigorous. They display scenes that are earthy, full of life: dancers, huntsmen, fowlers, animals and humans mating. In the later tombs, those of the decadence, the chambers are more opulent and the decoration increasingly morbid and affected. A horrific Cyclops loses his eye to the stake of Odysseus. Greek influence runs wild. On the sarcophagi themselves, the bloodier scenes from Greek mythology are favourite subjects: the Seven Against Thebes, the hunting of the Calydonian Boar, the murder of Agamemnon. Or the reliefs concern themselves with the journey to the Underworld – on horseback, by foot, by carriage. The sculptured effigies of the dead smile. Some find the smile sinister, and claim that it reveals something of the national character. Others see this aspect of the Etruscan enigma as simply the by-product of a sculptural technique, a traditional way of holding the chisel. Little is known about Etruscan statuary, though interest in the finds has been immense, and has readily attracted forgers. One scandal is of recent date: In 1916 John Marshall, purchasing agent for the Metropolitan Museum, bought some Etruscan statues in Rome. Growing doubts of their authenticity culminated, in 1960, in the conclusive proof that they were forgeries. Art historians had for some time been debating the distorted proportions of the figures on stylistic grounds. The true reason was much simpler. It turned out that the forgers had been working in a room with a low ceiling, which forced them to make the legs shorter than they had originally intended. This disclosure provoked others. The University of Kansas, almost simultaneously, discovered forgeries in its own collection.

It is easy, with hindsight, to laugh at the gullibility of art historians, but the fault was not theirs. It is the familiar problem of scholars being asked to make judgements in a field where evidence is scanty and grounds for reasoned criticism unsure. Etruscan art has provided many puzzles. One of the oldest and most famous concerns the statue of the wolf suckling Romulus and Remus, now to be found on the Capitol in Rome. There were several famous examples of this group in antiquity. In this case the she-wolf is now admitted to be of Etruscan workmanship, though the children were not added till the Renaissance. But earlier critics could not believe the work to be Etruscan, considering its techniques far too advanced for such an early civilization. The fact that the wolf was an Etruscan totem gives another dimension to the Romulus and Remus story, and provides one more tantalizing link between legend and history.

To the Etruscans the Romans owed many things. The architect-historian Vitruvius devotes considerable space to a consideration of Etruscan temple building and its influence on Roman styles. A number of Latin words – in particular, technical terms – seem to have been Etruscan in origin; the organization of the Roman army reveals a similar debt. On the darker side, it cannot be denied that several of the less attractive features of Roman life came from the same source. There was the passionate interest in divination, known in Rome as the 'Etruscan discipline'. Students of folk-lore have claimed to find clear survivals of Etruscan ritual in the beliefs of modern Tuscan peasants; by the same token, when the Romans drew portents from the sky, the behaviour of birds and the sacrifice of animals, they were practising an art far older than themselves. The Etruscans also seem to have bequeathed to Rome the idea of human combat as a public spectacle, and an elaborate and terrifying demonology which made its influence felt in diverse ways. The attendants who dragged the bodies of the fallen from Roman amphitheatres were costumed like the ghouls of Etruscan tomb paintings, and the early Christian concepts of Hell owe some of their more lurid imaginings to the same source.

NOTES TO CHAPTER ONE

1. Seneca the Elder, *Controversiae*, I. 6.
2. Livy, *A History of Rome from its Foundation*, I. 4.
3. Ennius, *Annals* fr. 33. 1–9, 14–21.
4. Ovid, *Fasti (The Roman Calendar)*, IV. 837–52, 857–8.
5. Dionysius of Halicarnassus, *Roman Antiquities*, I. 79. 11.
6. *Corpus Inscriptionum Latinarum*, VI. 36840.
7. Homer, *Iliad*, XX. 302–8.
8. Strabo, *Geography*, VI. 1. 12.
9. Geoffrey of Monmouth, *History of the Kings of Britain*, I. 17, old version; II. 1, variant version.
10. Virgil, *Aeneid*, VIII. 237–46, 251–5.
11. Herodotus, *Histories*, I. 94. 3.
12. Livy, op. cit., I. 2. 5.
13. Livy, op. cit., V. 33. 7–10.

Chapter Two

Greeks, Gauls and Carthaginians

AT the other end of the peninsula dwelt a people whose influence on the emergent power was to be even stronger and to provide Rome with a model for her culture. When Rome was still a collection of huts huddled round the Tiber, Greek colonies in Sicily and the south of Italy carried on a thriving and sophisticated civilization. The eighth and seventh centuries B.C. had seen one of the most remarkable achievements of the Greek world, the great wave of colonization which overran the shores of Asia Minor, extended north as far as the Crimea and pushed west to Spain. Greece was a poor country. Its growing population was forced to adopt the expedient that Herodotus attributed to the Lydians, and migrate. The settlers were attracted by merchants' stories of new grainlands and sources of mineral wealth. It was no haphazard process. Mother cities sent forth offshoots carrying fire from the sacred hearth which burnt perpetually to remind the colonists of their ties with home. Colonies spawned others in their turn, and bonds of affection were reinforced by ties of trade. Greece penetrated Italy to such an extent that the south became known as greater Greece. It is said with pride (by Italians) that there are now more Greek ruins in Italy than in Greece itself. Homer, in the *Odyssey*, already knew of Sicily as a source of slaves, and the wanderings of Odysseus touch at several points along the Italian coast. Finds of early pottery testify to Greek contacts in the area even before the eighth century B.C., though their sporadic nature suggests no more than a passing interest at this time, with no attempt at settlement. But colonists soon followed along the paths that the merchants had pioneered. The Greek interest in Italy was at first wholly, and always largely, commercial. They came to find what their own country did not readily provide, and settled in numbers where they found the soil good, the mineral deposits rich or the waterways affluent. Their first contacts were made with the Etruscans and the people of Latium, the district later to be controlled by Rome, and trade with the former was always lively. It was from the Western Greeks that the Etruscans adopted their alphabet, and the preponderance of Greek motifs in Etruscan art has already been mentioned.

It used to be believed that the first Greek settlement proper was in Cumae, near Naples, later to be famous for its prophetic Sibyl. More recently Giorgio Buchner, excavating under joint American and Italian auspices, has proved beyond reasonable doubt what many scholars had previously suspected: that the first colony was established at Ischia, a volcanic island at the entrance to the Bay of Naples, and a modern tourist paradise. Buchner thus supports the opinion of Livy, who placed the first Greek settlement there; the Greeks knew the island as Pithekoussai. In 1949 schoolboys levelling a soccer field turned up a number of Greek potsherds. Buchner went to work and, almost singlehanded, showed who had settled there, their provenance and the nature of their business. The colonizers came from Euboea, the sprawling island to the north-east of Athens. They left their own work on Ischia in the form of vases, together with imports from their trading posts in Asia Minor. And it is clear that they had come for iron. There are no ore deposits on Ischia itself. It was mined on Elba, up the coast in Etruscan territory. On Ischia the Euboeans established a harbour and a working base, where the Elban ore was smelted down (slag-caked crucibles and fragments of bellows have been discovered) and shipped back to the motherland. Payment to the Etruscans was in luxury goods – fine pottery and jewellery.

Cumae, though deposed from first place, is still venerable. Founded in 750 B.C., it rapidly prospered and acquired wide dominion. Its earliest historical figure is its ruler Aristodemus, who fought the Etruscans in 542 and again about 505. Cumae traded with Athens on the one side and Massilia (Marseilles) on the other, adopting Athenian coinage and standards of measure. Through Cumae Greek metalwork flooded southern Italy and created a local tradition.

In 720 another city was founded on the Gulf of Taranto: Sybaris, proverbial for wealth and luxury. Its name is perpetuated in the modern Sibari and less honourably in the adjective 'sybaritic'. The region then was highly fertile, though it is one of the poorest parts of Italy now, and the population of Sybaris was variously given as between one and three hundred thousand. Etruscans came to live there. Like Cumae, it grew rich on commerce. Goods were imported from Miletus, the principal Greek colony on the coast of Asia Minor, and reshipped to the cities of Etruria. Most important of these commodities was Milesian wool, the mink of the ancient world and the most luxurious of ancient fabrics until the silkworm arrived from the Far East.

Ancient writers lavished their hyperboles on Sybaris. Strabo tells us that it 'ruled over four neighbouring tribes, held twenty-five cities in subjection and campaigned against the people of Croton with three hundred thousand men'.[1] A Greek poet, preferring fancy to statistics, saw it as Cockaigne, the land of heart's desire, where fine food, already cooked, floated downstream into the fortunate inhabitants' waiting mouths. Many of the stories told about the city are patent inventions, born of envy. We hear of tax incentives given to dealers in luxury goods, of chefs encouraged in inventive *haute cuisine* by a year's monopoly on any new dish, and of women invited to public ceremonies with twelve months' notice to prepare an appropriate *toilette*. But through the fantasy we can discern a realization of the economic importance of such colonies, and the opportunity for the good life that they presented – an opportunity usually denied to the Greeks who stayed at home. But Sybaris, in the end, fell victim to a hereditary Greek disease, dissension between cities. It was not to survive for Roman eyes to see. In 510 B.C. it was destroyed by its neighbour Croton. Strabo saw this as a judgement. 'Because of their idleness and self-indulgence', he pontificates, 'their high fortune was taken from them in seventy days.'[2]

It seemed for a long time as though Sybaris had been completely effaced. Its location became a mystery. Time and topographical changes compounded the ravages of war. The river on which Sybaris had stood shifted its course. The ground level sank some twenty feet. Deposits from adjacent mountains were washed down to cover the site. Archaeologists explored in vain, tunnelling through likely-looking sand dunes to find only sand. Finally, in 1962, modern technology came to the historian's aid. With equipment similar to that used by oil prospectors, archaeologists sank test holes every hundred metres until they began to wash out fragments of likely material. Instrumental surveys followed, using the proton magnetometer to measure the strength of the magnetic field at various depths. Digging in the places indicated turned up fragments of a date compatible with Sybaris. It now seems likely that, given time and money, one of the richest cities of the ancient world will be exhumed and another archaeological riddle solved.

Although Sybaris must remain for the present invisible, enough is left of one of her own colonies to give an idea of what the settlements in Italy were like, and of the problems of relocation that the Greeks had to face. This is Paestum, south of Salerno on the west coast. Founded about 600 B.C., it was first called Poseidonia, after the god of the sea. When a road was cut through the region in the eighteenth century and the long-forgotten site rediscovered, the excavators naturally associated the largest and most impressive temple of the three that they found with the same deity; it is still popularly known as the Temple of Neptune. The city's closest religious ties, however, were not with the sea god but with Hera, wife of Zeus and goddess of fertility. A few miles away, on the coast, at the mouth of the river Sele, archaeologists discovered in 1934 a sanctuary to this goddess which may have marked the original settlement in the region. A Greek legend sketchily preserved in later writers gave it a mythic origin, claiming Jason, leader of the Argonauts, as its founder. The shrine was attacked by pirates in 62 B.C., and further damaged by subsequent earthquakes. Terracotta images have been found which portray the goddess holding a pomegranate, the ancient symbol of fertility, and authorities now generally agree that the so-called Temple of Neptune or Poseidon on the main site is really hers. So is the older temple close by, generally known as the basilica. The Hera-cult was perpetuated through the many vicissitudes of Paestan history, and some aspects of it still survive today. As so often, Christianity absorbed the pagan deities and involved their worship in its own. Already unpopular because of its malarious climate, the site was finally abandoned after the Saracen invasion of the ninth century. In the hills nearby the refugees founded Capaccio Vecchio, where there still stands a church dedicated to the Madonna of the Pomegranates. Twice a year tiny boats full of flowers are carried up the mountain path to the church. In just this way, we are told, the Greeks used to worship their Hera.

But the site was inhabited long before the Greeks came. In 1943, American troops building an airstrip nearby discovered a prehistoric burial ground. Over twenty tombs have been uncovered. Reconstructions of two of these, showing the skeletons in place together with the flint weapons and pottery buried with them, may be seen in the Paestum Museum. They are conjecturally dated between 2400 and 1900 B.C. When the Greeks came, it was as new arrivals in an already populated land. It is clear from the layout of their city that they faced hostility, and were forced to compromise between local necessity and their customary principles of town planning. The portion of the site now excavated and dominated by the three impressive temples is only a fraction of the original extent. Greek temples normally reached to heaven from the summit of a hill, which served both as sanctuary and citadel. Here there was no hill. The Greeks were forced to build on the plain and set their temples on puny artificial mounds. A strong wall pierced with four gates and armed with watchtowers, stretches of which may still be seen, surrounded the whole. The earlier and later temples of Hera stand to the south. To the north is the third temple, later in date and popularly associated with the corn goddess Demeter, though it was probably not hers but Athena's. Between the temples lay the city's heart, the civic and administrative centre. Some Greek remains can still be seen under the Roman accretions – cisterns, meeting-halls and other structures associated with religious worship. The Greek Poseidonia was a prosperous place. But its walls were not protection enough. In about 400 B.C. it fell to the Lucanians. In 273 B.C. the Romans became the masters, and established the colony called Paestum. As we see the site now, the Roman settlement has largely overlaid the Greek. Aerial photography has traced the grid plan of the Roman streets. The Roman forum, where the holes may still be seen that supported the awnings of stalls on market-day, occupied the site of the Greek agora. An amphitheatre, now bisected by the modern road, gave the citizens their pleasure. But the Greek temples still stand, one grey, one white, one golden in the sun, monuments of the Greek spirit transplanted to a foreign soil; and, though the outline of the coast has changed, one may still see the magnificent sweep of the bay that invited the Greeks of legend and history to seek their fortunes inland.

Returning to the Gulf of Taranto we find another Greek colony whose presence is still evident, and which was hardly less magnificent than Sybaris itself: the city that gives the gulf its name, known to the Greeks as Taras and to the Romans as Tarentum. This was the only colony founded by Sparta, a city that conspicuously distrusted foreign entanglements. Tradition said that it was settled by illegitimate children born to Spartan wives whose husbands were away at war and shipped off *en masse* to avoid embarrassment. Tarentum was almost as famous for wool as Miletus itself, and produced its own luxury commodities: a purple dye extracted from mussels, whose formula modern chemists have recreated synthetically, and a diaphanous fabric woven from the filaments of the shellfish *pinna marina*. This was the nearest that the ancient world could come to silk, and was highly prized. When Croton, the victorious rival of Sybaris, itself declined, Tarentum became the most important city in the region. Tarentine coins discovered in the Po Valley show the extent of its connections. It was to offer notable resistance to the spread of Roman power and introduce the Romans to the arts of Greece.

One other colony on the peninsula deserves mention, if only because it was untypical: Thurii, founded comparatively late as a rare example of panhellenic co-operation, near the site of Sybaris. Athens took the initiative, other cities associated themselves with the enterprise, and the new city was born in 443 B.C. Herodotus the historian and Lysias the orator were reputedly involved in its fortunes. Its streets were laid out by a distinguished town-planning expert. After surviving independently for some time it finally went over voluntarily to the Romans and joined with them in opposing other colonies that were more recalcitrant.

Rome exploded outwards. At the beginning of Chapter One we took a journey which reversed the course of history, peeling off layer after layer of the city until we arrived at its primitive kernel. To explore Rome's relationship with Italy we may reverse the process, take the capital as our nucleus and travel outwards as the early Romans did when they brought more and more of the surrounding country under their sway. The Romans today love to take to their cars and escape to the serenity of the surrounding hills. At weekends the roads are choked with them. They flee to the cool air of the mountains, the medicinal springs, the sea; they follow the paths their ancestors took when Rome first became conscious of its power and began to subdue the adjacent settlements. It was not an easy conquest. Rome had to compete with other cities of equal or greater antiquity, perched on hilltops behind the security of massive walls. In some places these hazards are still apparent; in Alatri, for example, the walls of which, built in the fourth century B.C., were still strong enough to protect a medieval castle, and whose squat presence commanding the valleys was typical of the obstacles the Roman armies had to face. And yet the cities fell. Italy, like Greece, is a mountainous country: but where in the older civilization the mountains often dictated the course of history and kept the development of individual cities within bounds, in the younger they were a condition of life, seldom an outright prohibition. The Apennines form an unbroken chain down the length of the peninsula, breaking up the land into pockets and discouraging any cohesion among the population. But the mountains were assailable, and, after the conquest, cultivable; it was still possible for a stronger power to assert its dominion over the country as a whole in a way that was never possible in Greece. In time, the various alliances and confederations of the Italic peoples yielded to Rome's superior strength.

We may look to Mussolini again for a modern boast with a historical ring to it.

> I am proud of one thing, it is to have led the Romans back to the seaside. They had forgotten it. It is just about twenty minutes' ride with the tram or motorcar. I trust that, by and by, the sailor's virtues will also flourish again. I must confess that Rome, in antiquity, had no exceptional naval qualities, but all the same she succeeded in beating Carthage, even at sea.

Mussolini refers to Ostia, which was Rome's first colony. Before the coming of the electric train and *autostrada* it was a two-hour carriage-ride from Rome or a four-hour walk. Roman tradition made it the landfall of Aeneas, and attributed the founding of a colony there to the city's fourth king. Certainly the location was inviting; lying at the mouth (*ostium*) of the Tiber, it provided salt, a much-sought-after commodity, and, in time, a coastal base for shipping. Archaeology places the foundation considerably later than the traditional date, between 349 and 317 B.C. At first it was no more than a fortified camp, a mere five and a half acres squared off and walled with tufa blocks which may still be seen as one approaches the later forum. It is often argued that the form of such a *castrum*, with its principal street as axis and the blocks of buildings symmetrically oriented about it, gave the impetus for the typical grid-plan of later Roman town construction. It is a tempting suggestion, since so much of Roman policy was coloured by the military mind. Alternative arguments derive the grid-plan from the Etruscans, or from the designs drawn up by Hippodamus of Miletus for the panhellenic colony of Thurii. Ostia was not a simple *castrum* for long. Under the Republic it developed into a sizeable city, governed by two chief magistrates (*duoviri*) who were the local equivalent of the consuls at Rome, assisted by a council. It acquired considerable naval importance. But it is imperial Ostia, the city revealed by the archaeologists, that is of greater interest to us, and we shall return to it in another place.

Some cities, though conquered by the Romans, retained a considerable amount of independence. We may look at Praeneste (modern Palestrina) some twenty-three miles from Rome. It too had origins that reached back into myth. According to one account it was founded by Telegonus, the bastard son of Odysseus; according to others by a son of the fire-god Vulcan (appropriately, perhaps, in this terrain) or by the son of a nymph. At the time of Rome's traditional foundation it was already flourishing, with a mixed population of various Italic tribes under strong Etruscan influence. In the fourth century, after frequent conflicts with Rome, it became her ally, and was permitted a number of special privileges. It was particularly famous for the oracle that resided there. Visitors to the modern town can see in the walls a testimony to its ancient strength, and in the remains of the temple above an indication of the magnificence that Praeneste attained in Roman hands. One of the happier by-products of the Second World War was the uncovering, through bombing, of more of the Temple of Bona Fortuna (Good Fortune), one of the most grandiose of Roman building projects, engineered by the dictator Sulla in the first century B.C. The cave in which the oracle dwelt became the nucleus of a vast architectural complex sprawling down the hillside in a series of ramps, stairs and terraces. It was a township in its own right, of which the upper reaches, now forming part of the Barberini Palace, can still be seen. The semicircular stepped terrace which now leads to the main entrance of the palace once accommodated the faithful assembled to watch the priests above. The palace is now a museum. The floors have been pierced to reveal the intricate and monumental Roman foundations, while the rooms contain relics, artwork and statuary discovered in the shrine, including a famous mosaic showing scenes from the River Nile. In this one site alone we can study the cosmopolitan nature of the Roman achievement, and the freedom with which it absorbed elements from other cultures. A primitive oracle – itself probably imported, at some remote period, from outside Italy – is venerated and consulted by them; it is housed within an edifice based on Hellenistic architectural principles, which in time is decorated with motifs from the more exotic quarters of the Roman Empire.

Descend from Palestrina to the Via del Sole, travel south through Frosinone and war-torn Cassino, and you will come eventually to Capua, a city which invited Roman intervention and lived to regret it. The modern city is some miles from the old site, now Santa Maria Capua Vetere. It was an Etruscan foundation, though it too claimed Aeneas as an ancestor. In the middle of the fourth century it requested Roman protection in a local squabble. Thus began an equivocal relationship between the two cities from which Capua tried several times to escape. Always brought back to heel, it finally resigned itself to its lot and enjoyed renewed prosperity under the Empire. As usual, the earlier foundations have been lost to sight, and only the imperial remains confront us; the enormous amphitheatre, begun in its present form under Augustus, is second in size only to the Colosseum in Rome.

From Capua the road turns east through the most difficult country that the Roman soldier had to contend with. It rises to cross the Appennines, and the hills close in; for two and a half miles it passes through a defile still known as the Caudine Forks, the site, in 321 B.C., of a humiliating defeat. The exact location of the disaster is uncertain, as the terrain has changed. It is still easy, however, to imagine the Roman army trapped helplessly between the hills, and the Samnites forcing them to pass under a yoke of spears as symbol of their degradation. Near Montesarchio, a castle looks down from the neighbourhood of the old Samnite capital of Caudium. The place is still forbidding.

So to Benevento, once Beneventum, which represents still another type of Roman involvement in the south. Originally a Samnite stronghold, it was turned by the Romans into a garrison town. Not long after the roads began to come through. In 312 the first of these great arteries was laid, the Appian Way, covering the 132-mile stretch from Rome to Capua. Good roads were good policy. They facilitated the movement of armies and linked the newly acquired territories to the capital. The modern motorist who is impressed by the engineering miracles of the Rome–Florence *autostrada* may reflect on the skill of the ancient builders who constructed roads hardly less excellent, for their time, with more slender technical resources. For a tribute to their prowess we may jump ahead in time to the imperial poet Statius, who writes of what Domitian's new highway did for the city of Naples:

> *In the old days, only a pair of wheels*
> *Stood between you and the ravenous*
> *Morass beneath. You ploughed your way*
> *By inches, clinging tight*
> *To the shafts for safety. Latins*
> *Knew all the horrors of shipwreck*
> *Without going near the water. . . .*
> *First surveyors came, to score*
> *The new road's limits. After them*
> *The excavators, packing firm*
> *The trench that they had dug, to stop*
> *The highway sinking, or the soil*
> *From shifting under the pavement. Then*
> *The laying of kerbs, the mating*
> *Of block with block. The gangs are busy*
> *Stripping the neighbouring hills of timber,*
> *Planing the wooden ties and smoothing*
> *Lumps of masonry; between each course*
> *Tufa to bind it, and fire-dried sand.*
> *The pools are drained, and culverts*
> *Turn the streams to other courses.*[3]

In Rome, the beginning of the Appian Way may still be traced at the Porta San Sebastiano, and the modern coast road partly follows the ancient course. Some stretches of Roman paving still survive in the hills, and in the small town of Itri houses have been built into the substructure. Before long the road was carried through Capua to Beneventum, which became an important junction. A triumphal arch, erected in A.D. 114 by the people of the town in expectation of the Emperor Trajan's safe return from the Parthian Wars, straddles the highway before it plunges into the hill country beyond. From its humble beginning, Beneventum, like Ostia, grew to great prosperity. The modern Benevento is a shadow of its former self. As soon as one leaves the main thoroughfare, one dives into a tangle of alleys that have sprouted like weeds around the ancient monuments. Families still live inside the Roman walls; a Roman archway, stripped to bare bricks, separates adjacent slums; the imposing theatre, still used for summer performances, seems likely to be crushed by the pressure of the population.

Thus the Romans spread into the south. Invited or uninvited, peacefully or with force, they infiltrated the country and made it their own. They were discriminating in their relationship with the cities they dominated. Some remained virtually independent, others suffered a harsher discipline. Each case was decided on its merits. It was at Beneventum that the Romans met the sharpest resistance from the Greek colonies. Tarentum had called for aid from the motherland, and the appeal was answered by Pyrrhus, King of Epirus, with a force of twenty-five thousand men and twenty elephants. Two victories brought his army within striking distance of the capital, but a diversion which took him to Sicily allowed the Romans to draw breath. The inconclusive battle of Beneventum in 275 left Pyrrhus so weakened that he was forced to return to Greece, and the remaining Greek colonies came more or less willingly to the Roman side. Tarentum secured a lenient treaty, Neapolis (Naples) became a favoured ally, and the colony at Paestum was established in 273.

For some time, Rome faced greater dangers from the north. The Alps, enclosing the continental plain and curving round the west coast to join the Apennines, afforded little real protection.

They had proved no barrier to the migrant tribes who had settled in the country at the beginning of Italian history, nor were they to shut out Rome's enemies. In about 408 B.C. a great migration of Gauls passed through the mountains. They came for plunder, not for empire, and swarmed over the fertile Po Valley. Marauding bands skirted some Etruscan cities and skirmished with others. Their impact further weakened an already failing power, and to this extent was beneficial to Rome. But the Gauls eventually penetrated to Rome itself, sacking the city and holding it to ransom. The Romans remembered this disaster as one of the blackest days in their history.

Nor could the Alps keep out a more dangerous opponent. The first major check to Rome's expansion, and her first serious encounter with a major foreign power, came when she collided with the African city of Carthage. It is appropriate to treat this conflict in some detail here, as it acquired heroic proportions in Roman legend.

Carthage had been founded by the Phoenicians, the earliest colonizers of the Mediterranean. Greek historians gave the date of the foundation as 814 B.C. Carthage was thus roughly contemporary with Rome, and the youngest of the Phoenician settlements; archaeological findings confirm the late date. The Carthaginians knew it as Kart-Hadasht, 'the new city', the Greeks as Carchedon; to the Romans it was Carthago, and its people Poeni, after the colonizers. It was situated on the Bay of Tunis, an outpost of civilization among the Berber tribes who were still living in the stone age; it was isolated by its own advantages, for in that region few such attractive sites were to be found. It stood on a peninsula which offered shelter for shipping. Appian compares it to a ship riding at anchor. Virgil, in a lyrical description which owes more to imagination than to geography, sees the harbour through the eyes of Aeneas and his companions when they have just survived a disastrous storm:

> *There is a place a long sea-reach behind*
> *The coast; an island, broadside, makes*

A harbour there, and parts the rolling waves
To send them scampering along the bay.
Its mouth is high and rugged. Neighbour peaks
Rise sheer to heaven, and the waters that
They lower upon are safe and still. Behind them
A vista of shimmering leaves. The trees
Hang like a mane, to keep the sunlight out,
And as you enter, in the great poised rocks,
There is a cave with a freshwater spring
And benches hewn by nature from the stone,
The home of nymphs.[4]

Carthage, like Rome, was traditionally founded by an exile. We know the legend first through the *History* of Timaeus, a Greek brought up in Sicily and thus close to Carthaginian sources. Elissa, a princess of Tyre, married her uncle Acherbas. Pygmalion, her brother, murdered Acherbas for his fortune, but Elissa was able to escape, travelling by way of Cyprus to Africa. There she founded a colony, was sought in marriage by a local chieftain, and threw herself upon a blazing pyre rather than accept him. In later versions the name Dido, perhaps a local variant, began to creep into the story, and eventually supplanted that of Elissa. The queen also acquired a sister, Anna. When the Roman writers took up the story, they pushed the date back several hundred years, to permit a meeting between Dido and Aeneas and create a legendary background for the confrontation between the cities that they founded. This may well have been the version used by Naevius, who fought in the first Carthaginian war and wrote an epic poem about it. The story of the Trojan involvement in the fortunes of Carthage was certainly current by the first century B.C. According to Varro, it was Anna who fell in love with Aeneas. In the *Aeneid*, of course, it is Dido herself, and Anna is relegated to a minor role. This may well have been Virgil's original contribution to the legend. When Aeneas is forced by the call of duty to leave Carthage, Dido, harking back to the earliest version of the story, commits suicide by burning.

In later Roman literature Dido appears as a genuinely sympathetic figure, a rare exception to the harsh criticisms levelled at her people in most ancient sources. Neither Greeks nor Romans had any reason to love Carthage, and their prejudice is reflected in their writings. For the most part, we must see the history of Carthage through the eyes of her greatest enemies, and allow for the inevitable distortion.

The legend of Dido, like that of Aeneas, contains some historical truth. Phoenician colonization was stimulated by the same hunger that impelled the Greeks. The quest for metal drove them west as far as Spain, where they formed trading connections and founded Gadir, the Roman Gades and modern Cadiz. Long before the Greeks appeared, the whole of the Mediterranean knew the Phoenicians as sailors, merchants and explorers. They are mentioned in the *Odyssey* where we see, perhaps, the earliest traces of anti-Phoenician sentiment. Solomon's 'ships of Tarshish' were probably Phoenician vessels from Andalusia, which they called Tartessus. Their system of colonies spread along the southern shore of the Mediterranean. The Greeks who followed them were interested in acquiring land, but the Phoenicians were solely concerned with trade at sea, and all the more uneasy when they saw that trade threatened. The Greek colonies, like their mother-cities, were autonomous, but the Phoenicians were not; they responded to directives for joint action, and thus presented themselves as formidable opponents to the younger powers who sought to establish themselves in the Mediterranean.

In historical terms Carthage was the last, and ultimately the most important, of this system of trading posts. The Dido story has features in common with foundation legends elsewhere. The settlers were said to have been granted by the natives as much land as they could enclose with a bull's hide. By cutting the hide into thin strips, they won for themselves a substantial amount of territory. In this case, the story seems to be a late attempt to explain the name Byrsa, 'bull's hide', given to the Carthaginian citadel; but similar stories are told of William Penn and the Delaware Indians, of the Dutch colonists in Formosa, and of the Spaniards in Manila. Elissa-Dido's rejected native suitor may represent abortive attempts at union between the local tribes and the newcomers, and the royal suicide may be a distorted memory of ritual self-immolation. We know that the Carthaginians practised human sacrifice at least as late as the fifth century: a surviving stone from that period shows a priest offering up a child. We know too that when the general Hamilcar lost the battle of Himera in 480 B.C. he perished in the way attributed to Dido. It has therefore been surmised that primitive Phoenician custom, as in other early societies, required the regular sacrifice of the spiritual or temporal leader to secure the divine blessing on a new enterprise; that Dido's legendary and Hamilcar's actual death preserve the memory of such a custom; and that the thousands of jars discovered in Carthage and containing the ashes of cremated children represent a later stage in the tradition, when the person of the ruler was replaced in the sacrifice by a substitute-figure.

Carthage seems to have adapted itself more than other Phoenician colonies to the resources of the land. We know that, like Tarentum across the sea, it engaged in the manufacture of textiles and purple dye. At its greatest period it had enough land to be self-supporting. Mago the Carthaginian wrote a farming manual in twenty-eight volumes, which was translated into Latin and Greek and became the prime source for later Roman writers. The Romans also used a sophisticated type of threshing machine whose name, *plostellum Punicum* or Punic cart, shows it to be a Carthaginian invention.

But the lure of exploration was still strong. The Carthaginians crossed northern Africa by land, reaching places which were not rediscovered until the nineteenth century, and then only with great difficulty. They traded with Egypt, and copied its architectural devices on their own temples. By sea the people of the New City traded with Spain; their commerce was chiefly with the western barbarians who were not interested in the quality market that the Greeks supplied. Carthaginian products have been found in Switzerland. The Carthaginians were, however, interested in trading with the Greeks on their own account, and were still importing luxury products at the time of the destruction of their city by the Romans.

Some of their voyages made maritime history. A Carthaginian explorer, Hanno, led an expedition to secure colonies along the Moroccan coast, reached Sierra Leone, within eight degrees of the Equator, and on his return posted an account of his wonderful voyage in the temple of Moloch. A Greek translation has survived for us to read. The Carthaginians also established contacts with western Europe, probably overland through Gades and Massilia, but at least once by sea. We have a second-hand account of this in a poem by Avienus, a Latin writer of the fourth century A.D. who had access to Massiliote and Carthaginian sources. He writes that beyond the Pillars of Hercules – the ancient name for the Straits of Gibraltar –

> There lies a wild infinity of waters,
> A vast expanse of ocean, sounding, still –
> So Himilco reports. A virgin sea,
> A tract unknown to vessels, for the lack
> Of blasts to drive them forward on the water
> Or heaven's breath to help the boat along.
> And more than this; there is a sombre cloak
> Of mist upon the sky: perpetual fog
> Lies on the waters, turning day to night . . . .
> But even off-shore, seas are shallow here
> And barely hide the ocean's sandy floor.
> Amid the swirl of waters, towering weeds
> Reach out to hold the vessels in their grip.
> Beneath the surface monsters turn and glide,
> Lending their terror to their ocean home.[5]

It may not be easy to recognize the coast of Brittany in this bleak and sinister Sargasso Sea, but this is where Himilco's voyage seems to have taken him, perhaps about 500 B.C.; the reference to the dark, limitless waters suggests that he may have penetrated the Atlantic.

The Carthaginians were not interested in acquiring an empire, and preferred to avoid foreign entanglements. It was inevitable, however, that they should be forced into contact with the other powers interested in exploiting the resources of the Mediterranean. It was on the fertile island of Sicily that Carthaginian met Greek.

Sicily has always been the meeting-place of nations. The modern visitor may trace the influence of Normans, Arabs, Italians and – most recently – of Americans on its architecture, customs and language. It was no less susceptible in antiquity, for its situation was inviting. Sicily is separated from Italy only by the narrow Straits of Messina, a notorious navigational hazard in the ancient world, and supposedly inhabited by the monsters Scylla and Charybdis. It also lies within easy sailing distance from Africa, providing, like Crete further down the Mediterranean, a convenient stepping-stone between continents. It was once believed, indeed, that both these islands were originally part of the African land-mass. The ancients knew Sicily as Trinacria, in recognition of its three-cornered shape, and the Romans gave it a symbol similar to the arms of the Isle of Man, showing three legs radiating from a common centre. These may have been intended to suggest the mountain ranges which divide the island and invite piecemeal colonization. The mountains are a continuation of the Apennine chain, and have the same volcanic characteristics. The ancients believed that the island lay on the body of a fallen giant, one of the primordial inhabitants of earth subdued and imprisoned by the younger gods. From time to time he would roll over, or vent his fury through the mouth of Mount Etna. At Sciacca, archaeologists have turned up the remains of human sacrifices, the bones of small children who had been offered up to placate the underworld volcanic gods. Belief in these chthonic deities persisted far longer in Sicilian folk-lore than elsewhere; the disastrous earthquakes of 1961 and 1968, which shattered Palermo, are witness to their continued hostility.

Virtually every movement of peoples in the ancient Mediterranean left its mark on Sicily, and the Phoenicians were not exempt. Panormus, the modern Palermo, in spite of its Greek name, was originally a Phoenician settlement; surviving Punic inscriptions are preserved in the National Archaeological Museum. Selinus, now Selinunte, shows traces of a Punic street plan. The Phoenicians brought their customs with them. In Motya, on the island of San Pantaleo, excavations have uncovered relics of human sacrifice. But the custom was clearly on the wane: together with the bodies of infants lie those of birds, dogs, cats and monkeys. Gelon of Syracuse, after his defeat of the Carthaginians at Himera, ordered the abolition of human sacrifice. The same process is observable in Carthage itself, where the relics of sacrifices contain an increasingly large proportion of animal bones. After the Roman conquest, these are the only kind found.

The Phoenician settlements, however, were small in number, and swamped by the newcomers. Sicily was rapidly colonized by the Greeks. Syracuse, founded in 734, rose under a succession of strong leaders to become the bulwark of Hellenism in the eastern Mediterranean, and a great patron of the arts. Pindar wrote his courtly poetry there, and Aeschylus, who was to die in Sicily, produced his own plays in the great theatre. Gela was founded in 688 and Himera some time after 650, while Selinus became a Greek city in 628. Greeks and Carthaginians established tentative trading relations. The produce of Acragas (now Agrigento) famous for its vines and olives, was sold in Carthaginian markets. Carthage, however, soon grew alarmed at the rapid expansion of Greek power, and fought to protect her interests in western Sicily. An alliance was formed with the Etruscans. Mercenaries began to appear in her army, drawn from Spain, Africa and Gaul. In 480, while the Greeks and Persians were joining battle at Salamis, the Greek colonists fought the Carthaginians at Himera. These two actions may be seen as part of a concerted movement on the part of the older powers to expel the upstart. In both cases the Greeks won, and six years later we find the Syracusan ships in the service of Cumae, defeating the Etruscans.

Continuing to infiltrate after its rebuff, Carthage controlled a third of Sicily by 370. At its strongest it stood alone. Alexander the Great, carrying Greek power into the East, had destroyed the other remnants of the Phoenician civilization. Carthage was the isolated but powerful survivor. Its population at its height was about four hundred thousand. It was widely respected as a trading centre, and it was in the hands of the great merchant families that power ultimately lay. Its social system and its religion retained some relics of the earlier savagery. It was not tolerant of failures, and the public executioner was a busy man. Its principal deity, Baal Hammon, was equated by the Greeks with their Kronos, father of Zeus, who ate his children. But even the Greeks found something to admire in Carthage. Aristotle found her constitution admirable, comparing it with that of Sparta to their mutual credit and describing it as 'justly famous'.

Relations between Carthage and Rome were at first amicable. The traditional love affair between Dido and Aeneas may represent this brief honeymoon period. In 508, shortly after Rome had expelled her Etruscan kings, the two cities signed a treaty of mutual recognition. A further pact was made in 348, and again in 278, when the Carthaginians sent a fleet to aid the Romans against Pyrrhus. But this harmony came to an abrupt end when Rome was invited by the Greek cities to intervene in Sicily. War broke out, and Rome was forced to acquire a fleet – one hundred quinquiremes, modelled, it is said, on a Carthaginian vessel captured in 264. The rapid growth of Ostia sprang from this new involvement with the sea. The port which had received the Carthaginian ships as allies in 278 was now the supply base for the Roman armies fighting the same Carthaginians abroad. Typically, the Romans designed their ships with boarding bridges and grapples to turn sea battles into land battles; they were always happier as infantry. The historian Polybius says that in the course of the war Rome lost seven hundred, Carthage four hundred ships; at the end of the struggle both powers were exhausted, but Rome was still able to exact a favourable settlement. Carthage surrendered all her Sicilian possessions and promised to abstain from further fighting.

For the next few years Carthage was occupied with internal troubles. A revolt of the mercenaries postponed any new military involvement, and the Carthaginians sought a neutral area for expansion by busying themselves in Spain. But they found that the Romans had interests there also; this was to be the next scene of conflict. At home, Rome took advantage of the hiatus to secure the north. In 220 the Via Flaminia was built, running to Ariminum on the north-west coast. Two years later the colonies of Placentia (modern Piacenza) and Cremona were founded. They were soon to be connected by the Via Aemilia to the existing system. Visitors to Parma can follow the course of this highway through the centre of the city and see the foundations of the Roman bridge preserved in a pedestrian underpass near its modern counterpart.

The resumption of the war in 218 brought to the fore the most successful general that Carthage produced, and a man the Romans looked upon as a combination of ogre and magician. This was Hannibal, whose operations in Spain so alarmed the Romans that they demanded his recall. The Carthaginians refused to disown him, and the fighting in Spain continued across the Alps. Hannibal's feat in crossing the mountains and attacking the Romans at the rear has become legendary. As Polybius pointed out, the Gallic tribes had frequently made the crossing before, but the Roman imagination – exaggerating, perhaps for propaganda reasons, the power of the opponent they were later to beat – attributed to Hannibal almost supernatural powers. He is represented as overcoming fantastic hardships as he struggled against the elements and local tribes:

> Forcing a way where feet had never trod,
> He was the first to scale the ridges, urging on
> His armies far below; and where packed ice
> Lay clamped upon the mountain, and the snow
> Rose sheer to mock their slithering steps, he hacked
> A stairway with his sword. An avalanche
> Of thawing snow would open up its jaws
> To swallow companies; the menace of the wind
> Would fly on black wings from the west and north,
> To splinter snow and drive it in their faces . . . .

> *Nor was the climb the sum of their disaster.*
> *There peered out from the rocks the matted heads*
> *Of men – or animals? – shaggy, caked with filth.*
> *The dwellers of the Alps came pouring from*
> *Their crannies in the rock, and with the ease*
> *Of long acquaintance, picked an easy way*
> *Through the tundra and the snow that was their home,*
> *Scouring the mountains for the trespassers.*[6]

The exact route that Hannibal took is still disputed by archaeologists and military historians. The pass of Mont-Genève and the Col de la Traversette have been suggested. Like Pyrrhus, he took elephants with him; the remains of their stables have been discovered in Carthage. Forty began the journey and only one survived. In 1777 what was thought to be the skeleton of an elephant was discovered in France, together with a small bronze medallion; it turned out later to be an aurochs. Similar discoveries made in 1938 were found to be a hoax. Several attempts have been made in recent years to test the practicability of Hannibal's supposed routes, by leading elephants over them. These have invariably been frustrated, either by the indignation of Humane Societies or by the unwillingness of the beasts themselves, who seem to be less hardy than their Carthaginian forebears.

Livy, in his account of the crossing, contributes another puzzle. He describes, in tantalizingly vague terms, how Hannibal dissolved the boulders in his path by some chemical means. Livy clearly did not know the details himself, and there have been many surmises about how this mysterious operation was conducted. An old suggestion, recently revived in all seriousness, is that the Carthaginians possessed some knowledge of explosives, which was not transmitted to the Romans and remained lost to the Mediterranean world for centuries until the Byzantines discovered 'Greek fire'.

Once he had reached the plains, Hannibal evolved further stratagems to dismay his enemies. A series of lightning victories brought him through Etruria and within striking distance of

Rome. He was eventually defeated by a Roman general who had the intelligence to depart from the customary strategy of pitched battle, and by lack of support from home. Many towns in Southern Italy, including Tarentum and Capua, had deserted Rome for Hannibal. But the Carthaginian foothold in Italy did not prevent the Romans from carrying the war abroad. Spain had been conquered in 205, and Publius Scipio was entrusted with the invasion of Africa. Hannibal, recalled from Italy, left a record of his achievements in the temple of Thurii; it is believed that this document was used by later historians. The battle of Zama in 202, fought on African soil, marked the end of the war. Carthage was forced to surrender most of its fleet and its remaining claims to Spain, and to pay a large indemnity.

Carthage survived for a while. It was not until 146 that it was finally destroyed, in a new outburst of Roman hatred fomented by rival African states. Excavations have revealed a sinister charred layer which marks its fall. The destruction was not total; new temples were later to rise on the old foundations. Although the site was cursed, it was too attractive to remain unsettled for long. In 123, Gaius Gracchus founded a colony there under the name of Junonia. This attempt failed, but a later settlement took root, and in imperial times the revived Carthage became the leading city of the Roman province of Africa. In A.D. 698 it was again destroyed by the Arabs. Its presence is still felt; raking the sands for Carthaginian relics is a favourite weekend occupation in Tunis.

The Punic Wars have been called, with justice, the World War of ancient times. They involved most of the Mediterranean – Sicily, Italy, Spain, Africa – and brought Rome to the forefront as a world power. The city of Romulus was irrevocably committed to foreign adventure, and the conquest of Carthage was rapidly followed by the domination of the old divisions of the Hellenistic world, Macedonia, Syria, and eventually Egypt. It was the beginning of Roman expansion, and of Roman wealth.

Italy was now completely pacified. The last flickers of resistance in the south had died with the defeat of Hannibal; the northern territory, where the Gauls had rampaged in the foothills of the

Alps, was to become, before long, the site of elegant resorts, much as it is now. But the increasing foreign involvement meant that the Romans were less inclined to use the resources available to them at home. The early Romans, like their Italian neighbours, had practised a simple agrarian economy, marked by the strong personal attachment of the individual smallholder to his land. Although the winters can be cruel in Italy – in the cold of 1962–3, there were wolves out south of Naples – the climate is, on the whole, moderate and the land fertile. Water was an abiding problem. There was either too little of it, or too much. Mention has already been made of the marsh on which Rome was built, and one of the earliest works of construction was the great sewer which spills into the Tiber. An increasingly elaborate drainage system helped to keep the city dry; when these pipes cracked and burst in the neglected Rome of the sixth century A.D., the site began to resume the shape in which its earliest builders must have found it. Other cities knew the same problem. South-east of Rome lay the malaria-stricken region known as the Pomptine Marshes, which the Romans made several attempts to drain and reclaim. The work was first begun in 160 B.C., perhaps earlier; it was not until our own century that it was finally accomplished. The traveller driving south from Ostia through the fertile flat-lands crisscrossed with locks and canals may reflect that it was Mussolini's boast to have accomplished what his ancestors failed to do. He is passing through a region where few Romans cared to set foot. Although the Via Appia crossed the marshes, ancient travellers shunned a road which was unhealthy and haunted by highwaymen, and preferred the longer route by ship-canal.

Conversely, there was equal difficulty in securing adequate fresh water. Providing supplies for the growing urban areas called for the extreme of Roman engineering skill. We may look at some of these problems later, in connection with the development of the imperial cities. In the country, as the farming manuals show us, one of the main concerns was irrigation. Travelling through Italy in high summer, one crosses bed after dry bed labelled *torrente*. In winter these may literally become torrents, as the catastrophic flooding of the Arno in 1966 has shown. But for a large part of the year the farmer was forced to find a supply for himself.

Nevertheless, farming was pleasant and profitable. We hear few of the curses hurled by farmers at the arid stony soil of Greece. Varro, writing a manual of agronomy in the first century B.C., compares Italy favourably with the gloomy lands beyond the Alps, praising its several regions and their products:

> Can you name any useful product which does not grow in Italy, and, what is more, grow better than anywhere else? Is there anything comparable to Campanian spelt, Apulian wheat, Falernian wine, Venafran oil? Is not Italy so richly wooded that it looks like one big orchard? Does Phrygia, Homer's so-called 'vineland', produce more vines than we do? Or Argos, his 'corn-land', yield more wheat? [7]

Even Sicily, barren today, was a rich island then; Cicero in prose and Ovid in verse praise its fertility.

In an Italy increasingly urbanized, and enjoying the economic boom which followed her commitment to foreign conquest, the attractions of farming palled. The old tie between the husband-man and his land survived only as a sentiment for poets, or a theme for moralists:

> As Marcus Varro complained in our grandfathers' time, the husbands and fathers have abandoned plough and sickle and crept inside the city walls. The only exercise our hands get is at the theatre or circus, not in the wheat fields and vineyards. . . . But, by heaven, in the good old days the sons of Romulus got their exercise by hunting, and working day in, day out in the fields. They were at the peak of physical fitness. Hardened by their peacetime labours, they found war no hardship when it was forced upon them. The ordinary countryman had a higher place in their affections than his city neighbour.[8]

The Punic Wars, with their exorbitant demands on the citizen manpower, took many farmers from the land, and the eastern conquests brought in large supplies of cheap slave labour. Distributions of the public land in the century afterwards brought about the rapid decline of individual smallholdings in favour of large capitalistic monopolies. Vast areas of land (*latifundia*) were worked by slaves, in imitation of Hellenistic and oriental practice. Some, particularly in the south, were turned over to pasturage. With the influx of foreign corn from the tributary states, the new type of Italian farmer found vineyards a more profitable investment. The peninsula lost both the desire and the ability to produce enough grain to feed itself.

From the earliest times, Italy had been known as good wine-growing country. The Greeks had called the southern half of the peninsula, and especially Calabria, Oenotria – 'the vineland'. These vines were still presumably wild; scientific viticulture may have been introduced by the Greek colonists themselves, or by the Etruscans before them. There is some evidence that the early Romans, for religious or social reasons, regarded wine with suspicion – they preferred to make their libations in milk – but by 350 B.C. it had already assumed considerable economic importance. Italian growths were still *vin ordinaire* in a luxury market dominated by Greek vintages, but the sound principles laid down by the early agriculturists resulted in a number of *grands crus* famous in the ancient world.

A notable document in this respect is the treatise on agriculture written by Marcus Porcius Cato, known to history as the Censor from his most significant public office. He was born in Tusculum, ten miles from Rome, in 234, fought in the Second Punic War and several foreign campaigns thereafter, and was an implacable enemy of all things Carthaginian; his insistence was largely responsible for the destruction of the city in 149, three years after his death. He went into the senate like a Daniel Boone, a cracker-barrel philosopher snorting his contempt for the foreign affectations that were rapidly polluting the old Roman austerity. His manual of farming is the earliest work of sustained Latin prose that we possess. It praises the farmer as the salt of the earth, and sets out in simple business-like language everything necessary to run a small estate. But even this champion of ancient virtues has to face economic reality. Listing the qualities of a good farm, he places a vineyard first, and grainland sixth. Later writers, using

Cato as their basic source and quoting liberally from him, were to agree; it is the universal assumption of the later Republic and the Empire that the farmer's principal concern is wine.

This emphasis contributed to the spread of the capitalist monopolies. Wine-growing involved a heavy initial outlay – particularly in slaves – and a slow rate of return. Smallholders could not hope to compete, and the years which produced the first great Italian vintages (the earliest was the celebrated Opimian of 121 B.C.) marked the end of the traditional methods of agriculture. Sicily, with its volcanic soil, became famous for its vineyards; so did Pompeii. Tastes have changed, and the areas chiefly prized today were not greatly esteemed by the Romans. They found the wines of Tuscany too sour, preferring sweeter vintages which must have tasted somewhat like Greek *mavrodaphne*, and were normally mixed with water: modern Italians still mix their wine with *acqua minerale*.

'The practice of *latifundia*', remarks the elder Pliny, 'has ruined investment values in Italy. Now it is doing the same for the provinces.'[9] Although the authorities continually urged a return to the land, it remained no more than a romantic dream. The young Octavian, at the end of the Civil Wars which shattered the Republic, was assigned the politically disagreeable task of resettling discharged veterans. He found himself faced with hostility on both sides, from the remaining smallholders he was compelled to evict, and from the new tenants who found rural drudgery unpalatable after the profitable adventures of campaigning abroad. Over-production in the wine market and competition from the provinces reduced the land values still further. Several of the emperors tried to improve the situation by requiring political candidates to invest in property; Domitian urged the restriction of provincial wine-growing as a protective measure, and talked direly of nationalizing the Italian industry. The capitalists themselves regretted the short-sightedness of their policies. In the letters of the younger Pliny, written under Trajan, we find a long list of complaints. One of his properties had depreciated to almost half its value as a result of the general agricultural depression; he was losing money on the vintage; his tenants' arrears were increasing; constant bad harvests forced him to arrange for the remission of rents.

It was evils like this that the agricultural writers clearly foresaw. There was always a small, vocal minority in the senate advocating a return to the good old ways, and prophesying that increasing foreign commitments spelt the end of Roman self-reliance. It was not heeded. The voice of Rome became increasingly the voice of the cities; the old simplicity was replaced by an eclectic cosmopolitanism, in which the earliest, and always the strongest, influence was that of Greece.

NOTES TO CHAPTER TWO

1. Strabo, op. cit., VI. 1. 13.
2. Ibid.
3. Statius, *Silvae* (*A Poet's Workbook*), IV. 3.
4. Virgil, *Aeneid*, I. 159–68.
5. Avienus, *Ora Maritima* (*The Shores of Ocean*), 380–9, 406–15.
6. Silius Italicus, *The Punic War*, III. 515–24, 540–6.
7. Varro, *On Farming*, I. 2. 6–7.
8. Columella, *On Farming*, I. pref. 15, 17.
9. Pliny, *Natural History*, XVIII. 6. 35.

Chapter Three

The Rome of Plautus

WE have a large body of inscriptions to help us reconstruct the social and legal systems of the Romans, and archaeology continues to provide new insights into their public and private lives. The vast bulk of our information, however, comes from literary sources; and most of Roman literature is, in a sense, a facade. The orators, poets and historians speak with an official voice and a sense of mission. They create their own style, and virtually their own language, which were not those of the man in the street. The Roman *paterfamilias* did not argue with his wife in the ringing periods of Cicero; to recite Virgil properly demanded special training. This might perhaps give pause to those who advocate the teaching of Latin by the direct conversational method. Most of the Latin that we read was never a living language in the sense that French and German are. It was a highly literary language cultivated by a relatively small segment of the population, and constructed on elaborate formal principles. The truly living Latin was rarely written down. It was the language of that vast, continuous subculture the existence of which we can only occasionally perceive. Its vitality appears in its Romance derivatives. Often it is the Latin vernacular, spoken by the soldiers in the provinces, which yields the modern word, not its official counterpart. French *cheval* comes not from *equus*, 'horse', but from its slang equivalent, *caballus;* Italian *mangio,* 'I eat', not from *edo* but from *manduco,* literally, 'I chew'.

Only at the beginning and end of the classical period – before the social structure had completely hardened, and when it was beginning to fall apart – do we catch the authentic voice of the people in literature. For the early years our source is Plautus, a playwright who made his living by giving the masses what they wanted, and for the later Petronius, a sophisticated novelist who went slumming for his material. Although three centuries apart, they are remarkably similar. They use the same kinds of characters, talk the same kind of language, subscribe to the same philosophy; amusements already old in Plautus's time were still known to Petronius, though our more respectable sources make no mention of them. Plautus gives us an insight into that period of compromise in Roman history when foreign customs and traditions were making their first real impact on native folkways. Petronius suggests the popular survival of these folkways in a country officially dedicated to Hellenism.

Roman literature proper began in 240 B.C. with plays – a fact which shows how instantly pervasive the Greek influence was, for they were Greek tragedies in Latin translation. The Romans had just had their first real exposure to foreign ways of life. Penetrating to the colonies of Magna Graecia, and to Sicily in the Carthaginian wars, the Romans received a cultural shock from which, for better or worse, they never recovered. Greece, as Horace was to remark, subdued its savage captors. The peculiarly Latin talent, vigorous but as yet unformed, yielded to the attractions of a culture that already had centuries of tradition behind it, and preserved, although in muted form, some vestige of the golden age of Pericles. Rome, for all its military strength, had the cultural diffidence of the *nouveau riche*. It did not know much about art, and had not had enough time to find out what it liked. Presented with a set of ready-made standards, it accepted them unhesitatingly. This enthusiasm for Hellenistic culture, though resented and resisted by some – including Cato the Censor – became a cult among a number of notable figures in the state, whose influence pushed artists and writers further along the path down which they were already inclined to go. Given new impetus by the conquest of Greece itself, the movement became all-pervasive. Though critics and propagandists continued to utter plaintive cries of independence, the literary and artistic world set itself to imitate Greek models, and emulate Greek standards.

The first translations were the work of Livius Andronicus.

According to tradition he was a Greek captured at the fall of Tarentum, brought to Rome as a slave and liberated by an enlightened master in recognition of his talent. The form of his name supports the story. Livius, adopted by the slave in honour of his master, is Latin, Andronicus Greek. The form of the story is another matter. It appears so frequently, in connection with artists from the Greeks to the Renaissance, as to create some doubts about its historical accuracy in every case. It may have been a metaphor for a cultural experience which crept into the biographies as fact. If so, it was particularly suitable for the Romans, who could use it to justify themselves as patrons, if not creators. Even if they were forced to borrow talent and ideas, they were sufficiently enlightened to give them scope to act.

The coming of Livius Andronicus to Rome, forcibly or otherwise, set a precedent. The number of major writers and artists actually born in Rome can be counted on the fingers of one hand. Rome was a cultural magnet, as Syracuse, Athens and Miletus had been before, as Berlin was in the 1930s, or as New York is today. It attracted artists from all over Italy and abroad, who found the city a stimulating place to work and a profitable market for their wares.

It was in the drama that early Roman literature found its most vital expression, though most of the writers worked in other fields besides. Livius Andronicus produced a Latin translation of Homer, in native metres considerably less sophisticated than the original, which was still in use as a schoolbook long after his time. Gnaeus Naevius, besides his comedies, wrote the epic on the Carthaginian war already mentioned. Quintus Ennius wrote tragedies, comedies and an epic history of Rome from the earliest times, the *Annals*. But it is the plays with which we are chiefly concerned here. The theatre, as usual, serves as a mirror of its times, and the content, structure and sources of the plays tell us a good deal about contemporary Roman life and manners.

They tell us, first, something about Roman taste. It is evident that the Romans had no real inclination towards high drama. The vibrant fusion of mythic stories and contemporary issues that the fifth-century Greeks achieved in tragedy seems to have been beyond them. Surviving fragments of Roman tragedies suggest that they were pompous and dull, self-conscious elaborations of Greek originals. Nor did the Romans, for all their national pride, succeed in creating a native tragedy. Historical dramas on Italian themes enjoyed a temporary popularity, and the number of plays composed around the Trojan cycle seems to indicate the growing Roman desire to associate themselves with the earlier legend, but the rapid shift of emphasis shows that if a dramatist wished to survive in the theatre he was virtually forced into comedy. This was what the people wanted. Tragedy survived as a cult-art, a recreation for dilettanti, and lost any vital relationship with the living theatre.

The mass audience preferred a theatre that was for entertainment only. This meant a sharp decline in the status of the art. In fifth-century Greece, playwrights had been held in honour and actors appointed to important diplomatic missions. They were servants of the state at the highest level. The theatre was a forum in which urgent issues could be discussed and the public stimulated and provoked. It was, in the most important sense, engaged. Nor was there any significant distinction between amateur and professional. The theatre was a community enterprise in which the citizen body was encouraged to participate on every level.

In the Hellenistic world of Alexander and his successors – the world accessible to the Roman adaptors – this picture had already begun to change. Tragedy became rhetorical, florid and uncommitted. The pungent social satire of Aristophanes became an innocuous comedy of manners. Drama moved out of the mainstream of cultural life. Its practitioners, by now wholly professional, were regarded solely as paid entertainers. Aristotle, in the fourth century, was already complaining about the decline in actors' morals. In the Hellenistic and Roman worlds, individual performers might enjoy the modish adulation of upper society – Cicero, for instance, writes ecstatic tributes to the actor Roscius – but this was no more permanent, and no more real, than the adoration lavished on popular singers in our own time. For the average performer, the profession was thankless, demanding, and poorly paid. It used to be believed that all Roman actors were slaves. We know now that this is untrue, but their condition was little better. The Roman acting company was known collectively as the *grex*, a word more commonly used of a flock of sheep. Their actor-manager was the *dominus*, master. Their dramatists wrote under constant pressure to supply public demand. A play was so much merchandise, sold for a lump sum and thereafter the property of the company to do with as they liked. The playwright had no dignity, and outside his own profession little status. Plautus, forced to consider himself a hack, would be very surprised to find his works studied for their literary value in universities. The theatre had become a commercial enterprise.

It was a system where the playwright had little time or incentive to work inventively. The pressures on him must have been similar to those on the television scriptwriter today: to provide a constant flow of material in a short time, and to play safe. Inevitably, he wrote by formula, and the models he chose were tried and trusted. The Greek comedies of the fourth and third centuries B.C. provided an inexhaustible source of plots, scenes and characters.

We know little of these scripts in their original form. It was the Romans who, by adapting them, preserved them. But we have a good idea of their nature. Designed for the inhabitants of the widening Hellenistic world, they excluded any appeal to local humour or sentiment. They could be equally appreciated in Corinth, Ephesus, Alexandria, Tarentum – in any city where the inhabitants spoke Greek. Their themes were the universal commonplaces of domestic life: marital difficulties, financial problems, parental anger, the tribulations of lovers. Characterizations were simplified to a range of familiar stereotypes: the angry old man, kindly old man, cunning slave, stupid slave, scapegrace son, all easily recognizable to the audience by their distinctive masks. It was undoubtedly the mask, also, that encouraged another familiar type of plot, that of mistaken identity. We know of a whole series of Greek plays dealing with twin brothers. These characters were manipulated according to a system of conventions so rigid as to reduce playwriting virtually to a mathematical formula. The playwright simply assembled a selection of his stock personages, introduced some arbitrary factor which set them in collision, and drew his humour from their predictable responses. Permitted a look into the future, he would have acknowledged a spiritual kinship with Molière at his worst and Sardou at his best; he would have hailed Viennese operetta as his legitimate descendant. Theatre was no longer action, but relief.

This was the legacy to which Titus Maccius Plautus fell heir. We know little of the man. He was born some time about 250 B.C.; his name, which means something like 'Titus the flat-footed clown' may indicate early theatrical connections. He lived through the first major crisis of the Roman state, though we could hardly deduce this from his plays, and his personal fortunes, if we may believe his biographers, fluctuated no less alarmingly. He is said to have lost his money in theatrical enterprises and been driven to work in a mill. While there he began writing comedies, the success of which restored his fortunes. Twenty-one of his plays have survived. He undoubtedly wrote more, but his success was so great that even the Romans did not know how much of the work attributed to him was his own. The name of Plautus attached to any playbill would guarantee an audience, and before the days of copyright managers had no scruples about using his name on someone else's work.

His plays were, in the convenient tradition approved by generations of Roman playwrights, patchwork adaptations of Greek originals. When the writers of *A Funny Thing Happened on the Way to the Forum* combined three plots to make a modern musical, they were applying to Plautus the same treatment he had applied to his own sources. Such adaptations were easy to do, when the plots and characters of the originals were virtually interchangeable. They do not always make good reading. There are many loose ends, and the endings are often, to say the least, perfunctory. When the plot seems to be flagging Plautus has no compunction about introducing another character out of the blue to initiate another set of complications. Whatever enormities the characters may perpetrate on each other during the course of the play are wiped out with a happy ending and general forgiveness. There is little to exercise the mind, and no problem that cannot be solved by a pratfall and a whack of the bladder. The plays belong to the erratic, often brutal world of vaudeville and burlesque. They are scripts for actors, intended to be filled out with a wealth of comic business.

Horace, writing cool criticism in a more sophisticated age, accused Plautus of being interested only in money. Plautus would probably not have found this assessment objectionable. He had the measure of his audience, and gave them what they wanted. There are occasional glimpses of a different Plautus at work, a man who would have liked to attempt something more subtle and escape from his monotonous, if profitable, rut. His prologue to *Amphritryon* contains a wry joke on the audience. The god Mercury speaks:

> First, the favour that I've come to ask,
> And then the prologue to this tragedy.
> What? Looking glum because I said this play
> Would be a tragedy? I am a god.
> If you like, I'll turn this tragedy into
> A comedy, and never change a line.
> Well? Would you like me to? How stupid of me,
> I know you would. The gods know everything.[1]

One can almost hear the audience roaring 'Yes!'

But *Amphitryon* is a comedy considerably more sensitive than most of Plautus's work. It is based on a Greek myth in which Jupiter, the king of the gods, assumes the likeness of the warrior Amphitryon to seduce his wife. Plautus compounds the confusion by having Mercury disguise himself as Amphitryon's slave Sosia. At the end of this comedy of errors, in a peal of thunder, the demigod Hercules is born. It is a familiar story, but significant in Plautus's hands because he does not give it the usual burlesque treatment. Alcumena, the wronged wife, is not the stock figure of farce but a character of considerable dignity and charm. When her husband accuses her, she replies in a moving speech:

> The dowry that a woman brings a man
> Means more to me than what it means to others.
> It is purity and honour, continence,
> Fear of the gods, love for my father and mother,
> Affection for my family. It means
> To know my duty, and to make you rich
> With the gift of my own virtue.[2]

In the same vein, *Prisoners of War* takes another stock commodity of Roman farce, the master–slave relationship, and extracts from it a plea for common humanity:

> I was once a free man, like your son.
> The war has cost us both our liberty.
> He is a slave in my land, I in yours.
> But I know this. There is a god above
> Who watches everything we say and do.
> As you treat me, so he will treat your son,
> And punish or reward as you deserve.
> You long to see your son again. My father
> Longs no less for me.[3]

But such sensitivity is the exception. For the most part, the characters of Plautus move in an amoral world, where the only good is material gain, where the sole function of a father is to be cheated of his money, and where gilded playboys seem to have no other occupation but to seduce girls at festivals, only to discover, by the end of the play, that they are long-lost heiresses or the daughters of their fathers' best friends. It is a world that reflects the cultural ambiguity in which the Romans were floundering. Even the language is in a state of flux. The political domination of the Greeks by the Romans did not mean the disappearance of the Greek language. It was the common tongue of southern Italy, and remained so for a long period; some authorities argue that it was in regular use as late as the thirteenth century

A.D., and point to the survival of Greek dialects in isolated regions of Calabria in our own time. The Greek *koine*, the *lingua franca* of the Hellenistic world, infiltrated Latin at all levels. In Roman comedy, Greek words appear frequently as slang, often with a significant debasement of usage: the prestigious Greek *logos*, for instance, which can mean speech, argument, the exercise of reason or, in the New Testament, the thought immanent in the mind of God, takes its plural form, *logi*, in the Latin vernacular and comes to mean mere words, babble, foolishness. It is a significant change, for it demonstrates the popular Roman attitude to one of the most admired Greek virtues. On a higher level of society, Greek was soon to be used, like French in the Imperial Russian court, as the mark of the educated man. Even in Plautus, we can see how Greek forms and constructions were beginning to modify the Latin language.

The environment of the plays shows the same ambiguity; the settings, as in the originals, are Greek. The characters, though they mostly retain their Greek names, talk sometimes like Greeks and sometimes like Romans. You may even find Roman actors, playing Greeks, referring to their compatriots in the Greek manner as 'barbarians'. Plautus inserts names and allusions familiar to his own audiences. In *The Pot of Gold*, which is supposed to take place in Athens, one character interrupts the action with a song on the Roman traffic problem. *Curculio*, named for the slave who is its chief character, is set in Epidauros, the famous healing shrine in southern Greece. This does not stop Plautus from interpolating a 'crook's tour' of the dubious delights of Rome:

> *Name any kind of man. I'll show you where he is,*
> *So you can find him easily when you want him.*
> *Vicious, virtuous, deserving or despicable.*
> *Want a man who can talk with hand on heart*
> *And tongue in cheek? Try City Hall.*
> *Tall stories? Try Our Lady of the Sewers.*
> *Husbands gambling their fortunes away? Try*
> *The Stock Exchange. You'll know it by the call-girls*

Waiting outside. You can pick up anyone
You want to, at a price. The dining clubs
Are by the fish-market. In the lower Forum
You'll find the respectable bourgeoisie
Taking their daily stroll. The upper Forum
Is the hang-out of the smart set. Scandalmongers
And gossip writers congregate above the lake.
(They'd do well to take a good look at themselves!)
Below the old shops are the moneylenders,
The con-men behind the Temple of Castor,
The Tuscan Quarter is the red light district
Where you can make a living, one way or the other.[4]

This topicality, however, is limited; we look in vain for references to the greater issues dominating the Mediterranean world in Plautus's time. At a period when Rome was fighting for her commercial life, Plautus could offer, in *The Boy from Carthage*, a sympathetic and affectionate portrait of a Punic salesman, travelling in spoons, drainpipes, walnuts and panthers (the Romans called them 'African rats') for the public games. The part was presumably so written in the Greek original, and Plautus has taken it over without change, blind to its incongruity in Rome's immediate circumstances. There are, admittedly, some crude jokes about the Carthaginian's costume and his slaves with rings in their noses, which may pander to popular prejudice. Political comment is conspicuously lacking. Although politicians found plays a useful vote-catching device, this is as far as their involvement went. Plautus's contemporary, and possibly his colleague, Naevius, had written a line in one of his comedies derogatory to the Metelli, an influential family in Rome: *Fato Metelli Romae fiunt consules* – 'it was by accident [not by merit] that the Metelli were elected consuls in Rome', or perhaps, 'It was a black day for Rome when the Metelli were elected consuls'. Romans of a later century, who knew the pasquinade, would have enjoyed the reply. The Metelli answered in a line of similar metre, threatening Naevius with punishment, and promptly threw him into jail.

Plautus alludes to the mishap obliquely in a comedy of his own.

The plays, then, are not social documents in the ordinary sense. Aristophanes, writing in the fifth century B.C., could use comedy to provide a running commentary on contemporary Athens. The conditions of his art and times deny such possibilities to Plautus. His work is still, however, a commentary in a wider sense. It reflects, although in a distorting mirror, characteristic Roman types and attitudes. Imported as a sophisticated novelty, Hellenistic comedy kept its place in Roman life because it possessed an affinity with its adoptive home.

The characters of Plautus, as we have seen, exhibit a simple pattern of behaviour. Each stereotype has his traditional line of speech and action from which he only rarely departs. The characters rarely seek or initiate change; when it comes it is thrust upon them, violently, by a deity or some arbitrary stroke of fortune. In Plautus, these two things are virtually interchangeable. The characters can hardly be said to interact with or modify one another. They are brought into sharp collision. Each has his own set of prejudices, his own particular obsession, his fixed way of looking at things. All, from the *paterfamilias* to the humblest slave cook, are egotists. The humour of Plautus, as in most farce, consists in bringing these conflicting prejudices into opposition. The prime mover in his plots is usually the parasite, a character who had as yet no real counterpart in Roman society (though this was soon to come) but was taken over from the Greek sources as a dramatic necessity. The parasite is an unemployed man-about-town, a sponger, a professional freeloader who lives by his wits, and attaches himself to anyone from whom he thinks he can benefit. Like the other characters he thinks only of himself, but his way of life necessarily brings him into contact with characters of all ranks in life, and every temperament. And so it is his manipulations that bring the others into collision. He is the random factor, the force of chance personified. Without him, one feels, the others would never meet. If they were left to themselves, there would be no play.

In a wider sense, the characteristic patterns of Plautine comedy are those of the society which favoured it with its attention. From early times it had been a society divided. The earliest and most deeply rooted schism was that between the patrician and plebeian classes. How this distinction first arose remains obscure. It may reflect the subjection of an indigenous population to an immigrant conquering race, or conditions of inferiority on which settlers were admitted into an established community. It may possibly derive from a racial distinction, such as that between Etruscans and Latins, or Latins and Sabines. The plebeians, or plebs, were originally excluded from religious and civil offices, from access to the law, and intermarriage with patrician families. With the expulsion of the last of the Etruscan kings in 509, the functions of the monarchy were transferred to elected officials. At the head of the state were two consuls, elected annually. They were empowered to nominate officials to assist them, notably the quaestors, who were responsible for financial administration. For some time the patricians had the monopoly of such offices. Bitterly resenting their inferiority, the plebs fought for their rights with the only weapon available to them, the witholding of their labour. Roman historians record five such strikes between 494 and 287, each resulting in some concession. After two centuries the plebs had some measure of representation, with their own assemblies and officers. They were already represented in the Senate, the advisory council which had been established under the monarchy and survived its fall, though there was a significant difference of title between the patrician and plebeian members. They won the right to stand for the quaestorship in 421, and for the consulship, at least in theory, in 367; for some time representatives of the two orders shared the office, and it was not until 172 that two plebeian consuls were elected.

Although the plebs had won official recognition, Roman society continued to maintain strict divisions. The various orders held themselves aloof. Rank and birth still had their privileges. Free birth did not automatically guarantee equal rights. Many were forced to put themselves under the protection of a more powerful citizen if they wished to enjoy full legal representation, paying for such patronage with their services and attentions. This patron-client relationship, alluded to frequently in the plays, is one of the distinctive features of the republican system. One may see Roman society at this time as consisting of a number of separate units, each jealously guarding its rights and privileges and wary of crossing bounds established by law or custom. Plautus catches the essence of this spirit in *The Pot of Gold*, where he studies the dilemma of a poor man asked to marry his daughter to a wealthy neighbour:

> *You want to know what I think, Megadorus?*
> *You're rich, with a position in society.*
> *I'm poor – the poorest man you ever saw.*
> *If I gave you my daughter, this is what I think;*
> *You'd be the ox, and I should be the ass.*
> *If we teamed up, I couldn't pull my weight;*
> *Down goes ass in the mud, and for all the attention*
> *I'd get from you, friend ox, I might as well*
> *Never have been born. It would be too one-sided,*
> *And my own sort would laugh at me. If anything*
> *Should come between us, then I wouldn't have a place*
> *To call my own, in your world or mine.*
> *The asses would chew me into little pieces,*
> *The oxen run at me and gore me. That's the risk*
> *You run, if you're an ass with ox ambitions.*[5]

The relations between the orders were carefully prescribed by law, and the individual seeking to advance his own career was compelled to follow paths hedged with protocol and regulations. Long before it officially established a civil service, Roman society was tending towards the bureaucratic. Yet in spite of this continued insistence on legality and propriety – or perhaps because of it – the history of Roman politics was one of violence. Change came sharply, and usually by force, as a result of the collision of the various elements of society. This is true not only of Roman, but of Italian history generally; there can never have been a society so concerned with rules and regulations which saw them broken more often. The inflexible system was, in the end, self-destructive.

The pattern of Plautine comedy, therefore, may be seen as a metaphor for the society which cultivated it. If there is any moral principle observable in Plautus at all, it is that the fabric of society must be maintained at all costs. Whatever changes of fortune may affect the characters, they return to their appointed orders in the end. The scapegrace son who steps outside his class to marry a slave-girl finds, inevitably, that she is of free birth and respectable parents and a fit candidate for his hand. Divided families are reunited and long-lost sons discovered. In *The Pot of Gold*, the old man whose peace of mind is threatened when he discovers buried treasure gives it away in the end; he is happy again, for he can go back to being what he was. It is fitting that there should be in this play a character called Eunomia, whose Greek name means 'law and order'. She is a fussy but kind-hearted matron who bustles about setting all to rights, and redeeming the errors of the younger generation. Her spirit presides not only over this, but over many plays.

If the comedies reaffirm the restrictiveness of contemporary society, they also offer temporary release, by ridiculing the institutions of domestic life. Republican Rome prized the domestic virtues, and saw the family as a state in miniature, with its members subject to the same overriding discipline. This too is something that has perpetuated itself in modern Italian life. But the Latin *familia* had a wider meaning than its modern derivatives. It embraced not only those we should now call the family, but relatives, slaves and freedmen, who took their master's name on regaining their liberty and accepted his protection. The word is still used in its ancient sense to describe the papal household in the Vatican. Over this group the *paterfamilias*, the father and the head of the household, reigned supreme. He was given absolute authority over them by law. He had the right of life or death over his children, and there are several stories from the legendary days of the early Republic which show this power being exercised with its full severity. In practice, it was usually tempered by religious sanctions or the restraining influence of the family council. The power of the *paterfamilias*, however, was still awesome. He could, if he wished, sell his son into a state analogous to slavery, or compel him to marry whom he pleased. He was entitled to receive his son's military pay, but not liable for any debts the boy might incur. In Roman comedy, the sons are often at their wits' end to find money; they have great difficulty in borrowing from a moneylender, for he knows he has no legal means of restitution if the son chooses to renege on his debt. The *paterfamilias* in Plautus is usually a figure of fun, but one senses the real power behind the comic image. The very news of his appearance is enough to make sons tremble and slaves hide in corners. Comedy practises wishfulfilment in so frequently frustrating his plans, allowing him to be robbed and cheated, and letting his sage advice fall on deaf ears.

The chief restraining influence on the *paterfamilias* was his wife. Rome placed the matron on a pedestal, and gave her enough rights by law to allow her to take a firm position when the need arose. Marriage was a matter of prudence and arrangement rather than affection; the sons in the comedies are frequently revolting against their father's choice of bride. The marriage ceremony could take several forms. *Coemptio*, the oldest, was a survival of primitive bride-purchase; the husband received his wife in return for a token sum of money. Common-law marriage was also recognized, with the stipulation that the couple must live together for one year before the union became official. A third and more elaborate form, *confarreatio*, involved sacrifices and the eating of a sacred cake. This may have been restricted to patricians, and was insisted upon for certain orders of the priesthood.

Divorce involved even less ceremony than marriage. It required only a simple verbal formula, and no other grounds but boredom. The husband had only to tell his wife to take her things and go. Roman law, however, in its providence, had given the woman one strong safeguard. She was entitled to take her dowry with her. This was usually substantial, and might well either have been spent or so involved in her husband's business that he could not let her go without financially crippling himself. In comedy, this matter of the dowry is the husband's greatest complaint. In *The*

Pot of Gold the millionaire Megadorus philosophizes on the problem:

> It's my opinion that if all our richer citizens
> Followed my lead, and married girls
> Out of the poorer families, without a dowry,
> There'd be more concord in the body politic,
> We wouldn't be so keen to spite each other,
> Our women would be more afraid of trouble
> And we should see the cost of living fall.
> Yes, that'd be best for nearly everyone.
> But there's always a minority of troublemakers
> Who only see what's in it for themselves,
> So greedy and impossible to satisfy
> That neither law of land nor rule of thumb
> Can take their measure. And if anybody says
> 'Who will the rich girls marry, then,
> The ones with dowries, if this poor-law passes?'
> They can marry whom they please, always providing
> Their dowry doesn't go along with them. If things
> Were done this way, our girls would see to it
> That they provide themselves with better dispositions
> Than they have now; and that would be their dowry![6]

In comedy, if the son is always in terror of his father, the father is always in terror of his wife. The archetypal figure of the hen-pecked husband is more immediately meaningful in a parody of Roman society. The wife's sphere of influence was limited to the household – a famous epitaph reads *domum servavit, lanam fecit* – 'she kept the house, and worked at her spinning'–but the Romans, at least in the Republic, practised the cult of 'momism' hardly less than the modern Americans. Plautus shows us the more dignified side of Roman womanhood in Alcumena and a few others like her. But the eternal cry of the nagging wife rings out across the centuries:

CLEOSTRATA: *Insect! Good-for-nothing! It's all I can do*
> *To keep from telling you a few home truths.*

> Look at you! Gadding about, reeking of scent;
> You ought to know better, at your time of life.

LYSIDAMUS: But dear, I was only helping a friend
> Buy a bottle of perfume.

CLEOSTRATA: A likely story!
> Aren't you ashamed?

LYSIDAMUS: Whatever you say, dear.

CLEOSTRATA: You've been with another woman, haven't you?

LYSIDAMUS: Who, me?

CLEOSTRATA: Yes, you! I know more than you think.

LYSIDAMUS: And what does that mean?

CLEOSTRATA: That there's no fool
> Like an old fool. And you're the worst of the lot.
> Where were you? With some woman in a bar?
> Ugh! You're drunk! And look at your clothes!
> What a mess!

LYSIDAMUS: Damn it all – and damn you, too –
> I haven't touched a drop all day.

CLEOSTRATA: Go on, don't pay any attention to me.
> Drink us out of house and home.

LYSIDAMUS: Shut up!
> Enough is enough, woman. Save your voice.
> You'll need it to nag at me tomorrow.[7]

Many a Roman in the audience would have trembled in sympathy with Lysidamus.

The voices of the slaves sound loudly too – cocksure, plaintive, whining, acrimonious. They were as much a part of the plays as of Plautus's daily environment. In Rome, as in Greece, slavery was seen as part of the natural order of things, and justified by the philosophers on the grounds of racial supremacy. It had been an integral part of the Roman system from the earliest times. In an agricultural community, the citizen army came home with prisoners of war and set them to work on the land. The great wars of expansion in the second century B.C. flooded the market with slaves; Julius Caesar was later to bring back fifty-three thousand from one Gallic town alone. Piracy was another source. So was the exposure of children. A familiar situation of comedy is that of the slave-girl who turns out to be a free citizen, and is promptly allowed to marry the young master. Great slave-markets, of which the most famous was the island of Delos, came into existence to deal with the growing traffic. It was a brutal business. 'He must have been a slave dealer' grumbles a character in *The Rope*, after experiencing particularly savage treatment; and the pimp Labrax, who appears in the same comedy chasing some slave-girls from whom he hopes to make a substantial profit, is treated, like all his kind, as odious. Slaves could be bred like livestock. A child born to slaves was automatically the property of his parents' master.

A slave was *instrumentum vocale*, talking furniture; in law he was considered *pro nullis, pro mortuis, pro quadrupedibus*, as having no more existence than dead men or animals. Cato can talk of slaves as casually as his modern counterpart might talk of tractors: while it was more economical to work them to death, it was always possible to trade them in, when their productive value had diminished, to a dealer who would fatten them up for resale. Columella estimates that the cost of a farm slave would be written off in a working life of twenty years. Employers welcomed this source of cheap labour. Cato staffs his model farm with twelve slaves to fifteen free men. Their use contributed to the growth of *latifundia* and the disappearance of the independent smallholder from the land. In the cities they were no less welcome, for they made possible the large-scale manufacture of handicrafts. The proportion of slave to free population in the peninsula of Italy has been estimated as 3:5. The equivalent figure for the United States in 1850 was 1:100.

A slave was the absolute property of his master, who had the power of life and death over him. His evidence could be secured under torture in a court of law. He could be fettered to his labour or forced to work under privileged slaves, 'trusties', who appear in the comedies as whip-cracking, cudgel-bearing thugs. Varro writes of the necessity of having humane slave-overseers. Plautus's picture is probably more accurate. Masters were obliged to care for their property, as they would for any stock, if they wished to protect their investment. Plautus shows us what slave life could be at its worst. If his biography is true, he spoke from personal experience. The master enters cracking his whip:

> Outside! Come on, keep moving! I was a fool
> To buy you, and a bigger fool to keep you.
> Can't you get it into your stupid heads
> To do just one thing right for a change? (whack)
> That's the only treatment you understand;
> The only way I'll get my money's worth.
> Look at those ribs. They're all over welts,
> More like donkeys than human beings.
> A waste of good rawhide, that's what you are.
> Give you a chance, and you're picking and stealing,
> Guzzling my wine, and running away.
> It's safer to use a wolf as a sheep-dog
> Than leave this lot in charge of the house.
> They don't seem too bad when you look them over.
> Making them work is another matter.
> All right! Pay attention! Your master's speaking!
> Wipe the sleep out of your eyes! Look lively
> Or I'll beat you till you look like patchwork quilts.
> You'll be prettier than a Persian carpet.
> I gave you all your duties yesterday,
> But your skulls are so thick you need a thrashing
> To refresh your memory. That's the way you're made. (whack)
> This is wearing me out. The whip's broken, too.[8]

Many employers far surpassed the minimum requirements of good treatment. We have ample testimony from Roman history of the friendly relations that could exist between slave and master. Plautus shows us many households where the discipline is, to say the least, lax; Terence, in the next generation, shows us slaves entering on familiar terms into the intimate affairs of their masters. They still grumble, but more like old retainers than slaves. We have to contribute, they say, to a wedding present for the young master; there will be another gift due when the first baby is born. Is this an accurate representation of Roman slave life? The influence of the Greek sources must be taken into account. Both Plautus and Terence are reproducing, at least in part, descriptions of a society where the life of the slave tended to be less rigorous than it was in Rome. Nor must we forget that the reversal of normal social standards is a familiar comic device. The Roman audiences would have found it just as amusing for a slave to triumph over his master as for a son to defy the power of the *paterfamilias*. Both things belonged to the acceptable world of comic fantasy. The Victorian novelists describing the doings of their servants, and James Barrie when he wrote *The Admirable Crichton*, exploited the same possibilities. Their audiences enjoyed the fictitious antics of a class who in real life were faceless and anonymous. It is doubtful how far Plautus and Terence or the later writers intended their work as social criticism.

In one respect at least Plautus touches on a genuine feature of Roman slavery. He regularly shows us slaves who are wittier, more intelligent, more resourceful and often more moral than their masters. It is Pseudolus, in the play of that name, who engineers a series of plots with hairsbreadth dexterity, and controls the actions of the other characters like a puppet-master. It is Messenio, in *The Twin Menaechmi*, who throws up his hands in horror and lectures his master on the evils of going into a brothel. It is Tranio in *The Haunted House* who invents a phantom to scare the angry father away from the house where the son is carousing. Once again, such a relationship has an obvious comic value, akin to that between Jeeves and Bertie Wooster. We know, however, that it often represents an actual state of affairs. In their conquests the Romans brought home as slaves people far more literate and cultured than themselves. Livius Andronicus was traditionally such a one; Terence, who is said to have been brought to Rome as a slave from Africa, was another. The Romans did, as the stories suggest, often recognize their talents, and give them positions where they could use their skills to the best advantage. They were employed as tutors, or doctors; Plautus shows us a slave doctor in *The Twin Menaechmi* who is threatened with a flogging when his professional questions grow tiresome. Slave-girls bred for prostitution enjoyed some advantages. They were often highly trained in music and the arts to enhance their value. But, however high the status that a slave could reach by the exercise of his particular skill, he could never forget that he was still a slave. In Plautus the amiable bickering between slave and master is interspersed with moments of casual brutality. Messenio philosophically lists the punishments he can expect – 'beating, chains, the mill, exhaustion, cold, starvation'.[9] *Prisoners of War* adds the stone quarries, a punishment considered tantamount to torture. The terrifying power of the master, like that of the *paterfamilias*, is always present behind the fooling.

Plautus shows us also something of the gradations of a slave's life – as rigid, in their way, as those of the masters. The comfortable jobs were in the city, where the slave could work in the town house as cook, butler or running footman. To be sent to work in the mills, where the heavy stones had to be pushed round by hand, or in the country, was the equivalent of being sold down the river. Plautus catches the flavour of these social distinctions of the sub-world in the opening dialogue of *The Haunted House*:

GRUMIO: *Come out of the kitchen, damn your hide!*
      Think you're smart, don't you, with your pots and
        pans?
      You'll be my master's ruin! Come outside!
      If I can only get you in the country
      I'll get my own back, as I live and breathe.
      I'm talking to you, stinker! Out you come!
      What are you skulking in the kitchen for?
TRANIO: *What the devil are you shouting at?*
      At the front door too! Do you think you're on the farm?
      Clear off! Get back to the country, and be damned!
      (hits him)
      Take that! Is that what you were waiting for?

GRUMIO: *Ow! Why are you hitting me?*

TRANIO: *Because you're there.*

GRUMIO: *I won't defend myself. But just you wait.*
Just wait till master comes back safe and sound.
You're eating him out of house and home.

TRANIO: *Why, nothing could be further from the truth,*
You numbskull. How can you eat a man
Out of house and home when he isn't in it?

GRUMIO: *You city slicker, you street-corner idol!*
So you don't like the country! I can guess why, Tranio.
You know you'll soon be heading for the mill.
You haven't much more time to go
Before you join the chain gang on the farm.[10]

In such conditions it was hardly surprising that the slaves revolted. In the comedies the revolts are farcical, and resolved in the general aura of forgiveness and well-being at the finale. In real life, they led to desperate and suicidal attempts which, as the authorities realized, posed a serious threat to national security and could only be crushed by military action. In 198 a conspiracy was fomented by the slaves of Carthaginian hostages at Setia. Slaves in the near-by communities were roused and Setia taken. The city magistrate marched hastily from Rome, conscripting an army *en route*, and defeated them without much trouble, but the fear was a real one, and Rome was for a time put under martial law. Another uprising took place two years later. In 135 a slave war broke out in Sicily, and lasted three years, sparking other outbreaks in Italy. Four hundred and fifty slaves were crucified in one town alone. A second war erupted on the island in 104. Again it took three years to restore peace. On this occasion the authorities were hampered by the lack of troops, but whenever the slaves revolted the owners themselves had to be reckoned with; they resisted any wholesale slaughter of their chief means of profit.

The most famous revolt occurred in 73 B.C., under the leadership of Spartacus. It began in Capua, with a riot in the gladiatorial school where slaves were trained to fight. Seventy-eight escaped, and became the nucleus of an army which Roman historians numbered at ninety thousand. They beat the Romans on five occasions in the march towards the north, where Spartacus hoped that his followers would disperse across the mountains and find safety. They preferred, however, to remain in Italy and plunder. Spartacus led his followers south again to inevitable defeat. It is difficult to find any consistent policy in his actions. Whatever his ideals may have been, his followers did not accept them. In our own time, Spartacus has been hailed as the prototype of the social-ist hero revolting against capitalist oppression. His name was adopted by the revolutionary groups in Germany in 1918, and the Russians celebrated him in a ballet. But there was certainly no such thing as an organized freedom-movement among slaves or any hope – except among a few isolated visionaries – of founding a new, more liberal society. Both slaves and owners accepted the inevitability of the system. The slaves who revolted were only protesting against their own bad fortune. Their principal con-tribution was a negative one. Their revolts contributed, hardly less than the conditions which produced them, to the gradual im-poverishment which reduced southern Italy and Sicily from their early prosperity to the barren condition in which they still exist today.

In Plautus, every slave has the hope of freedom in his heart. Sometimes he achieves it. Roman slaves usually received – by custom, not by law – a small stipend. In theory, they could save this up to buy themselves out. In practice, freedom was more frequently granted as an act of favour. The master could release his slave by a tap on the shoulder and a simple verbal declaration. Messenio, in *The Twin Menaechmi*, is liberated in this manner, though he does not completely trust his master, and prefers a written guarantee. The freedman remained within the *familia*, under his former master's protection. Only a limited range of jobs was available to him, and he normally had to take work that was shunned by respectable society. He could become an undertaker or an auctioneer. Messenio seizes the latter employment eagerly, and ends the play by selling off his master's property:

> The auction of Menaechmus' goods will be held on the morning of today week! Sale of slaves, furniture, estate and property! All to go to the highest bidder, ready money only! Sale of wife too, if anyone wants to buy her! I doubt if the whole lot will fetch five million sesterces![11]

Such work could be highly profitable. The situation of freedmen in Rome was somewhat similar to that of European Jewry, and for the same reasons. Ostracized by polite society, they turned their talents to work that others considered beneath their dignity. We shall see, in the early Empire, how freedmen could become millionaires in their own right. We shall see also how the gradual breakdown of the old social orders advanced several of them to important administrative positions in the state.

Plautus shows us, with healthy vulgarity, something of the daily activities and preoccupations of the average Roman citizen. His successor on the comic stage, Terence, was a man of a different calibre. A comparison of the work of the two men shows how sharply, even at this early date, the levels of Roman taste were beginning to diverge, and that the popular arts were being over-shadowed by works appealing to the cultivated minority. Terence's full name was Publius Terentius Afer. His cognomen, meaning 'African', seems to support the ancient biographical tradition that he came to Rome as a slave. We have seen reasons to doubt this type of story, but it is not necessarily untrue. An argument often advanced against it is that a man to whom Latin was a foreign language could never have become the acknow-ledged stylist that Terence was. There are ample examples from later literature to show that such a development is possible. Joseph Conrad, a Pole, became a master of English prose; Samuel Beckett, an Irishman, prefers to write in French. In the Roman world itself, the cities of imperial Africa produced several writers of high reputation – Apuleius, Tertullian, Augustine; though the comparison is not quite accurate, for these men came from pro-vinces which had already been permeated with Roman culture, and wrote a Latin which was a lively fusion of classical and local styles, much as the French colonies in our time have produced.

their distinctive literature in African French. Nevertheless, it is not inconceivable that Terence had the career that tradition attributes to him. We know, from his own admission, that he found patrons in Rome, though it is not clear who these were; they may have been the influential family of the Scipios. He died young, while travelling to collect more Greek manuscripts for translation.

He left six comedies, enough to show that he did not work under the same pressures as Plautus and wrote for a different type of audience. Although he used the same sources, and cites Naevius and Plautus as precedents for his own methods of collation and adaptation, the resulting products are completely different in mood and treatment. This difference is obvious even before the play begins, when we compare the prologues that the two writers used. There is some argument as to whether Plautus wrote his own prologues or not. This is irrelevant here, as they were clearly aimed at a certain type of audience and, whoever wrote them, designed to perform an elementary function. They take the form of monologues spoken by a member of the company, in or out of character. He warms up the audience before the play begins, cracking jokes with individual spectators and rambling on, sometimes incoherently, about anything that will create a warm and friendly atmosphere. He is like the barker at a carnival side-show, luring the customers inside. Once he has their attention, he outlines the plot. Plautus's opinion of the mental agility of his audience was apparently not high. Not only does the prologue give away the main lines of the action in advance, but the plays labour to explain the obvious. Modern directors, reviving the comedies for more sophisticated audiences, often feel the need to cut these redundant explanations.

Terence's prologues are aimed at a smaller and more cultivated group. He discards Plautus's careful exposition. He can assume that his audience has probably read the Greek originals already: at any rate, they are alert enough to follow a complex plot without assistance. The Terentian prologue is a literary manifesto, a defence against his critics. He talks about his aims and methods, protests against the charge of plagiarism and accuses his rivals of academic pomposity. Translators sometimes omit these prologues, considering them too topical to interest modern readers. It is a pity: they give us a glimpse into the literary salons of the Republic which has its own particular fascination.

Terence also complains, with a genuine note of grievance, about the public indifference to his work. Audiences walked out of his plays, finding acrobats or rope-dancers more amusing. This did not prevent him from having his work performed. It was here that patrons proved themselves useful. His *Mother-in-law* failed twice, and achieved a qualified success at the third presentation. No actor-manager, in the harshly competitive world of the Roman theatre, would have revived a proven failure unless the performance was subsidized. Terence was in the happy position of being able to write as he pleased, without the stress of financial necessity. But like all artists he craved applause. This he did not have from the masses in his lifetime.

It was perhaps the delicate sensitivity of his plays which appealed to the *cognoscenti* but bored the greater public. Though we do not have his sources, we may conjecture that his plays were far closer to the Greek than those of Plautus. He does not compromise, even in small things; his title for *The Brothers* is *Adelphoe*, the Greek word, not *Fratres*, the Latin. There are no local allusions, no Roman topicalities. And, though he uses the same stock plots and characters, his treatment of them is more human. His errant sons have a conscience, and show genuine regret when necessity drives them to act against their fathers' wishes. The fathers show a similar desire for understanding. Terence's comedies explore constructively the no-man's-land of family relationships, and suggest that many problems may be solved by mutual tolerance. In an age increasingly concerned with the generation gap, his plays might well be revived more often than they are. Audiences who have learned to enter the delicately shaded emotional world of Chekhov might find Terence more accessible than the Romans did.

And yet it is Terence who can boast the more continuous tradition. It was scholars who preserved plays, not audiences. Plautus's scripts, like all good farces, do not read well. Terence was another matter. His polished style made him popular with educators; his plays were the European schoolboy's introduction to Latin, until the Victorians found him morally unsuitable, and substituted Caesar, a less fluent and far duller writer. His morality, though pagan in inspiration, was acceptable to the nunneries and monasteries of the Middle Ages. One can see why; he is prolific in proverbs. One is tempted to remark of him, as the old lady said of Hamlet, that his plays are full of quotations. 'He whom the gods wish to destroy, they first drive mad.' 'Fortune favours the brave.' 'I am a man; I think nothing human alien to me.' All these make their first appearance in Terence.

And so Terence was carefully preserved, to inspire Christian imitators and performers; the medieval manuscripts are decorated with pictures of masks and stages which may represent contemporary revivals, or possibly the medieval idea of what the Roman theatre looked like. Plautus, so popular in his own time, survived largely by accident. A number of his plays were discovered after several centuries on a manuscript that had been reused to transcribe the Second Book of Kings. Both Plautus and Terence were used as sources by later writers, and helped to form the shape of modern domestic comedy. Shakespeare took *The Comedy of Errors* from *The Twin Menaechmi;* countless lines of Ben Jonson are Plautine reminiscences; Molière's *Les Fourberies de Scapin* is an almost literal translation of Terence's *Phormio*; Giraudoux wrote what he thought was the thirty-eighth version of *Amphitryon,* but miscounted, for there have been several more. Plautus has now been gloriously rejuvenated on the musical stage. Visitors to Italy may still see the comedies performed in an approximation to their original environment. His words ring out from the theatre in Ostia, as lively in colloquial Italian as in the Latin of the streets in which they were written.

NOTES TO CHAPTER THREE

1. Plautus, *Amphitryon*, 50–7.
2. Ibid., 839–42.
3. Plautus, *Captivi* (*Prisoners of War*), 310–16.
4. Plautus, *Curculio*, 467–83. The place names have been modernized to keep the point of the joke; City Hall is the *comitium*, where the representatives of the people met; Our Lady of the Sewers is the temple of Venus Cloacina; and the Stock Exchange is the basilica.
5. Plautus, *Aulularia* (*The Pot of Gold*), 226–35.
6. Ibid., 478–93.
7. Plautus, *Casina*, 239–49.
8. Plautus, *Pseudolus*, 133–51.
9. Plautus, *Menaechmi*, 974–5.
10. Plautus, *Mostellaria* (*The Haunted House*), 1–19.
11. Plautus, *Menaechmi*, 1157–61.

Chapter Four

Gods, Philosophers and Others

IF we take the plays of Plautus as evidence for their times, one element is conspicuous by its absence: a sense of religious purpose. The trappings of religion are there. Slaves seek sanctuary on altars, the miser hides his treasure in a shrine, characters swear by deities both Greek and Roman. But of religion as a vital force in community life there is little sign. It may be objected that such manifestations have no place in comedy, but their absence is even more remarkable when we compare the plays of republican Rome with those of democratic Athens. Aristophanes shows us a number of major and minor deities – Poseidon, brother of Zeus and god of the sea; Hermes, the divine messenger; Dionysus, the patron of wine and drama; Ares, god of war; Iris, the female counterpart of Hermes; Pluto, the god of the Underworld; the demigod Heracles, and various subordinate members of the Olympian personnel. His travesties are, in their own way, a testimony to the importance of these figures in everyday life. The Greeks lived on sufficiently familiar terms with their deities to make jokes about them, as old friends. Plautus does not pay his gods even the tribute of abuse. In only one play, *Amphitryon*, do major deities appear, and perhaps in this only for topical reasons; it is possible that Plautus wrote his comedy as a parody of a tragedy on the same theme that had been performed in Rome shortly before. The comedies before his time contained an element of religious burlesque. The tragedies retained the traditional divine apparatus. But in popular comedy there is a meaningful silence. The supernatural figures who sometimes appear at the beginning of a Plautine comedy to initiate the plot and put the characters into motion are, like the corresponding figures in their Hellenistic sources, vague, allegorical, and virtually anonymous, like the

Household God in *The Pot of Gold*, or the constellation Arcturus in *The Rope*. They are little more than the spirit of chance personified. The Household God leads the miser to discover buried treasure, Arcturus raises a storm which scatters the characters and begins the complications. Once they have set the action going, they disappear from sight, for their function is over. Once again, the plays stand for their society. They show us a Rome in which religious interest was at best perfunctory, and concerned more with form than substance.

The vitality of Greek religion is seen in its mythology. The Greeks made up wonderful stories about the gods and their intervention in human affairs – stories which, in spite of the unifying effect of the Homeric poems, continued to survive in numerous local variants and were constantly being added to. The major myths, particularly in the hands of the dramatists, served as a basis for creative reinterpretation, and old stories became a vehicle for new truths. This ready flow of imagination has proved a continuous delight and inspiration to artists, but an embarrassment to scholars. It is often hard to disentangle the various accretions to a story and trace the myth back to the nuclear belief or ritual observance that started it on its snowball course. In Roman religion, less difficulty exists. The Romans, more prosaically, borrowed stories, as they borrowed gods, from others. Mythologically speaking, their divinities are barren. It is comparatively easy to distinguish the various strata in Roman religion and trace its development from primitive beliefs to a cosmopolitan system whose supreme tolerance betrays its fundamental lack of conviction.

Any religion, in its formative stages, reflects the most pressing needs of its society. The early Romans, like the early Greeks, were bound up with the soil. They saw spirits at work in the vital functions of the earth and sky; they believed that growing things were inhabited by forces which had to be placated if the work was to go well and the life of the community be assured. The Romans, however, developed very early in their society a fondness for system and particularity which the Greeks lacked. Where the Greek deities were often vaguely defined and overlapping in their functions, the Romans created a divine bureaucracy in which the major gods were surrounded by a number of smaller figures, precisely distinguished in function but not in character. This tendency may have been innate in them; it was certainly encouraged by their association with the Etruscans, whose own religious practices show the same insistence on precision. One of the most interesting Etruscan finds is a model liver, perhaps used to instruct initiate diviners. It is marked with the names of many deities, each located in his exact region in the sky. On the same principle, the Romans imagined the gods of the corn and crops as attended by a host of subordinates, each in charge of his own department: the breaker-up of fallow land, the renewer of the soil, the maker of furrows, the grafter, the plougher, the harrower, the weeder, the reaper, the gatherer, the storer, the taker of corn from the storeplace to the mill.

A few of these rustic deities have minimally distinct personalities. Priapus was a fertility god originally worshipped in Asia Minor, passing to Italy by way of Greece. He was considered to be the son of Aphrodite, or of a nymph, and had a lustfulness appropriate to his parentage and function. He disliked asses, because one had once brayed and alarmed a nymph he was stealthily pursuing; his image, grossly obscene, stood in fields and gardens. Poets amused themselves by celebrating him in verse, such as the trifle attributed to Virgil:

> They bring me roses in the spring
> And apples in the fall;
> In summer, corn; but winter's rough
> And brings no joy at all.
> I hate the cold; and I'm afraid,
> Although I am a god,
> I'll end on some dull peasant's fire –
> My statue's made of wood.[1]

Priapus has his direct descendants in the gnomes still used to decorate gardens. A slightly more sinister figure was Silvanus, the god of the untilled land. His domain thus began where the civilized community ended, and he represented the spirit of wild nature, who had to be propitiated. He is thus somewhat akin to the Greek satyrs whose mythological buffoonery conceals a more dangerous quality.

Similar spirits watched over the hearth and home. When a child was born, a multiplicity of spirits attended him – one to watch over his first cries, another over his first teeth, another over his first steps. The household god, or Lar, was originally the spirit of a departed ancestor. He had his niche in the family dwelling, where it was customary to leave small offerings. Plautus sums up his attributes in the prologue to *The Pot of Gold:*

> *In case somebody's wondering, I'll briefly*
> *Introduce myself. I am the Household God*
> *Belonging to the family you saw me leaving.*
> *I've kept a watchful and proprietary eye*
> *On this establishment for many years now,*
> *For the father of the present occupant*
> *And his before him. . . .*
> *He has one daughter. Every day she comes*
> *To pay her respects, and always has*
> *A pinch of incense for me, or some wine –*
> *Something, anyway – and hangs me round with garlands.*[2]

The Lar was the guardian of the home in the widest sense – of the comings and goings of its inhabitants, of the surrounding property, of relations with the neighbours. He could also preside over crossroads, including those of city streets; thus cities, as well as individual households, could have their Lares. A small temple to the Lares of Pompeii may be seen in the forum, erected to propitiate the guardian powers after the earthquake which foreshadowed the eruption of Vesuvius in A.D. 79. There is a similar structure at Ostia, in the form of a courtyard containing several niches arranged around a central fountain. The individual home also recognized the Penates, who were the guardians of the larder and watched over the food supply of the household.

The life of the average man was beset by such spirits, whose favour he had to preserve to ensure his own success. Roman religion is prolific in spells. We know of one to rid the house of ghosts, to be performed on three nights in May. The householder put nine black beans in his mouth and walked round the house spitting them out one by one. The ghosts were supposed to follow to pick them up. This done, the householder washed his hands and spoke the formula, 'Good folk, get you gone.' He addressed them as good in the same way that the Greeks gave propitiatory titles to the night, the Furies, and other powers they dreaded, not because they were good, but in the hope that they might be. Such euphemisms are part and parcel of early magical and religious observance.

The official gods of the state had more personality. Their chief was Jupiter, who like his Greek counterpart Zeus was primarily associated with the sky and its phenomena. Their names are related – Jupiter means simply 'god the father' – and derive from a common Indo-European root. The sky god was worshipped by the early migrants from the north who imposed their religion, as well as their racial characteristics, on the first inhabitants of the Mediterranean basin. Zeus is regularly 'the cloud-gatherer' in Homer, and presides over the daylight in opposition to his brother Hades, who rules the darkness of the underworld. In the same way, Jupiter is the god of thunder, lightning and weather in general; of light as a potent force; of the full moon. His priest enjoyed particular sanctity, and was restricted to a carefully prescribed range of activities. He was not permitted to see men at work; an attendant walked in front of him to clear the way and ensure that the people were standing idle. He was allowed no contact with war, or with elections. This was not because the Roman elections were violent (though in fact they often were) but because the voting system followed the lines of the military organization. He was not allowed to look on death, for fear of pollution. There was a whole list of unlucky things that had to be avoided.

Jupiter was worshipped on the Capitoline Hill together with the goddesses Juno and Minerva. Juno, the consort of Jupiter, may be equated with the Greek Hera; like her she was primarily a fertility goddess, and in one of her functions, as Juno Lucina, presided over childbirth. Minerva was the goddess of handicrafts. She was regularly identified with the Greek Athena, and had similar functions. Some scholars have argued that she is in fact Athena, imported to Rome through Etruria, but it is more probable that she was of native Italian origin. She had another important temple on the Aventine Hill, which served as the headquarters of a guild of writers and actors during the second war with Carthage. Ennius was one of its members.

Another important native god was Mars, popular all over Italy under various names – Mavors, Marmar, or, in Etruria, Maris. He was the god of fertility and of war. Scholars have argued endlessly over which function came first. It is an unprofitable discussion; the two things had equal importance in the life of the early peoples. He was particularly associated with horses, which were made to race in his honour. He, Jupiter and Quirinus (the deified Romulus) were worshipped by the Salii, a group of priests who performed a war-dance of great antiquity, wearing Bronze Age armour. The shields they carried were supposed to be patterned after an original which had fallen from heaven. Their song, fragments of which have been preserved, was almost totally unintelligible, even to the priests of the Republic.

The god Janus was, like many Roman deities, a personification – in this case of the gate or door (*ianua*). He presided over entrances and exits, comings and goings; since to enter a house one must first go through the door, he became the god of beginnings. As such his name regularly occurs first in the list of deities, taking precedence even over that of Jupiter. The month named after him was first in the reformed calendar, and he was recognized as god of the new year. He was represented with two faces looking in opposite directions. A monument to Janus stood in the Forum, its gates closed in time of peace, and open for war.

With the other gods there is considerable confusion. The rapid spread of Roman contacts with other races led to the adoption of their deities, or at least the names of those deities. It is often impossible to say whether any given god is a native Italian deity or a foreign importation. Several times the functions associated with one deity in Greece reappear in Italy associated with another name. Are we to say that there were originally two gods, one Italian and one Greek, with exactly identical functions, or that the Greek god has been taken over into the Roman system and given a Latin name? Sometimes the transformation is obvious. The Greek name is retained, or slightly altered in transliteration. Roman tongues found occasional difficulty with Greek sounds.

Certainly the idea of the gods as a family derives from Greek influence. In the earliest period the Romans did not attempt to relate the gods to one another. But the family concept, once acquired, had an obvious appeal for a people so much concerned with family unity. The Greek pattern was reduplicated in the Roman religion, with the same general division of functions.

We have already seen Jupiter as the father of the gods and Juno as his wife. Ceres, the corn goddess, was the Roman equivalent of Demeter, the earth-mother, though her primal importance to an agricultural community suggests that she may originally have been an independent figure. Flora, her attendant, is essentially the same goddess in another aspect. Venus, originally an Italian goddess, was identified with Aphrodite. She therefore came to have a special connection with Rome, as the mother of Aeneas by a mortal father; in Virgil she appears as his guide and protector.

Hestia, goddess of the hearth, was a nebulous figure in the Greek pantheon in spite of the fact that she presided over the social centre of the community. Her Roman equivalent, Vesta (the names come from the same root, the Indo-European *wes*) had more prestige. Her shrine in the Forum contained a fire that was never allowed to go out. Tending this fire was one of the chief duties of the Vestal Virgins, a college of six priestesses selected under rigid conditions at an early age, and compelled to renounce marriage for their term of office. On retirement – at about forty – they were at liberty to seek a husband. Few did; Plutarch reports the superstition that it was unlucky. Though they enjoyed considerable power and prestige, and were in frequent attendance at festivals and processions, their life was an onerous one. If a girl let the sacred fire go out, she was whipped. If found unchaste, she was buried alive for the crime of incest, for the Vestals were the daughters of the state. On several occasions they were made the scapegoats for political and military disasters. When Hannibal defeated the Roman army at Cannae in 216 B.C., it was decided that two of the priestesses were to blame.

The shrine of Vesta was a circular building. Plutarch gives the shape a mystical significance – it symbolizes the universe, with the eternal fire at the centre – but Ovid was in closer touch with popular belief when he related it to the primitive huts such as those that Romulus and Remus had built:

> *This brazen roof that now you see was thatched by peasant hands*
> *In olden days; the walls were made of thickly woven bands*
> *Of osier. This little spot, which now supports the hall*
> *Of Vesta, was where bearded Numa's palace stood up tall.*[3]

Numa Pompilius was the traditional successor to Romulus, and the second king of Rome. Some would argue that the first Vestals were the daughters of the royal house.

The shrine of Vesta is one of the most fascinating monuments of the Forum, for it shows the continuous Roman regard for tradition from the earliest times to the late Empire. Destroyed by fire on several occasions (ungracious behaviour, one might think, on the part of its resident goddess) it was always rebuilt in its original shape. One such fire occurred in 241 B.C. The consul Metellus violated the taboo forbidding men to enter the sacred precinct, and broke in to rescue the sacred objects. As a result, he lost his sight. The present form of the building dates from the last restoration, after the fire of A.D. 191 in the reign of Commodus.

The Vestals lived near the shrine in their own house. The ruins now visible show the building as it was restored by several emperors. It had a large central court lined with busts of former heads of the order, and, originally, with columns. Archaeologists discovered several honorific inscriptions to leading Vestals. One reads:

To Flavia Publicia, the most devout and sacred head of the Vestal Virgins, who after passing through every grade of the order and serving the altars of all the gods and the eternal flame, with pious mind day and night, deservedly succeeded to that office in the fullness of time. Erected by Boreius Zotius and Flavia Verecunda his wife, in recognition of her extraordinary kindness, on 30 September in the consulship of our lords the Augusti Valerian and Gallienus.

The house of the Vestals was a self-contained unit, with its own mill, baths, kitchen and dining-room, together with a private chapel for the Lares. Its storehouse was, symbolically, the storehouse of the state, and opened periodically for public inspection. The Vestals' rooms surrounded the courtyard. Even now, the ruins have a cloistered air. It is not difficult to recreate the convent-school atmosphere that the place must have had in antiquity, and to imagine the Vestals, matronly seniors and, as history records, frequently restless novices, strolling around the pools, with the busts of their predecessors glowering down like Distinguished Old Girls, and reconciling themselves to their enforced spinsterhood. They were wealthy enough – the state gave them a dowry in lieu of a husband – but must have been very bored; the festivals which gave them a place of honour among the citizens of Rome must have been red-letter days in their calendar.

The Greek Apollo, god of harmony in all its aspects – in music, health and the body politic – was taken over into the Roman system with his name and functions unchanged. Hermes, the messenger god, was the Roman Mercurius. Mars was identified with the Greek Ares. He was the only native deity who lost by the association. The Greeks had little love for Ares, and exiled him to barbarous domains. Of all the major deities he was the least attractive to the mythmakers. Mars, whose functions were originally much wider, came to share this unpopularity.

To the perplexing hinterland between Greek and Roman belongs Saturn, whose temple stood on the Capitoline Hill. It eventually became the Roman treasury, and portions of its massive structure may still be seen. Scholars have suggested a connection between the god's name and the Latin *satus*, sowing, which would argue him to be an early Italian agricultural deity. The ancients, however, unhesitatingly identified him with the Greek Kronos, the tyrannical father of Zeus. Himself an expatriate, he was a suitable deity for a people who believed themselves descended from an exile: Zeus had expelled Kronos and taken the throne of Olympus in his stead.

Some importations are a matter of precise date and historical record. Asklepios, or, as the Romans called him, Aesculapius, is a prominent example. He was the son of Apollo, and inherited one of his father's functions as the patron of the healing arts. He figures variously in Greek sources as a god, demi-god or mortal – in one story he was killed by a jealous Zeus because he had the power to raise the dead – and had his principal shrine at Epidauros. This was the Greek equivalent of Lourdes, and a popular place of pilgrimage. Thousands came there to be healed; mementoes of their visits and thank-offerings for their cures, which appear in many cases to have been genuine, have been discovered. In 293 B.C. Asklepios came to Italy. A plague had broken out and the authorities, acting on prophetic suggestion, sent to Epidauros, where, according to the tradition, the god appeared to them in the form of a sacred snake and promised to accompany them to Rome. The snake was undoubtedly genuine; it was a regular feature of the healing shrines. When the boat sailed into the Tiber the snake slipped overboard and swam to the island now known as Isola Tiberina. This spot had mystic associations of its own: according to Livy, it had been formed originally by the dumping into the river of corn grown on sacred ground and so unsuitable for human consumption. Livy suggests that the silt collected around this nucleus, and that the Romans eventually strengthened it artificially to make the basis for a temple. The cult of Aesculapius had its Roman centre here. In the Roman imagination the island was shaped like a ship, and accordingly decorated: part of the stone poop may still be seen. Later still, and most appropriately, the hospital of San Bartolomeo was built on the same site.

The Roman religion thus absorbed most of the major and minor figures of the Greek pantheon. This ready acceptance of foreign deities betrayed a fundamental spiritual dissatisfaction. The Romans, as we have seen, were not a readily imaginative people. Their native deities were humdrum, workaday figures compared to the vivid personalities with which the Greeks invested their gods, nor were they able to use the traditional divine framework as a frame of reference, as the Greeks had done, within which to conduct philosophical investigations. The Roman religion was spiritually barren, and the greater part of it came at second hand. Why, then, did it have such importance in Roman society? To what extent did the average Roman believe in it? It is important to clarify what we mean by belief in this context. Obviously, few Romans believed in their gods as a Christian believes in Jesus Christ and sees him as a saviour and redeemer. Equally few, on the other hand, dismissed their religion as a hollow sham perpetuated by the upper classes for political purposes – though this argument is occasionally raised. The state religion can most usefully be seen as an emanation of the principles of social order and moral restraint that guided the people in their everyday lives. The temples and their attendant ceremonies were visible manifestations of the spirit of republican Rome. Religion, morality and political well-being were intimately connected. It is for this reason that most educated Romans gave the gods their willing adherence; it is for this reason, too, that the Emperor Augustus was able to conceive of social and moral legislation as parts of the same programme, and couple both with a religious revival.

Roman religion was largely a matter of propriety and state-ordained observance. The priestly offices were sought, like political appointments, as a means of social advancement. In the increasingly elaborate apparatus of the state religion the presiding body was composed of the *pontifices* – originally three, but increased to sixteen by the time of Julius Caesar – under the leadership of the *pontifex maximus*. In historical times the latter was an elected official who also controlled the fifteen *flamines*, each responsible for the cult of one god, the Vestals, and the *rex sacrorum*, who had inherited some of the religious functions of the early kings. These functionaries were chiefly concerned with the complex ritual which proliferated as any genuine religious feeling waned.

Most Romans would have been conscious of religion mainly as a social function. The number of festivals expanded alarmingly. As Ovid was later to remark, 'It is expedient that there should be gods.' The authorities undoubtedly found it expedient to use the gods' festivals to boost public morale. Celebrations could take various forms. They usually involved processions. One example, interesting because it shows how elements of primitive folk ritual remained embedded in the elaborate state system, is the familiar *lustratio* or ceremony of purification, which involved a rite rather like the 'beating the bounds' occasionally surviving in Christian usage. Cato gives the formula for purifying farmland. A sacrificial pig, ram and bull were led around the desired area, and various prayers offered, including one to Mars:

> Mars, our father, I pray and beseech you, look kindly on me, my home and all that dwell herein: for which purpose I have bidden these animals to be led around my land, my ground, my farm, that you may ward off, avert and keep away sickness visible and invisible, barrenness, devastation, and all malign and untimely influences; that you may permit my harvests, my grain, my vines and plantations to grow and bring forth fruit, preserve the well-being of my shepherds and my flocks, and give good health and strength to me, my house and all that dwell herein. To this intent, to the intent of purifying my land, my farm, my ground, and of making expiation, as I have said, for my wrongdoings, deign to accept the offering of these sucklings, who are given to you.[4]

On a public level, the same ceremony could be used to purify a people, a city, an army: every five years the censors conducted such a *lustratio* of the city of Rome.

The favourite public festivals were those which, in the Greek manner, involved athletic contests or the performance of plays. One may catch something of their flavour in the garrulous prologues of Plautus, addressed to a jolly holiday crowd, or in Terence's complaints about the events with which he had to compete. The Romans added the less desirable attraction of gladiatorial games, which were borrowed from the Etruscans. They appear first in a religious association, as part of a funeral ceremony in 264

B.C., and may have originated in memory of the custom of human sacrifice. Acquiring rapid popularity, they soon lost, like many of the other elements of Roman festivals, all traces of religious usage, and survived as an all too familiar blood sport.

In its public manifestations, therefore, the Roman religion tended to lavish ceremony which had a mass appeal, and could, in the wrong hands, easily be manipulated for political purposes. In its language and liturgy, it relied on elaborate and precisely worded formulae. Cato's prayer, quoted above, shows an almost legalistic concern to cover all possible eventualities. Correctness in phraseology is of the utmost importance. In other aspects of their religious behaviour the Romans exhibited the same concern with ritual. The sacrifice of an animal could only be carried out according to rigid rules. First, the victim had to be unblemished, with no mark or deformity that might make it unsuitable in the eyes of the god. Its head was sprinkled with wine and fragments of a sacred cake. The sacrifice was then conducted in an atmosphere which has been described as 'religiously sterile'; no distraction was allowed to intrude upon the ceremony. A flute-player played throughout to drown improper noise. The priest's head was covered to keep evil influences from his own eyes. If anything went wrong, the whole ceremony had to begin again. After the sacrifice, the beast's internal organs, especially the liver, were examined for omens.

The Roman emphasis on the forms of worship is particularly obvious in divination. The art of reading the future by signs was, as we have seen, another Etruscan legacy; it may also be regarded as a further example of a primitive belief surviving in a sophisticated urban culture. There were a number of recognized methods of divination in the ancient world – Tacitus, for example, mentions the German custom of tossing strips of bark in the air and foretelling the future from the pattern in which they fell – but the Etrusco-Roman system was divided into three principal branches: the observation of heavenly phenomena, the observation of bird-flight, and the interpretation and explanation of the entrails of a slaughtered animal. In primitive societies, where the senses were more closely attuned to nature, the first two of these, and to a certain extent even the third, may have had some basis in empirical observation and even have achieved a certain measure of success. The survival of this pseudo-science, and the enormous importance it achieved in historical times, is none the less extraordinary. It is as if the reading of tea-leaves were taught at the doctoral level in universities, maintained at state expense and allowed to influence government policy; it is as if a whole civilization followed the personal foibles of Napoleon and Hitler, and allowed its decisions to be governed by astrologers.

In Etruria the diviners were members of the priestly nobility, educated with care – probably in special schools – in the various branches of their profession. Even in the late Roman Empire the Etruscan diviners were still famous. In the second century B.C. the senate decided to select and train ten boys of noble family in each Etruscan city. A diviner accompanied each army: chickens accompanied the troops into action, and battle-plans were decided in accordance with their behaviour. Rome had its College of Augurs, whose responsibility was not so much to foretell the future as to look for signs of divine favour, or otherwise, in regard to any given plan of action. As late as the fourth century A.D., the Code of the Christian Emperor Theodosius decreed that if the imperial palace or any other public buildings were struck by lightning, the diviners were to be consulted. No business could proceed without taking the auspices, and the necessary ceremony became a clog on every public activity, offering obvious opportunities for trickery and deceit. Seneca, in his Latin dramatization of the Oedipus story, gives, albeit in fictional form, a sense of the awesome ceremony which surrounded the undertaking; it is noteworthy that in this play the blind prophet Teiresias of Sophocles' Greek version, who speaks from his own god-given intuition, is accompanied by the full apparatus of Roman divination. The heifer is slaughtered and dire predictions read from the entrails:

The natural order of the parts is changed.
Nothing is seated in its proper place

But all lies backwards. The lungs are on the left
And full of blood, not air; the heart is where
The lungs should be, and where the folds of fat
Should wrap and shield the entrails, there are none.[5]

We see the other side of the coin in the comic writers who tend to use the word *hariolor*, literally 'to foretell the future' as an equivalent for 'to lie, to talk nonsense'. But, whether credited or not, the art of divination remained a powerful political force. Notable portents were published in the annual calendar. An unfavourable reading of the omens could have the same effect as a filibuster in the American Senate, and delay business indefinitely. Conversely, a favourable reading might be engineered to sway public opinion in favour of a dubious project. In 200 B.C. Rome was debating the probable success of a war with Macedonia. The consuls were directed, on the first day of office, to sacrifice to such deities as they might select. The diviners were presumably primed, the omens were favourable, and war was declared. Similar circumstances attended the beginning of the war with Syria some years later. The intellectuals scoffed. Cicero has some caustic things to say about portents:

> It was reported to the Senate that it had rained blood; that the river Atratus had run blood; that the images of the gods had sweated. Do you think that Thales or Anaxagoras or any scientist would be impressed by such announcements? Sweat and blood can only come from the human body. . . .
> Then are we to be terrified by stories of portents from some animal or human source? Let me be brief; such cases are susceptible to the same explanation. Any phenomenon, of any sort whatever, must have a natural origin. To say that it is unusual does not mean that it is unnatural.[6]

But the voice of reason had as little effect as the hoots of the comedians. Archaic, ponderous, irrational, outmoded, the divining art remained entrenched in Roman public life.

The Romans sought supernatural assistance in other ways, notably from the treasured collection of the Sibylline Books. These were Greek in origin, being a compilation of random prophetic utterances attributed to a mystic female figure, half human, half divine, inspired by Apollo and known as the Sibyl. In the sixth century B.C. she was located in various parts of Greece, and as the legends of her wanderings spread she came to be regarded not as one figure but as many. Her name became generic. Varro listed ten Sibyls resident in Persia, Libya and various parts of Greece and Italy. The most important for the Romans was the Sibyl of Cumae. In the local tradition, probably modelled on the Greek story of Cassandra, she had been pursued by the god Apollo. Ovid makes her tell her own story as she deprecates the honours offered to her by Aeneas:

> 'I am no goddess,' said the Sibyl. 'Do not be misled.
> You must not lay the sacred incense on a mortal head.
> I could have had eternal light. I could have lived for ever
> If I had taken Apollo, when he sought me as my lover.
> For while he still had hope he tried to bribe me to give in,
> And said in his desire to me, 'Sweet maiden, you may win
> Whatever favour you may ask.' I took a heap of sand
> And asked him for as many years as I had grains in hand.
> Oh, what a fool! I should have asked to keep my youth as well.
> But I forgot. He gave the years, and promised he would sell
> Eternal youth for my virginity. I told him no.
> No man has ever had me. But that was long, long ago.
> And I am wretched now, and sick; and this I must endure.
> But seven hundred years have passed. There are three hundred more.'7

And Petronius writes the sad epilogue:

> I even saw the Sibyl of Cumae with my own eyes, hanging in a bottle; and when the boys shouted 'Sibyl! What do you want?' she used to answer, 'I want to die.'8

Virgil also describes the meeting between the Sibyl and Aeneas:

> Cut in the great rock face there is a cave
> That has a hundred entrances, a hundred
> Mouths to utter when the Sibyl answers.
> They had reached the threshold, and the virgin cried
> 'It is time to ask the fates; the god is here,

Behold the god!' And as she stood before the gates,
Even as she spoke, her features were transformed,
Her colour changed, her hair fell wild upon
Her shoulders, and her breast heaved as the fury
Swelled and possessed her from within. She grew
Before their eyes, and spoke in a voice
That was no longer human.[9]

Her cave may still be seen at Cumae. It is a long, narrow passage carved out of the rock, with a series of side-passages providing air and light, and ending in the small square chamber of the oracle. The ruins of a temple to Apollo stand nearby.

In the Roman tradition her utterances were written down – at first on palm leaves – collected and consulted. Nine books of prophecy were offered to the last king of Rome, Tarquinius Superbus. When he refused they were gradually burnt before his eyes, until at last his curiosity overcame him and he bought the last three. These were kept in the city, and frequently studied; they were destroyed when the Temple of Jupiter on the Capitol, which housed them, was burnt down in 83 B.C. The senate ordered a new collection to be made to replace them. This seems to have been done haphazardly, with no attempt to distinguish between material of genuine antiquity and the spurious prophecies which by that time were circulating in considerable numbers. Fourteen books are still extant, containing a number of blatant forgeries inspired by Jewish and Christian sources.

The Sibylline Books were consulted in times of national crisis. As many of the oracles came originally from abroad, they were interpreted as instructions to bring foreign deities into Rome, and contributed to the existing tendency to look outside Italy for religious stimulus. Their form – the new collection seems to have consisted mostly of short Greek hexameter pieces – had some influence on the Roman poets, notably Catullus and Virgil. They have also had a strong fascination for Christian writers. Virgil, in his fourth Eclogue, combined a conventional ode on the birth of a child with Sibylline prophecy to produce a cryptic poem that has become widely known as the 'Messianic' Eclogue, and has been piously interpreted by some as a mystic foresight of the birth of Christ:

And now the world ends, as the Sibyl has foretold
And the cycle of the ages recommences.
The Virgin comes again, and Saturn's reign,
And earth receives a Child conceived in heaven.
Holy Lucina, look with favour on him
At the moment of his birth; before his sway
The iron race shall vanish, and across the world
Another Golden Age shall see the light.[10]

We do not know who the child was, though several possibilities have been suggested from the distinguished families of the time. But the heralding of a new Golden Age struck a sympathetic chord among Christian apologists, and gave both Virgil and the Sibyl a standing considerably higher than that usually enjoyed by denizens of the pagan world, protracting the influence of the Sibylline Books long after their last official consultation in A.D. 363.

What the state system failed to provide was satisfaction for the individual. For this reason the mystery cults, which promised a more intimate relationship between the worshipper and the divinity, exercised an early attraction. The spiritual hunger of the Romans, which led them constantly to seek for new deities, attracted them to the more exotic foreign cults. In 205 B.C., while Hannibal was still in Italy, the Sibylline Books were consulted and interpreted as urging the importation of the Great Mother from Phrygia, in Asia Minor. This goddess, also known as Cybele, was a survival of the earliest fertility cults of the Mediterranean, and worshipped in conspicuously un-Roman ways. The authorities took care to provide against the more sensational aspects of her cult, in particular her attendance by eunuch priests – it was forbidden that these should be Roman citizens – but the emotional reaction to so exotic a deity can be gauged from the later poem of Catullus, an account of the mythic Attis who became her acolyte:

> But hasten one and all, and follow me
> To Phrygia, to the home of Cybele
> Deep in the forest, where the cymbals cry
> And the deep drum answers, where the curved pipes play
> Their eastern melodies, where Maenads dance
> Their mad revel with ivy in their hair
> And moan in ecstasy to celebrate
> The coming of the Goddess, as she haunts
> The woods with her wild company.[11]

Cybele arrived in the form of a black stone, was brought ashore by a young Roman of unimpeachable character and carried to the city by a procession of matrons. In local tradition, her arrival was attended by miracles: the ship ran aground, and seemed to be irremovably stuck until a Roman wife, about whom there had been some scandal, prayed the ship to follow her if she had been chaste. The ship moved, confuting the gossip-mongers, and the anniversary of its arrival became one of the major Roman festivals. Cybele's arrival produced rapid results – a bumper harvest and the expulsion of Hannibal from Italy.

The scandalous possibilities inherent in the worship of Cybele were kept under control. This was not so easy in the case of another, far better known deity, the Greek Dionysus. Originally an Asiatic god, he had come late into the Greek pantheon, and always retained strongly marked eastern characteristics, even after he had infiltrated into established cults. His worship, like that of Cybele, was of a type foreign to both the Greeks and Romans, involving orgiastic celebrations by women who were drunk both with wine and with religious ecstasy. It is clear from the Dionysus myths that the early Greeks regarded him as a social menace. There are frequent stories of resistance offered to the new god by a local ruler; it is always the god who wins, and his opponents who are punished in horrible ways. The same social disruption that these myths reveal attended the god's arrival in Rome.

The Romans already had their Liber, a fertility god of corn and wine. It is unlikely that many of them recognized the identity of

Liber and Dionysus, for the native god was comparatively respectable. His worship lacked the more degrading features of the cult in Greece. Rome had a temple to Ceres, Liber and his female partner Libera, built in 496 B.C. and dedicated three years later. It was not until three hundred years afterwards that the full impact of Dionysus worship hit the city. Livy gives the story:

> A Greek, a man of no rank or birth, entered our country by way of Etruria. He was possessed of none of those many arts which his people, with their unequalled reputation for learning, have brought to us for the cultivation of our minds and bodies. He was an amateur diviner and fortune teller, and spread his pernicious creed not by frankly disclosing his beliefs and advertising his profession in public, but by rites performed in secret, and under cover of darkness. The initiation ceremonies, which were at first carefully restricted, began to attract increasing numbers of adherents among both men and women. Any religious element in these ceremonies was made more attractive by the orgies which accompanied them. Under the influence of wine, mixed company and the mingling of age groups, all vestiges of modesty were abandoned and every variety of debauchery was practised. Everyone found his own particular vice catered for. Nor were these confined to sexual licence. Out of this devil's workshop came false witnesses, forged wills, seals and evidence, and even poisoning and murder of relatives. Often the bodies disappeared before they could be buried. A number of crimes were committed by guile, and even more by violence. The latter passed unnoticed, for amid the howling and the crash of drums and cymbals the cries of the sufferers could not be heard as the debauchery and murders proceeded.[12]

The extent of the cult and the nature of its practices were revealed to the senate by informers. Terrified, the authorities acted with unusual good sense. As was to happen later in the case of Christianity, they were concerned, not so much with the appearance of a new deity, but with the undesirable social manifestations of the cult; they were particularly alarmed by anything that smacked of secrecy, and of an inner group owning other allegiances than to the body politic. In a decree of 186 B.C. (which has the additional interest of being one of our best pieces of evidence for early Latin) they refrained from banning the cult outright; this would only have driven it underground, and made martyrs of its adherents. Instead, they hampered it with so many rules and regulations that only the most determined celebrant would consider it worth the trouble. If anyone considered himself bound by necessity or tradition to worship this god, he could make a declaration before the city magistrate, who would consult the senate before granting permission. A quorum of one hundred was required for the decision. If the permission was granted, the applicant was allowed to celebrate the rites provided that not more than five people – three women and two men – were present. The pernicious influence was thus contained, if not eradicated, and senatorial scruples satisfied. We may ascribe this particular manifestation, perhaps, to the lax morality of the post-war years. It was by no means the last. The Bacchic scandal was followed by other cults no less curious. The popular hunger for colour in religion, and emotional satisfaction, was unappeased. We shall see further examples under the Empire.

The intellectuals sought satisfaction in more austere and recondite ways by taking refuge in philosophies that either denied the existence of the gods, or relegated them to a position where their influence on human affairs was minimal. A sceptical attitude reveals itself in the earliest Roman philosophical works that we know, two poetic treatises by Ennius. His *Epicharmus*, a study of nature and the elements, seems to have been influenced at second hand by the Pythagoreans (who had settled in Italy and practised their curious blend of mysticism and mathematics in the south) and it offered a physical interpretation of the universe. His *Euhemerus* was named after a Greek writer who had, somewhat in the manner of *Gulliver's Travels*, used the form of the wonder-tale to attack certain popular attitudes of his time. He had described a fabulous journey to the island of Pancheia in the Indian Ocean, where he found a golden pillar inscribed with the deeds of the three generations of rulers of Olympus – Uranus, Kronos and Zeus. This revealed that the gods had originally been mortal kings, deified by their subjects in gratitude for their achievements. Ennius popularized in Latin a work which seems to have had little effect in the original Greek.

The official attitude towards foreign philosophers was, at best, unfriendly, though individual Philhellenes welcomed them and responded to their teaching. It is here that the Roman ambivalence with respect to things Greek most clearly reveals itself. In 155 B.C. the philosophers Carneades, Critolaus and Diogenes arrived in Rome as ambassadors from Athens. They were met with coldness by the senate, especially by Cato, and ordered back home. Some ten years later another philosopher, Panaetius, who had studied in Athens and Rhodes, arrived; he was given a cordial welcome by the Scipios (the same family which, it is believed, had supported Terence) and thereafter divided his time between Rome and Greece. It was not until later, when the military campaigns of Pompey, Caesar and Antony had begun to broaden Roman minds and make them more receptive to foreign ideas, that the Greek philosophy took root in Italy.

Speculative philosophy enjoyed little vogue in Rome until Cicero. 'Philosophy has been a neglected field,' he says, 'until our time.'[13] When they eventually accepted the Greek philosophy, the Romans imparted to it their own practical tendency. The Romans were apt to select what was most easily assimilated, and to modify this by giving it a more practical character. They were not metaphysically inclined, nor did they share the Greek delight in abstract discussion. The classical philosophy of Socrates, Plato and Aristotle had been deeply concerned with the well-being of man, with the nature of true happiness, and with the study of how man could attain to such happiness by the rule of reason. Above all, it had been a critical philosophy, devoted to the stripping away of false preconceptions. It recognized no easy solution, and offered no convenient formula for the attainment of happiness. On the contrary, it had demanded a long process of study and self-examination, full of difficulties and with no promise of ultimate success.

With such matters the Romans had little to do. Their philosophical attitudes reveal their natural traits. They sought systems that were practical in their ends, and subordinated theory to laws of conduct. For this reason the later Hellenistic philosophies were more immediately attractive. Their schemes were easy to grasp and readily assimilable. They offered what appeared to be infallible formulae for the attainment of inward security.

Panaetius, the friend of the Scipios, was a Stoic. He belonged to a school which had been founded in Athens about 300 B.C., and enjoyed a continuous existence as an organized body until at least A.D. 260; which was to number Roman soldiers and statesmen, as well as professional philosophers, among its devotees; and which was to influence men of such diverse character as Cicero in the moribund Republic, Seneca in the turmoil of the early Empire, and Marcus Aurelius in the first decline of Roman power. The Stoics took their name from the *stoa poikile*, or painted colonnade, in which Zeno, the first head of the school, had taught. They had a widespread following. Among their disciples were Aristos of Chios, Herillus of Carthage, another Zeno of Tarsus, and Diogenes of Babylon. The writings, though voluminous, were extremely dull, lacking Plato's dramatic immediacy and sense of style, but they appealed to the Romans because they came to be more and more concerned with matters of practical conduct, and seemed to prove by reason things in which the average Roman was already inclined to believe by instinct.

For the Stoics, as for Socrates, virtue was knowledge, but they admitted the existence of nothing which was not perceptible to the senses. Plato's concept of an ideal world transcending its material counterpart, which the soul could contemplate only after long and arduous spiritual discipline, had no meaning for them. They considered the soul to be a body like other material bodies. Blank at birth, it received impressions from the objects perceived, and gradually acquired a store of such impressions which, when grasped firmly enough, could be called 'knowledge'. The Romans, who preferred hard facts to abstractions, found such a doctrine acceptable. Increasingly prone to deny the existence of any immaterial factor operating on human affairs, the intellectuals, by virtue of their temperament and upbringing, also found it easy to accept a philosophy that taught that virtue was, in fact, conformity. In Stoic eyes, the aim of the philosopher was to adjust himself to the world about him, to effect an agreement between his mental capacities and the physical universe, and to live in uniformity with nature.

Stoic physics saw the world as permeated by the cosmic principle of *pneuma*, or divine fire, which gave nature its form and order. Matter was eternally generated from this fire, and periodically re-absorbed in it. The popular idea of early Stoicism was that of a cyclic conflagration, in which the universe would periodically be consumed and born anew. But there was no concept of progress. Each cycle would be an exact repetition of the last. Although later Stoics tended to discard this aspect of the theory, it continued to have some currency in Rome, where it blended with the mythic view of the world as a succession of ages, progressively degenerating from the Golden, through periods denoted by baser metals, to the corruption of the writer's own times. Tacitus, composing his history of the early Empire, saw a steady decline of morality from the golden days of the early Republic: when Vesuvius erupted in A.D. 79 many a good Stoic thought that the end of the world had come.

Such a philosophy necessarily involved a deterministic view of the universe. All things were predestined, and doomed to eternal repetition. Nothing could be changed by human prayer or divine intervention. Man's whole end and object in life was to arrive at an understanding of the divine reason and to live in conformity with it. He was ultimately forced to accept the decrees of fate, and had liberty only insofar as he could choose the willingness or otherwise of his acceptance. The best adjustment could be made by following the voice of reason and refusing to be misled by the passions.

Stoicism, which urged the individual to regard himself merely as one element in a larger pattern, assigned man a unique position in the universe. He differed from the animals in that he was formed by nature for social union, and thus had a daily incentive to the right use of reason; the circumstances of his environment encouraged him to think of himself as a member of a greater body. This emphasis on the potentialities of man flattered the

Roman conception of themselves as a *herrenvolk*, a master race.
So Cicero:

> Nature has given men hands. What ready instruments they are,
> and how many arts they serve! The flexibility of the joints allows
> them to be opened and closed with ease; and so, with a simple
> movement of the fingers, the hand may paint, model, carve, sculpt,
> and play strings or flute. As with the pleasures, so with the necessities
> of life: I mean agriculture, housebuilding, the weaving and stitching
> of clothes, the various ways of working bronze and iron. And so it
> is obvious how the inventions of the philosophers, given practical
> application by manual skill, provided us with cities, walls, houses
> and shrines. So, by the work, or rather by the hand of man, we have
> food in abundant variety. It is the hand that gathers the bounty of
> the fields, for immediate consumption or storage against later need.
> We trap or breed the beasts of earth and air and water, and by this
> means are fed. We tame the four-footed beasts to carry us, and make
> their strength and speed our own. We lay yokes and burdens on the
> backs of animals; we turn the super-sensitive instinct of elephants,
> and the keen scent of hounds, to our own purposes; we draw from
> the caverns of the earth the iron we need to cultivate the land; we
> have found the buried veins of copper, silver and gold and harnessed
> them to our own use and pleasure.[14]

Similarly, the emphasis on community obligation gave theo-
retical support to a society which already placed enormous stress
on social duties, urged citizens to compete for the elective magistracies and seek honourable advancement in public service, and
supported with moral encouragement and legal sanctions the
virtues of family life.

As a sop to the traditional religion, Stoicism found room for
the gods by a process of allegorization. For an educated public
that was already in revolt against the old theology on both scientific and moral grounds, the philosophers proposed to make the
myths symbols of scientific truths, and ritual an incentive to
honest living. Jupiter, in this argument, stood for the most important element, the fiery heaven. The affiliations of Vulcan, the
god of volcanoes, smiths and forges, were similarly obvious.
Neptune stood for water. Other deities were regarded as personifi-
cations of acts or feelings. Once again, this was readily acceptable
to a society where, as we have seen, the gods lacked personality

and tended to be little more than everyday actions given a proper name. Prayer, instead of an appeal to a supreme power, became a daily process of self-examination, and the virtue of a man was seen as his ability to adapt his behaviour to the circumstances in which he found himself and which he was unable to control. In popular terms, this was translated into imperturbability in the face of misfortune, and gives us our modern sense of the word 'stoic'.

The chief rival to Stoicism, and a philosophy which appealed to many Romans on both rational and emotional grounds, is known to us chiefly through the strange, tormented personality of the poet Lucretius. He was born perhaps some time between 99 and 94 B.C., and was probably a member of the patrician family of the Lucretii whose names appear in the records as holders of a number of magistracies. He came into contact, at least indirectly, with a number of the leading figures of his time. He was a friend or dependant of Memmius, the patron of the poet Catullus. His ancient biography claims that he was an intimate of Cicero and the tyrannicides Brutus and Cassius. Cicero had certainly read his work and found it to have considerable merit. It was probably not published until after its author's death – a far from happy death according to the ancient tradition, for Lucretius was believed to have been driven insane by an aphrodisiac administered by his wife. But ancient biographers held as a cardinal principle that a man's life could be deduced from his works. The story of insanity may rest on nothing more substantial than the violent diatribe against the passion of love in Book IV.

Lucretius's work, *The Nature of the Universe*, is an exposition in six books – probably not composed in the order in which we have them, and certainly unfinished at the time of his death – of a theory which can be traced back, in part, to the early Greek scientist-philosophers. The medium, like the argument, had a venerable tradition. It had been common Greek practice to use poetry for didactic purposes, and for subjects which we should now relegate to the bleakest scientific prose. But in the hands of Lucretius, for such a subject, the poetic form has certain obvious disadvantages.

There are passages of noble poetry which bear comparison with the finest that the Romans produced – the death of Iphigeneia in Book I for example, or the eulogy of Epicurus that forms the proem to Book III. They may occur in unlikely places, where Lucretius uses poetic insight to illuminate a scientific principle. In Book II he is describing how apparently solid objects are in reality composed of atoms in perpetual motion:

> Imagine now a green and pleasant hill
> Where sheep graze placidly, and roam to taste
> The dew-bright invitation of the grass;
> And how, their bellies full, they prance and play.
> But from a distance we can only see
> A spread of white upon a hill of green.
> Or see the legions practising the arts
> Of war, manœuvring across the plain.
> The earth shines with their armour, and the gleam
> Reaches to heaven, while their marching feet
> Wake thunder. The surrounding hills receive
> Their war-cries, and project them to the stars.
> The horsemen wheel and turn across the plain
> Which shudders at the fury of their passing.
> Yet from a vantage you can only see
> An iridescence on the quiet plain.[15]

But science and poetry make an uneasy marriage. Lucretius's frequent reiterations, made for the sake of clarity, end by wearying his audience. The denser his argument becomes, the more it defies transmutation into poetic form; in attempting to combine a complex technical vocabulary with a strict metre, the poetry often lapses into a meaningless jingle. Translators have been made particularly aware of this problem, and have tried to make the ambivalence acceptable by rendering the more technical passages into prose and the rest into verse. Their attempts have not been completely successful; but the fault lies not in them but in the material.

Lucretius was the self-appointed exponent of the teaching of the Hellenistic Epicurus, who had lived from 340 to 270 B.C. The philosophy to which the latter gave his name was in great favour at Rome for the last three centuries before Christ, keeping up a steady rivalry with Stoicism, and usually surpassing it in popularity until Christianity began to have its effect on the upper classes. But Epicurus himself had taken over arguments which were already old in his time. In its physical theory Epicureanism reverts to the speculations of earlier Greek philosophers who had sought a material origin for the universe: in particular, to the work of Leucippus of Miletus and his pupil Democritus of Abdera, in Thrace, who had jointly formulated a theory that matter was formed from small particles called atoms (Greek *a-tomos*, uncut) uniting in various combinations. It is this theory that we see defended and elaborated in Lucretius.

The development of the atomic theory in Greece somewhat resembles that in modern physics. Before Democritus, Greek theories of matter had involved the assumption that the ultimate particles were already invested with the characteristics of the matter they were going to produce. (Anaxagoras, for example, had argued that for corn to grow from the earth, the earth must itself contain some corn-substance in its own material composition.) By the same token, modern analytical research was for a long time limited to the study of the molecule, which wore the characteristics of the individual phenomenon and gave a purely qualitative explanation to the formation of matter. Democritus, like Newton and Dalton after him, introduced the concept of a smaller unit which permitted the explanation of phenomena in quantitative terms. In Democritus there still exists a tension between his own and the earlier attitudes; he insists on a quantitative theory for physical phenomena, but in talking of the soul is forced to return to an idea of different *kinds* of atoms, some being larger than others. This discrepancy is perpetuated, as we shall see, in Lucretius.

The atoms were conceived of as first falling in straight lines in a void. An arbitrary disturbance – the 'swerve' or 'vortex' – brought them into random collision, as a result of which the atoms coalesced to form bodies. Thus, all existence depends upon absolutely undetermined movements. What initiates the swerve is not explained. In the material universe, the atoms remain in perpetual motion, though they are too small for the eye to detect and the bodies which they form appear to be solid. On the dissolution of the body, they go off to form new combinations. Nothing is made from nothing, nothing is dissolved into nothing. Thus Lucretius holds the two fundamental laws of physics: that the sum of matter and the sum of energy remain the same. But to account for differences in physical phenomena he is forced, as Democritus was, to postulate different kinds of atoms. Water is made of light, smooth, swiftly moving atoms; olive oil of those that are heavier and more sluggish. In hard objects the atoms are tightly compressed, in soft objects smoother, looser and rounder. There is an amusing explanation for the bitter taste of some substances:

> *Thus, when you take a taste of milk or honey*
> *It leaves a pleasant feeling on the tongue.*
> *But* centaurea *and* absinthium
> *Are bitter. You will pucker up your mouth.*
> *So we observe that substances which yield*
> *A pleasant taste are made of smooth, round bodies,*
> *While those we judge to be unpalatable*
> *Are made of particles with hooks in them,*
> *Which causes them to tear into our senses*
> *And leave a lesion at the point of entry.*[16]

Sense perception, like the formation of bodies, occurs from the collision of atoms. Material objects cast off successive sheets of fine atoms which make a physical impression on the sense organs. Thought takes place when atoms which are particularly small and fine penetrate directly to the mind. One of the important differences between Epicureanism and Stoicism is seen in the stress which Lucretius lays on the fallibility of our observations. Distortions may occur; we may be misled by what we see. Imaginary creatures derive from mixed images – the centaur from a blend of man and horse, the mermaid from fish and woman. But the two philosophies were alike in paying only token respect to the gods. Stoicism had turned them into allegories, Epicureanism relegates them to a passive function: they are seen as eternal outlines into which the streams of atoms continually flow, and constantly give off new shapes. They are thus immortal but inactive, and can exercise no intervention in human affairs. Lucretius would probably have written more on the gods had he lived to finish his work. He promises a discussion of them which never appears.

Where the Stoics had assigned mankind a higher place in the scheme than animals, Epicureanism saw both as part of the same continuum, originating from an identical source. Lucretius would have been sympathetic to Darwinism, for he sets out what is in essence an evolutionary theory. The first men came, not from any divine origin, but from the earth, and were much hardier than their descendants. They developed human speech out of animal sounds. They learned to build huts and form societies for mutual protection. Then came the invention of money and, with the spread of wealth, anarchy; out of this evolved constitutional government.

Lucretius becomes most violently doctrinaire when he discusses religion and the supposed immortality of the soul. The opening of Book I is a condemnation of popular superstition:

> When human life lay grovelling on the earth
> Oppressed and overmastered by religion,
> Which showed her face from the abodes of heaven
> And cast her baneful glance upon mankind,
> It was a Greek who was the first to venture
> To raise his eyes, and take a stand against her,
> Undaunted by the stories of the gods,
> Or thunderbolts, or heaven crying out
> For vengeance. These things only spurred his mind
> To greater daring. He desired to be
> The first to unlock nature's mysteries.[17]

He returns to the attack in his praise of Epicurus in Book II, exalting him as a champion of reason.

Both Stoics and Epicureans sought tranquillity, but where the former urged its attainment by identification with the life-force, the latter sought it by denial. Their view was largely negative. Tranquillity consisted not in any positive action, but in freedom from pain and trouble. The worst of troubles was fear, and the worst of fears was fear of the gods, of arbitrary divine interference and of the punishments supposed to await the sinner in the afterlife. Liberated from such apprehensions, the wise man could live in peace. Lucretius thus applies his physical theories to the disproof of the soul's immortality.

In the ancient world we may trace three distinct attitudes to death, though these sometimes overlapped, and were championed at different times by various groups and social classes. The most primitive was that seen in Homer, where the heroes conceive of death as the gateway to a grey and joyless existence, a barren mockery of life on earth. In opposition to this, the Greek mystery religions developed a more optimistic view of the afterlife which offered some consolation for unhappiness on earth. The spiritual element of man would survive. 'The aether received their souls and the earth their bodies', says a funerary inscription from Potidaea. And, finally, we see the more blasé and sophisticated attitude, held certainly by the upper classes in fifth-century Greece and increasingly prevalent in Roman times, that life was irksome and death annihilation, a welcome release from the imperfections of the universe. Sophocles, in a chorus of *Oedipus at Colonus*, argues that not to be born is the finest thing of all; Catullus talks of death as perpetual night; Julius Caesar, when *pontifex maximus*, argued strongly against the immortality of the soul; and for Horace, as for others, the only sort of immortality was fame.

It is this view to which Lucretius subscribes, and which he seeks to support with scientific arguments. To some extent he was flogging a dead horse. The nobility, to whom his work was addressed, would already have agreed with him. Lucretius must have been aware of this. It has therefore been suggested that he writes with a socialist impulse, and that he is protesting against the deliberate fostering of superstition as a means of controlling the lower classes. There is some support for this in Roman history, and in other writers. We may look, for example, at the frequent abuse of the auspices for political purposes. We may consider the events of the year 207 B.C. when the senate, to allay popular fears of a series of bad portents, commissioned Livius Andronicus to write a hymn which was sung through the city by twenty-seven maidens in procession. We may cite the historian Polybius who, eighty years before Lucretius, had suggested that the apparatus of the state religion was maintained to bemuse the populace. But such things seem to spring more from the hereditary temperament of the Italian yeoman farmer than from any manipulations on the part of the authorities. And it would be strange to find an Epicurean going out of his way to support the oppressed masses. The school to which Lucretius belonged was, on the whole, aristocratic in its affiliations, with a strong tendency to hold itself aloof. Lucretius's protests may stem simply from a personal obsession. His violent denunciations of religion and his opponents, and a lack of order in his arguments, suggest a certain unbalance on this point, if not the insanity attributed to him by his biographer. The following passages are typical:

> No longer will your happy home enfold
> Its warmth about you, or your peerless wife
> And children run to you to snatch a kiss
> And touch your heart with silent joy. No longer
> Will you have power to prosper in your ways
> Or guard your own. 'Unhappy man,' they say.
> 'Now one black day has taken all you worked for.'
> They do not add 'But it has also taken
> Your desire for it.' If they could see this clearly
> And let this knowledge guide their tongues, their fear
> Would vanish, and their minds would be at peace.[18]

> Death is the end. It cannot be denied
> Or wished away. Moreover, every day
> Is like its neighbour. We can never mine
> New pleasure out of this monotony.

But it is always what we do not have
That we desire most. When we have it
We long for something else. This constant craving
Besets us all our life. We never know
What fate tomorrow brings, what chance, what outcome
Is waiting round the corner. Though we live
Beyond our span, we cannot borrow time
From death. It will be every bit as long.
Live four score years, and then another four,
And everlasting death will still await you.
The man who dies this evening will be dead
As long as he who died this twelvemonth past.[19]

Shorn of its protestations, the argument is essentially a simple one. The soul cannot be immortal, for it is composed of the same substance as the rest of us. Death comes as an absolute ending. As the body decays and forms new substances, so the soul is returned to the atoms from which it came.

Though the Epicureans taught the pursuit of pleasure and the avoidance of pain, they were not outright hedonists. Epicurus himself led an austere life (though he embarrassed his followers by his praise of the pleasures of the belly) and his disciples were by no means selfish. One of the most admirable characteristics of the school was the deep friendship of its members for each other, and the almost religious devotion with which his followers regarded the master; we see this throughout Lucretius's work. The modern sense of the word 'epicure' is as great an oversimplification as the modern sense of 'stoic'. But Epicureanism urged the shunning of social and personal obligations which could only cause the loss of tranquillity. Epicurus advised against marriage and politics, both being sources of strife. Lucretius says that the wise man will not fall in love. A family can only be a burden; it is better to live obscurely. The Epicureans developed the metaphor of the garden, the spiritual refuge into which the wise man could retire, leaving the pressures of the world outside.

Why should a philosophy which opposed so many traditional

Roman attitudes have appealed so strongly to the Roman people? It was easy and attractive, and the notion of pleasure as the sole good was open to obvious distortion. The admission of Cicero, who disliked the Epicureans intensely, that the philosophy was adopted for lack of anything better emphasizes the fundamental weakness of the Roman position. Any solution to the increasing problems of daily life was welcome. And, in the last resort, the hectic political activity of the dying Republic, when Epicureanism acquired its greatest strength, made tranquillity desirable at any price. Philosophies, like religions, succeed because they answer a need. Many a Roman in the age of Julius Caesar must have longed heartily for simple peace and quiet.

For those who found the state religion dull and the philosophers unsympathetic, there remained magic and its kindred arts, particularly astrology, to which the Romans were attracted by instinct, and which was a natural extension of the official interest in divination. In an indirect way, it received additional support from Stoicism. The concept of predestination encouraged attempts to predict a future which was already determined. Although the authorities discouraged such attempts – particularly under the Empire, when it became a capital offence to cast the emperor's horoscope – astrology remained as popular a pastime in ancient Rome as it is in modern California. The astrologers – or Chaldaeans, as the Romans called them – were frequently expelled, and as frequently returned. Petronius testifies to this popular interest in the *Satyricon*, where the *nouveau riche* Trimalchio offers his guest a huge *hors-d'œuvre* plate decorated with the signs of the zodiac, each accompanied by an appropriate food.

For magic proper we must look mainly to the poets, who exploit its dramatic values in their works. Yet these aesthetic exercises derive from a strong foundation of popular superstition. Virgil, in his Eighth Eclogue, describes the rites performed by a Thessalian girl to bring back a truant lover. She goes to an enchantress (Thessaly was a favourite abode of witches) who enacts a ritual reminiscent of the voodoo cult. Images of the unfaithful youth are made of wax and clay, and broken and baked respectively; fragments of his old garments are buried beneath the threshold. Virgil's poem is a direct imitation of an earlier poem by Theocritus, which in turn shows the influence of Greek magical papyri, and obviously represents contemporary beliefs. Horace, in his Fifth Epode, shows a more horrifying witch, Canidia, who does an innocent youth to death so that she may use his spleen and marrow in a love charm. And Lucan, in his epic on the Civil War, offers the most horrifying treatment of all when he describes the consultation of a witch by Sextus Pompeius. She performs ghastly rites over a corpse, raises him to life, forces him to prophesy the future, and then allows him to walk to his funeral pyre to die a second death.

But the most vivid testimony is one which derives not from poetry but real life. It comes from the experience of Apuleius, a Roman African of the second century A.D. A university man, educated at Carthage and Athens, he wrote one memorable novel, the *Metamorphoses*, or, as it is better known, *The Golden Ass*. He was also something of a mystic and a dabbler in esoteric philosophies, interests which contributed to the predicament in which he found himself. Intervening, at the request of a friend, in a family dispute, Apuleius contrived to involve himself so deeply that he married his friend's mother, a wealthy widow. Her disappointed relatives promptly accused him of winning her affection by magic, and brought him into court. Apuleius has left us the speech he made in his own defence. We hear the voice of sweet reason arguing against prejudice and superstition; but we also see how powerful that superstition was. In one paragraph Apuleius distinguishes between the popular conception of magic and its serious religious associations (which, for the Romans, were always strong: the borderline between magic and folk religion was, to say the least, obscure); shows what a powerful hold the false conception had on the public minds, and turns its very strength to his advantage; and accuses his accusers of using the belief to further their own mercenary ends.

Do you hear, you who so rashly accuse the art of magic? It is an art acceptable to the immortal gods, replete with knowledge of their prayer and worship; a devout art, wise in things divine; a noble art since Zoroaster and Oromazes first established it, high priestess of the heavenly powers. . . .

But if these accusers of mine fall into the vulgar superstition of defining the magician as one who communes with the immortal gods, who can perform marvels at will by the power of his incantations, I am surprised they are not afraid to accuse a man they credit with such great powers. If you prosecute a murderer, you take care to come into court with an armed escort. If you prosecute a poisoner, you are careful of what you eat. If you accuse a thief, you keep your hand on your wallet. But when a man brings a magician, a man believed to have such awful powers, into the criminal court, how can guards, watchmen or any precautions save him from unforeseeable and inevitable disaster? They cannot. Nothing can. The man who believes in such practices should be the last to accuse someone of them in court.[20]

A society which was fundamentally irreligious needed urgently to believe in something.

NOTES TO CHAPTER FOUR

1. *Appendix Vergiliana*, Priapea, I.
2. Plautus, *Aulularia*, 1–5, 23–5.
3. Ovid, *Fasti*, VI. 261–4.
4. Cato, *On Farming*, 141.
5. Seneca, *Oedipus*, 366–70.
6. Cicero, *De Divinatione* (*On Divination*), II. 27, 28.
7. Ovid, *Metamorphoses*, XIV. 130–46.
8. Petronius, *Satyricon*, 48. 8.
9. Virgil, *Aeneid*, VI. 42–50.
10. Virgil, *Eclogues*, IV. 4–10.
11. Catullus, *Poems*, 63. 19–25.
12. Livy, *History*, XXXIX. 8. 3–8.
13. Cicero, *Tusculan Disputations*, I. 6.
14. Cicero, *De Natura Deorum* (*The Nature of the Gods*), II. 150–1.
15. Lucretius, *De Rerum Natura* (*The Nature of the Universe*), II. 317–32.
16. Ibid. II. 398–407.
17. Ibid. I. 62–71.
18. Ibid. III. 894–903.
19. Ibid. III. 1078–94.
20. Apuleius, *Apologia*, 26.

Chapter Five

The Rome of Cicero

IF one man may stand for an era, it is Marcus Tullius Cicero. His life covered the dying spasms of the Republic and its last convulsive bursts of energy; his death was a prelude to its dissolution. He shared in its last triumphs, and its greatest tragedy. Though he saw himself, in his proudest moments, as the saviour of his country, his career was flawed and his life a series of near misses. His inquiring mind and the breadth of his perceptions led him to see too many sides to any question for him ever to commit himself unreservedly to one. He was an indifferent poet, a formidable orator who sometimes lacked the courage of his convictions, a philosopher who explored all schools with equal enthusiasm, a statesman whose nerve failed at the moment of crisis, an idealist doomed to perpetual disappointment. He could be querulous, vain, complacent, pompous, cowardly; he lacked the quality of simple fanaticism of which heroes and martyrs are made. Sufficiently ambiguous to be elbowed aside from the crucial decisions, he was still dangerous enough to be assassinated. And yet his life touched that of his times at every important point. He was intimate with the leading figures of his day, arguing, infuriating, influencing; he has left us a continuous record of his involvement, fully documented, in his speeches, treatises and letters. He is a man who is better known to us, perhaps, than any Roman citizen before or since.

Cicero was born in 106 B.C. in the town of Arpinum (modern Arpino, in the hills near Cassino). His father was an *eques*. The word means 'knight', and derived originally from the Roman practice of classifying the citizen-body according to the position they could afford in the military system: the knights were those wealthy enough to contribute a horse and armour, and so ranked above the infantry in the non-professional citizen-army. But the word had long since lost its military significance, and the equestrian order no longer had any connection with horses. In a very broad sense, it was the equivalent of the modern middle class. Its members were largely those who had an interest in the financial administration of the state. Up to the third Carthaginian war, the senate and the *equites* had been in close alliance against the common enemy – the rural proletariat, who formed the popular party, and the increasing urban mob, swelled by displaced farmers demanding land and Italians demanding the vote. This convenient balance was not to be maintained. The postwar period saw the beginning of unrest among the orders which became so pronounced that some writers have characterized the second and first centuries B.C. as the age of social revolt and the establishment of the middle class. The revolt showed itself on one level in the great slave wars; on another, it produced the political fire-brands, Tiberius and Gaius Gracchus, who used their positions as spokesmen of the plebs to push through reforms designed to weaken senatorial control by strengthening the power of the *equites*. Gaius gave them a larger measure of representation on the standing judicial bodies; he also helped them to secure the contract for the taxation of Asia under favourable terms.

The *equites* were thus a powerful and influential group. Gaius Gracchus had excluded senators from the order. In 67 B.C. the *equites* were given special seats in the theatre. Their new prominence and more precisely defined duties brought them into rivalry, and often into outright opposition, with the senate. Cicero's fondest dream, when he became a powerful figure in political life, was a *concordia ordinum*, or restoration of the old unity. It was never re-established. The split only helped to further the ambitions of individual leaders who built their personal followings on the national divisiveness.

Cicero's father, whose poor health made it difficult for him to take a practical interest in farming, moved the sixty miles to Rome so that Marcus and his brother Quintus, four years his junior, could enjoy a city education. The Greek biographer Plutarch, who saw Cicero as the Roman equivalent of Demosthenes, paints a glowing picture of his schooldays, and shows him already marked out as a future leader of men. 'When the time came for him to go to school, his natural ability made him a shining example, and he won fame and title among his fellows. Their fathers used to visit the classes to see this Cicero with their own eyes, and observe the rapid and intelligent grasp of his studies about which they had heard so much. The more boorish among them grumbled when they saw their sons giving Cicero the place of honour in their midst.'[1]

Plutarch idolizes out of hindsight. We do not have a more objective description of Cicero's schooldays, but we know what his education must have comprised. Like any boy of his class and times, he learned Greek. His later works show a close knowledge of Demosthenes, Plato and Xenophon, and a few poetic fragments have survived which may date from his schooldays – translations from the *Iliad* and *Odyssey*, and a Latin version of an astronomical poem by Aratus. He would also have become familiar with the national poetry. He quotes frequently from Ennius and Terence, and criticizes the latter in a short verse usually attributed to Julius Caesar but now accepted as a work of Cicero's early days. It is a criticism which seems to reflect the popular viewpoint, praising the playwright's style but regretting his lack of comic force.

The principal subjects taught in Roman schools were rhetoric, philosophy and law. Of these, the first was of great practical interest to anyone seeking advancement in public life, and its development into an elaborate discipline is one of the more important ways in which the Romans were influenced by Greek traditions. The art of speaking had always been important in a society where most of the state's business was conducted by public discussion. In Athens, it had received new stimulus from the arrival of Gorgias as ambassador from the Sicilian city of Leontini in 427 B.C. Gorgias demonstrated to his audiences the persuasive effects of carefully structured prose. By exploiting the rhetorical devices in which the Greek language was already rich, he encouraged closer attention to speechmaking as a conscious art responsive to rules and systems which could be taught. His pioneering efforts were taken up by the sophistic philosophers of the later fifth century who, in their growing concern with the material, saw rhetoric as a key to political power and social success. By the fourth century, the golden age of Greek oratory, the rules of rhetoric had already been precisely formulated. Plato, gravely concerned with its public influence, denied that it was an art; Aristotle, opposing him in this as in so many other things, offered in his *Rhetoric* a detailed analysis of the forms of argument, the means by which a speaker could arouse emotion in his hearers, and the various ways of conveying a favourable impression.

Many of the Greek orators led a double life, both speaking themselves and writing speeches for others, sometimes on both sides of the same question. The subject began to develop an academic fascination, apart from its practical utility. In the fourth century we see an increasing number of rhetorical textbooks dealing with both theory and practice. The orator's stance and gestures were analysed as carefully as his delivery. Ancient oratory always contained a strong element of the theatrical; speakers were regarded as giving a performance in which everything contributed to the total effect, and many of them had either been actors themselves or gone to actors for their training. Once again, the art was built on existing national characteristics. It is virtually impossible for a native of the Mediterranean to speak without using his hands and the maximum of facial expression. The teachers simply codified these things to allow the speaker to convey the finest shades of expression with his body no less than with his voice.

The elaborate Greek art was introduced to Rome in the first half of the second century B.C. Greek teachers of rhetoric visited the Greek colonies in Italy, and Rome itself. They were made welcome, for Rome, like Greece, gave importance to rhetoric in the practical conduct of affairs. There was some opposition to Greek professionalism, notably from Cato the Censor. He was the first Roman to publish his speeches, though none have survived in full. Cicero knew of 150, and speaks of them with some admiration. Cato distrusted the rhetorical elaboration practised by the Greeks. *Rem tene, verba sequentur,* he advised: 'Master the subject matter, and the words will take care of themselves.' It was valuable advice in an art where style was often preferred to content and, particularly in Rome, produced highly florid manifestations. But Cato's insular prejudices, as usual, went unheeded; the Romans adopted the Greek system entire. And even Cato, it appears, was not entirely immune to Greek influence. The fragments of his speeches show more polish than his work on agriculture.

In Cicero's time, elementary education was conducted by the *litterator,* who taught the basic skills with, Horace informs us, particular emphasis on arithmetic. From there he proceeded to the *grammaticus,* whose field was, generally speaking, literature, though he taught with a strong emphasis on rhetoric and ranged wide in preparing his pupils for advanced studies. Cicero gives an idea of what this branch of his education comprised. 'We must train our memory by learning by heart as many pieces from native and foreign writers as we can . . . we must acquaint ourselves with poetry, study history, read and familiarize ourselves with the published authorities in the liberal arts, and practise our own art by praising, expounding, emending, criticizing and confuting them.'[2] The student also worked on 'problems, paraphrases, addresses and character-sketches' before going on to the *rhetor* for the final stage of his education.[3]

Cicero must have taken kindly to the discipline; he emphasizes in his later works the need for the speaker to be a well-rounded man, versed in history and philosophy. He justifies the former on the grounds of usefulness, in suggesting analogies and precedents to the speaker; with regard to the latter, he attempts to heal the breach between rhetoric and philosophy which was as old as Plato.

On this basis the student would construct his own speeches and arguments. In Cicero's time, this type of education gained cogency from being related to persons and issues of the day. The rhetor's school became a miniature senate-house, in which the student would be asked to discuss hypothetical cases, or deliver practice speeches on topical themes. It was an instructive and exhaustive discipline. Cicero, in his maturity, discarded most of it, but it gave him a firm base on which to build his audience appeal.

The teaching of law was more haphazard – strangely so, in a society where the entry to politics was often through the bar. It seems from Cicero that many speakers were ill-advised on matters of legal procedure. But the law itself, in his time, was still in a formative state. The first Roman code was the Twelve Tables, drawn up in the mid-fifth century to formulate what had previously been left to custom and patrician privilege. Displayed in the Forum, they made the law public and removed one of the chief plebeian grievances; although chiefly concerned with stipulating penalties, they were the basis on which all subsequent Roman law was founded. In Cicero's day schoolboys still had to learn them by heart. Cicero was lucky in attaching himself to a family of distinguished jurists. He was admitted as a pupil of Quintus Mucius Scaevola, attending his consultations, taking notes and following him to court. Scaevola's son, who had been consul when Cicero was eleven years old, published the first systematic treatise on civil law.

Cicero was therefore well-qualified to make his debut in the law-courts. But it was a dangerous time for a young man to draw attention to himself. He grew up in a Rome where the traditional liberties were being eroded by dangers inherent in the constitution. As the Roman interests expanded, the elective system, with its inbuilt safeguards of shared responsibility, proved increasingly cumbersome. The year after Cicero was born, the Roman army had received a crushing defeat because the two consuls who divided the command were at loggerheads. Nor could any continuous military policy be established when the officials changed yearly. The system had long recognized the necessity for occasional extraordinary commands. It began to break up when those who had achieved such authority, sometimes by means that were barely constitutional, refused to resign the power and prestige that it brought them.

The immediate problem was solved by Gaius Marius, a soldier of wide experience who, in a series of consulships, dedicated himself to the reorganization of the army. He succeeded brilliantly. Before his time the Roman fighting force had been composed of amateurs. Only those with sufficient property qualifications could enlist, and were grouped according to their means; the richer citizens provided the cavalry and the poorest the light-armed troops. Marius opened enlistment to all Roman citizens irrespective of income, and replaced the conscript militia by a voluntary professional force. He introduced new weapons and rigorous drill, creating virtually singlehanded the superb fighting machine that was to show its merits in the later wars of conquest.

The military success that Marius achieved brought him enormous popularity. He was a countryman, born not far from Cicero's home town; he had no connection with the old Roman families and was hailed as a prospective leader by the popular party. Like many successful generals, he was less happy in politics, and the promised leadership failed to materialize. Subsequent events in Italy produced a rival for Marius. The Italian allies were claiming the rights of Roman citizenship. Their demands were resisted, and general revolt broke out in the centre of the country, spreading as far north as Etruria. It was quelled partly by propitiatory legislation, and partly by the military actions of Lucius Cornelius Sulla, who suddenly, and late in life, arose to prominence from high-born obscurity.

War was threatening in the East. Mithridates, king of Pontus in Asia Minor, had built up a strong kingdom modelled on the vanished Hellenistic empires. His spreading power threatened Roman vassal states. Neither side wanted war, but it was urged in Rome by the tax-gatherers; in 88 B.C. fighting broke out, and Mithridates occupied Roman Asia. Sulla, as consul for the year, was given the eastern command. He was out of Rome at the time, attending to the revolt. Marius, whose political failures were beginning to smart, badly wanted the command, and took the opportunity to have a bill forced through the assembly conferring it on himself. Sulla promptly returned to Rome to crush this new threat, and Marius fled to Africa. The next year Sulla left to fight Mithridates. As soon as Rome lay open, Marius returned, and with his associates inaugurated a reign of terror. Leading members of the aristocracy were murdered and their property confiscated. After a few weeks, Marius died, but his colleagues fortified Rome against Sulla's return. Although he was fighting a victorious war against Mithridates, he was declared an outlaw, and another army sent out to act independently of him. Peace was made with Mithridates in 83 on terms extremely advantageous to Rome, and Sulla returned. He found the Marians disorganized, and after a series of battles up and down Italy occupied the capital. He had himself declared *dictator*, an office which had some faint pretext of legality; it had been added to the constitution soon after the expulsion of the Etruscan kings, to grant extraordinary, but strictly temporary, powers in times of crisis. The dictator had supreme military authority, and was beyond appeal. But the last time the dictatorship had been conferred was in 216 B.C. The senate saw the dangers of awarding such power to a strong leader who might not be prepared to resign it when the appointed time was up. Sulla's seizure of the office made him virtually king of Rome, and he proceeded to inaugurate his own reign of terror.

The confrontation between Marius and Sulla set the pattern for the years to come. It brought the inner workings of Roman politics into the open. Under the shadow of the constitution, real power had long been in the hands of a few important families who had controlled the offices and appointments and, occasionally, formed a coalition to prevent outsiders from getting in. They were fiercely concerned with their *dignitas* – pride, face, public image, more or less what their Italian descendants imply by their concept of *un gran signore*. And now a more sinister element had been added to their manipulations; a professional army, more loyal to its general than to the constitution. Military supremacy was to be the key to Roman politics in the future.

It was against this background of near-anarchy and martial law that Cicero made, not his debut, for he had delivered one speech already, but the appearance which first brought him to the public attention. He was later to recall the year of 80 B.C. with smug satisfaction: 'My defence of Sextus Roscius, which was the first case I pleaded, met with such a favourable reception that from that moment I was looked upon as an advocate who ranked with the best, and as capable of handling the most important and demanding cases. After this I appeared in many others, which I prepared with all the care and accuracy of which I was master.'4 At the time he must have been less sanguine, with good cause. The writing had, literally, been on the wall. The early days of Sulla's power saw the posting of lists of the proscribed, those who had been declared hostile to the Sullan regime. Their lives were forfeit, and their property seized. Informers and profiteers had a field-day, for the political purges opened the way for private gain. And the case in which Cicero was involved brought him into direct opposition to the regime. Although the proscriptions were now officially closed, the old threats to personal security remained. Sextus Roscius was accused of murdering his father, a crime which struck at the foundations of the Roman social system and for which early custom had prescribed a particularly abhorrent penalty: the condemned man was sewn into a leather sack together with a dog, a cock, a viper and an ape, and thrown into the river. The symbolism of this punishment is obscure, but it seems to indicate the alienation of the criminal from all true human feeling. In the case of Sextus Roscius, the charge was certainly false. At the most there had been ill feeling between father and son. The accusation had been fostered by Chrysogonus, a former slave and Sulla's henchman, who had designs on the property of the deceased.

The opening of Cicero's speech shows the atmosphere of terror which still hung over Rome. Self-deprecatingly, he represents himself as having undertaken the case only because of his own unimportance.

What was the reason that impelled me, rather than any of these others, to undertake the defence of Sextus Roscius? It was this. If any of my learned colleagues who occupy these benches, men whose distinguished contributions command the public attention, had introduced one word of politics into this case – and it is impossible to keep politics out of it – his statements would be given undue weight and importance. It is otherwise with me. I can say anything that needs to be said, without attracting the same publicity. Their rank and dignity transform their slightest word into a public statement; they are inhibited by age and experience. If I say anything beyond the bounds of propriety, it will either be ignored as coming from a political nonentity, or pardoned on account of my youth – though the idea of pardon, like the custom of judicial inquiry, has now been abolished from the state.[5]

The challenge of the last sentence is tempered, in the rest of the speech, by the adroitness with which Cicero distinguishes Chrysogonus from his master. It is the freedman's cupidity he attacks, not Sulla's:

Here is Chrysogonus coming down from his mansion on the Palatine: for recreation he has a pleasant country seat in the suburbs, as well as a number of farms, all of them excellent properties within easy commuting distance; a house packed with vases from Corinth and Delos, including the famous samovar for which he paid such a high price at the recent auction that when the bystanders heard the bids they thought a whole estate was being sold. And what quantities of embossed silver, draperies, paintings, statues, marble, do you think he owns? As much as a single house could hold without bursting: the plunder accumulated from many illustrious families in these troubled times.[6]

Cicero won his case and established his reputation. In 79 he went abroad – according to Plutarch, from fear of reprisals by Sulla, but on his own explanation for reasons of health. While abroad he continued his studies in rhetoric and philosophy at Athens and Rhodes. Sulla surprised Rome by laying down his power voluntarily in the same year. His rule, which had begun so tyrannically, was not without its altruistic side. By a number of reforms he had strengthened the power of the senate, and tried to create a system which would work smoothly while frustrating any personal ambition. But the precedent which he had set in seizing the dictatorship was to be followed by others. 'Sulla could,' Julius Caesar was later to say. 'Why can't I?'

Returning to Rome, Cicero resumed his work at the bar. In 76 he entered public life in the customary way, by securing the quaestorship, a financial office which was the recognized stepping-stone to higher things. In 75 he went to Lilybaeum, in Sicily, on the staff of Sextus Peducaeus, and had his first experience of provincial administration. This could be a haphazard business, as the Roman interest in the territories they acquired was strictly limited. Their first concern was to establish military occupancy, their second to collect taxes. As long as the province gave no trouble, it was usually not disturbed in any other way; the existing constitution was allowed to continue, and the Romans only intervened in the native way of life when they had to. The taxes were important. Up to the third Carthaginian War Rome had financed her army by a customs duty, a salt tax and war indemnities or the plunder from conquest. After the defeat of the Seleucid Empire in 190, Antiochus III had been made to pay an indemnity of fifteen thousand talents. Carthage was still paying two hundred talents a year when it was destroyed in 146. Macedonia paid a thousand. Generals grew rich, not only from plunder but from the companies they formed to procure military supplies. Senators were in theory forbidden to engage in commerce; thus most of this business fell to the *equites*, who emerged as prosperous middlemen, though many senators were sleeping partners in their operations.

In 146 the senate made the popular move of abolishing all income tax. What was good for Rome was bad for the provinces, which now became the sole source of revenue. Roman governors disgraced themselves by unrestrained plundering. Though a senatorial commission was set up to investigate the governors' peculations, abuses continued. The senate was powerless against the financial establishment. Senatorial governors and equestrian tax-gatherers worked in collusion. The most notorious case was the province of Asia, which had been bequeathed to Rome by King Attalus of Pergamum in 133. Using every conceivable device, legal and otherwise, the tax-collectors established a banking monopoly in the country and so impoverished it that Sulla had to cancel part of the debt to ensure that the system carried on at all. Governors could be tried, but were invariably reprieved by a court of their peers. Rutilius Rufus, who had attempted to prevent extortion, was accused by hostile elements and forced into exile. It was cynically remarked that a provincial governor needed three years to make his fortune: one to pay his debts, one to provide a nest-egg for himself, and one to make enough to bribe his judges on his return to Rome.

In 70 Cicero further enhanced his reputation by involving himself in such an extortion case. His target was the ex-governor Verres, and his client the Sicilian people, claiming restitution of money illegally extracted from them. But the case had considerably wider implications. It was, in effect, a criminal prosecution for misgovernment and oppression; it was also an attack, by an *eques*, on the senatorial monopoly. We have Cicero's speech, expanded into a monograph: it gives a vivid impression of conditions in the provinces, and how little hope of immediate redress the subject population had under the republican system.

So long as Verres was governor of Sicily the people had no protection either from their own laws or from the decrees of the Roman senate. No man has anything that he can call his own, except what Verres happened to overlook in his lust for plunder, or left untouched when even he was sated. For three years no one could be awarded anything by the courts unless Verres gave his assent. There was no right of inheritance so strong, no testamentary bequest so clear, that the courts would not cancel it if Verres said so. Countless contributions, under a new and unprincipled regulation, were extracted from the pockets of the farmers. Our most loyal allies were treated like enemy aliens. Roman citizens were tortured and executed like slaves. Men steeped in guilt purchased their own acquittal, while men of unimpeachable integrity would be prosecuted and sentenced to banishment without even being allowed to plead their case. Harbours bristling with defences, and mighty and impregnable cities, were thrown open to freebooters and pirates. Sicilian soldiers and sailors, our friends and allies, were starved to death. A navy which was the glory of the seas, outfitted with the most modern equipment, was destroyed and lost to us; Rome might well be ashamed of herself. And then there were the historical monuments, some donated by wealthy monarchs, others by our own generals, who gave or restored them to the Sicilian communities to celebrate their victories; every one of them has been stripped and despoiled by this same governor. He did not confine himself to statues and public works. There is no shrine, no temple, no place of sanctity that he has not ransacked. He left the people of Sicily no god that he considered to. have any artistic merit or historical interest.[7]

It is impossible to convey in English the full torrent of Ciceronian rhetoric, or the way in which he piles superlative on superlative, and reaches a magnificent crescendo of invective. Insult was a recognized and approved weapon in the orator's armoury. It was his duty to blacken the character of his opponent. If this could be done without departing too far from the truth – as, apparently, in the case of Verres – so much the better. If not, a ready imagination would remedy the limitations of truth. This licence was common-place in Rome; it is helpful to remember the fact, when we read the harangues directed by rival speakers at each other. Unfortunately – perhaps inevitably, since rhetoric was so important in Roman education – the same attitude has coloured other branches of literature. Historians and biographers, if unsympathetic to their subjects, included in their accounts long, slanderous passages in which half-truths, distortions and outright lies can only with difficulty be disentangled from the facts. Even friendly accounts may include old scandals, started perhaps for propaganda purposes, or deriving from an opponent's speech and current for so long that by the writer's time they passed for truth. And yet these same writers would be highly indignant if accused of bias. They were writing in the way that they knew – the rhetorical way. It makes the reading of ancient history more interesting, but considerably more confusing.

The successful prosecution of Verres gave Cicero added professional lustre. Even after his involvement in politics, he continued to plead at the bar. He preferred the defence: the Verres case is the only one on record in which he appeared for the prosecution. It was a lucrative profession. Although the law forbade a fee, substantial rewards in money or property could be expected from a satisfied client. The grateful Sicilians sent Cicero a cargo of grain. Hortensius, Cicero's chief rival who spoke in Verres' defence, was a prominent art collector. Cicero himself was a rich man. He did not, certainly, reach the level of the financial wizards of his time, like Marcus Licinius Crassus, who sacrificed a tithe of his estate to Hercules, gave a banquet to the whole population of Rome, provided every citizen with enough to live on for three months and was still able to boast that he had a thousand talents left. But he was wealthy enough. We can see from his voluminous correspondence how a rich man of his times lived. From his father, he had inherited the property at Arpinum and a town house. He gave the latter to his brother Quintus, and built himself a mansion on the Palatine, Rome's 'nob hill'. He owned several blocks of apartments in central districts. Outside Rome he had several country houses besides the one at Arpinum. One had previously been the property of Sulla. Others stood near the coast and the fashionable resort areas – Formiae, Antium, Pompeii, Cumae. There he could meet new clients, bask in the congratulations of old ones, and talk politics with the Roman élite more freely than was possible in the capital. His letters also show him as possessed of a large amount of capital, the income from which he was constantly reinvesting. He had an interest in a tax-gathering concern, lent out money at a good rate, and was an implacable creditor. Cicero the businessman was as proficient as Cicero the orator.

The talents which kept him in the public eye were undoubtedly powerful. His tactics were unorthodox but successful. Later critics recognized that his chief strength lay in his emotional appeal, and praised him for it. Cicero himself was well aware of this. In a profession which always had a large element of the histrionic, he had mastered all the tricks. The courts were theatres, in which the speakers and their clients vied for the sympathy of the audience. A defendant's weeping family would appear beside him at the trial. A veteran soldier would bare the scars won in the service of the Republic. Cicero reports that he once spoke with a child in his arms. Roman practice differed from Greek in that it permitted a whole series of speakers to be heard on the same side. In such a case, Cicero always spoke last. He wanted to be sure that the jurors were left with his thunder ringing in their ears.

He continued to advance up the political ladder. In 69 he was elected *aedile*, or superintendent of public works. This was a useful office for a politician; as well as the more mundane duties of supervising traffic, ceremonials, public buildings and weights and measures, its connection with the games offered valuable publicity. Three years later he became *praetor*, or city magistrate. He was able to use this position, as he had used the prosecution of Verres, to act as spokesman for the *equites*, and to throw his weight into a power-struggle which was potentially as dangerous as that between Marius and Sulla.

Once again, the question was that of the Asian command. Mithridates, only temporarily subdued, had used the lull to stabilize his kingdom. After a conciliatory approach by his envoys at Rome had been rebuffed, he entered into collusion with Tigranes, King of Armenia, to infringe upon the neighbouring Roman vassal states. The senate chose to ignore the threat and the two kings made preparations for a major war, hiring dissident Roman officers expatriated during the recent squabbles to lead their troops. Lucius Licinius Lucullus and Gaius Cotta, consuls at the time, were sent out with their armies. Lucullus was a man of high culture and refined tastes, as well as a capable soldier; taking the initiative when Cotta was defeated, he forced Mithridates into exile and devoted the following winter to the administration of the province of Asia, proposing a new and more equitable financial system. Inevitably, he fell victim to party politics. As the senate's man, he was resented by the *equites;* as a reformer, he was resisted by those who had financial interests in the province. He also lost the affection he had once had from his men, because he failed to realize the new conditions under which the army was operating. Since the days of Marius and Sulla, the troops had expected their commander to identify himself more closely with them than with the senate. Lucullus was too conservative to play this game, and his allegiance to the home government cost him the loyalty of his army. He was forced to abandon his conquests. This failure had important political repercussions in Rome, and opened the way for the rapid rise of Pompey.

Gnaeus Pompeius, later to be called Magnus, 'the great', was born in the same year as Cicero, and as a constant supporter of Sulla had performed distinguished military service in Italy and abroad. Sulla had sent him to Sicily, Africa and Spain, from which he returned to hunt down the fugitive slaves fleeing to the Po Valley after the defeat of Spartacus. His success led to his being given, in 67, an extraordinary command to deal with a perpetual menace to Roman security, the operations of the pirates. Piracy had been endemic to the Mediterranean from the earliest times, and was now organized to a point that threatened a major crisis. The eastern Mediterranean was, to all intents and purposes, under pirate control. The market at Delos was plundered; Syracuse and even Ostia were invaded; and during the recent fighting, the pirates had even acted as a link between Spartacus and revolutionaries abroad. Rome was hit where it hurt, in the stomach. The interruption of the wheat supply from Egypt caused a dangerous food shortage in the city.

Pompey was given all-embracing authority to deal with the situation. He had supreme power in the Mediterranean and over a distance of fifty miles inland on every coast, his own choice of subordinates, and a fleet of five hundred ships. Contrary to the fears of those who remembered Sulla, Pompey did not abuse his command. He took only what forces were necessary, and cleared the seas in forty days, making a grand sweep from west to east. The only hard fighting was over the last strongholds of the pirates along the rocky coast of Asia Minor. He treated his opponents with a clemency surprising in a Roman and in marked contrast to the behaviour of Crassus, who had crucified slaves by the thousand after the defeat of Spartacus. Many were resettled in different areas. The menace of the pirates abated, though it did not entirely disappear. They were to return as a political force in the civil wars soon to come, and to remain active in the Mediterranean for hundreds of years, making a last grand appearance in the Greek war of independence in the nineteenth century. The Mediterranean coast provided too many convenient hiding-places; it was impossible to wipe them out completely. But Pompey had done well, and success bred success. In 66 he was given the Asian command in which Lucullus had blundered, on terms which made him virtually dictator in the east.

This war is no light matter, gentlemen. We are faced with a crisis. Who is to be put in charge? I heartily wish that we had a large enough supply of valiant and upright men to make it hard for you to decide. But Pompey's transcendent merits stand alone. There is no one alive today to equal him. There is no one in the history of our country to equal him. The case is clear, gentlemen; what reason is there for any of you to hesitate?[8]

Thus Cicero. He saw the appointment of Pompey as a means of realizing his cherished dream, the *concordia ordinum*, the common front, the political alliance of the moderates of all parties with the *equites* as the core. This did not imply any concession to democratic programmes, especially not to revolutionary policies. No doubt Cicero had already recognized Pompey's essentially conservative character.

Once again Pompey justified all the hopes that were placed in him. His eastern campaign was a series of sensational victories. Mithridates was driven to the Caucasus, while Tigranes surrendered and was allowed to keep his throne on payment of a large indemnity. Syria became a Roman province. Pompey proceeded south to Judaea, to deal with local unrest which the Romans considered inimical to their interests. In 63 he besieged and captured Jerusalem, treating its inhabitants with his customary toleration: the monarchy was abolished but the office of High Priest retained. The effect of Pompey's conquests was that all the Roman possessions on the Mediterranean seaboard were now, with the exception of Egypt, linked together. In the interior, local monarchies under Roman protection acted as buffer states. Greek cities were given a special dispensation, and granted charters of independence within their boundaries. Instead of paying tribute to the local king, they now paid it directly to Rome. Pompey, in the manner of Eastern conquerors before him, founded a city with his own name, Pompeiopolis. He returned to Rome rich in prestige, loot and gratitude.

During Pompey's campaigns the popular party made an effort to seize power in Rome. Their method was to propose revolutionary laws in the public assemblies; their hope, that the extraordinary powers given to Pompey had sufficiently weakened senatorial authority for these measures to be let through. Gaius Julius Caesar identified himself with the popular party. A relative of Marius and four years Cicero's junior, he had come to public life by the same route – a publicity-attracting prosecution in 77, the quaestorship in 68, the aedileship in 65 – and he went so far as to associate with the anarchist Catiline, who was, like himself, heavily in debt. Sallust's monograph gives us a picture of the man:

> Lucius Catilina was of noble birth and endowed with notable physical and mental qualities. But these were marred by a depraved and vicious nature. From his youth he had delighted in civil war, murder, looting, rioting: this had been his apprenticeship. He could survive without food, clothing or sleep for incredible periods of time. He was reckless, cunning, shifty, capable of any form of pretence or concealment. He lusted for the possessions of others and squandered his own. When he wanted something, there was no holding him. He could turn a fair enough speech, but lacked discretion. Only excess could feed his grandiose ambition; only enormity past belief could satisfy his dementia.[9]

Cicero had his eye on the consulship for 63. Catiline also intended to run, and Cicero saw him as a dangerous rival. Nevertheless, Catiline was about to stand trial for extortion, and Cicero thought that he could buy his support by offering to defend him: 'At this moment I'm thinking of defending my rival, Catiline. I have the jury I wanted, and the prosecution is with me all the way. I hope that if he's acquitted, we can make some better arrangement about the election campaign. If things turn out otherwise, I won't let it worry me too much.'[10]

Cicero became consul in 63. With any other opponent he might not have been elected. Catiline, foiled, resorted to force, and withdrew from Rome to Etruria, where a small army had been raised on his behalf. Outnumbered and ill-equipped he fell in battle near Pistoria (modern Pistoia): a small street in that city, near the Ospedale del Ceppo, bears the name of 'The Street of Catiline's Tomb'. The remaining conspirators were imprisoned in Rome, where Cicero, who saw the whole movement as a deliberate affront to himself, urged their deaths:

You have a consul who has been preserved from the plots and snares which beset him on every side; who has been snatched from the very jaws of death not for his own salvation but for yours. Highborn and humble, rich and poor, we come with one will, one heart, one voice to save our country. As the swords and blazing torches of a godless conspiracy gather menacingly round her, she holds out her hands to you and asks your aid. She entrusts herself to you. The lives of her citizens, the citadel and Capitol, the altars of her guardian deities, the eternal fire of Vesta, the shrines and temples of her gods, the walls and dwellings of our city, all these things she entrusts to you, to you, to you. On the decision that you make today will depend the fortunes of every man here, your very hearths and homes.[11]

At Cicero's insistence, the conspirators were sentenced to summary execution. He saw this as the crowning achievement of a consulship he was to memorialize in a much-derided poem.

The course you followed from your early youth
And sought again with honest zeal as consul,
Pursue for ever, and increase your fame
Upon the tongues of honourable men.[12]

The fame, unfortunately, was to prove evanescent. At this point, with Cicero at the height of his power, we may try to reconstruct something of his daily environment. His private house, as we have seen, was on the Palatine. Plutarch says that he lived there to be nearer his clients, but the real reason was surely prestige; it was the best residential quarter in Rome, with powerful historical associations.

Stranger, this place, where Rome lies spread before you,
Was grass and hill, before Aeneas came.[13]

Thus sings Propertius, linking the site with the meeting between the Trojan founder and the local king Evander. The hut of Romulus stood on the Palatine, and so did the temple of Cybele, the Great Mother. Private citizens built their houses here, prizing the privacy that they could buy – for a large price – so close to the administrative centre of the city. The lucky occupants haggled over land and trees, and built houses of appropriate ostentation. Lucius Licinius Crassus, one of the great orators of his day, erected six marble columns in his courtyard at a time when such things were rare in Rome. This was in 92 B.C. Forty years later, Marcus Scaurus had a number of similar columns, thirty-eight feet high, removed from the theatre they had adorned, carried up the Palatine and installed in his hall. It was such a difficult enterprise that the drainage contractor forced Scaurus to insure him against damage during the hauling operations. Cicero tells us that Chrysogonus, Sulla's freedman, lived here, and a man who thought as highly of himself as Cicero could scarcely live anywhere else.

He bought a property on the hill in 62 B.C. As he is never tired of telling us, it did not stand for long. It was destroyed in his absence by a political opponent four years later, and the land was acquired by the state as a temple site. Cicero complained that the proffered compensation was inadequate, and after much argument succeeded in persuading the authorities to allow the land to be restored to private use. 'I am certain', he says, 'that no public work, no historical monument, no temple has ever had so many senatorial decrees passed about it as my house.'[14] It is difficult, now, to find out what these great republican houses looked like. They were overbuilt by the vast architectural complexes of the imperial palaces which have left the Palatine a maze of brick walls and crumbling arches. At the lowest levels, excavators have occasionally uncovered frescoes or mosaics dating from before Augustus's accession. But there is one more valuable clue, which comes to us through the activities of Augustus himself. According to his biographer, the first Emperor preferred to live on a modest scale:

He had originally taken up residence near the Forum, above the Ringmakers' Steps, in a house which had once belonged to Calvus the orator. He later acquired the house of Hortensius, no less modest for all that it stood on the Palatine. It was an unostentatious building of average size, with a short colonnade only, made of *peperino*. There was no use of marble for interior decoration, no fancy pavements. . . . If he wanted uninterrupted privacy for his work, he had a study on the top floor.[15]

Hortensius was, of course, Cicero's wealthy rival at the bar, and a house which seemed modest in comparison with the palaces of the later Empire was not necessarily so by republican standards. It has been identified with the so-called House of Livia, one of the simpler buildings on the Palatine, a split-level construction of which the lower rooms have been excavated. If this was once Hortensius's house, we can assume Cicero's to have been similar.

It is of a type with which we shall become more familiar at Pompeii, with rooms opening off a central court, or *atrium*. This was perhaps decorated with two statues, whose bases have been preserved. Across the court from the principal entrance lies the *tablinum*, or principal reception room. On its right-hand wall, framed in an architectural composition, is an illustration of the myth of Io, who was changed by Hera into a heifer in punishment for innocently attracting Zeus's amorous eyes. The painting shows Io at her moment of deliverance. She is seated at the foot of a column while her jailor, Argos, watches her jealously. Hermes, Zeus's emissary, approaches from the distance. He has been appointed to kill Argos, and is looking up to heaven, perhaps, for inspiration. Another illustration shows a street-scene, with balconied tenement-houses of the kind from which Cicero derived a considerable income. These pictures and others in the *triclinium*, or dining-room, are intended to give the effect of windows, a familiar Roman device to lend an air of spaciousness to rooms whose all-enclosing walls proclaim the need for privacy.

From such a house, then, we may imagine Cicero coming down from the Palatine to attend to the business of the day. He would have been accompanied by his freedman and secretary Tiro, who had invented a system of shorthand and was to act as his master's literary executor. In the Forum below were the buildings which Cicero graced with his oratory. State business would have taken him to the western end, past the *lacus Curtius*, a small pond that, in republican times, reminded the citizens that the whole valley had once been a marsh, to the seats of office overshadowed by the Capitoline Hill. Films and novels have given an exaggerated idea of the spread of the Forum. It was impressive, but not large. When the producers of the film *Cleopatra* wished to represent the

Queen of Egypt's entry into Rome, they had an exact historical reconstruction made only to find that it was far too small for their purposes. The Senate House in which Cicero spoke was of considerable antiquity. Tradition attributed it to one of the early kings, and Sulla had enlarged and embellished it. It was destroyed, like Cicero's house, soon after his consulship. Julius Caesar began a new structure the building of which, interrupted by the civil wars, was not completed until 29 B.C., when it was dedicated by Augustus. Restored by Domitian, it was destroyed again in the fire of A.D. 283 and rebuilt by Diocletian, in the version that still stands, to the same dimensions. And even this was swallowed up in the Church of San Adriano, from which it was not disengaged until the 1930s. It is thus difficult to reconstruct a picture of the building as Cicero knew it; difficult, even, to see it as Domitian restored it, though sculptured reliefs found by the *rostra* show a pillared façade which may be the Senate House as it looked in the second century A.D. But it is safe to assume that piety and tradition preserved the internal arrangements more or less the same through their various external transformations. Its present appearance is appropriately solemn and monumental, with windows looking out onto the Forum and, inside, three tiers of seats – or steps on which the senators' chairs could be placed – running down each long side.

In front of the Senate House was the *comitium*, or place of assembly, where Plautus said the perjurers could be found. Here the representatives of the thirty divisions of the population met for discussion and the election of magistrates. This was the centre of Roman political life; its successive repairings date from the early Republic to the late Empire. Here the *rostra*, or speaker's platform, originally stood. It acquired its name from its ornament of ships' prows captured from the Latins at the battle of Antium in 338 B.C. Decorated with statues of noble dead, changed from time to time and in some cases of great antiquity, it must have inspired every orator to think of himself as the living mouthpiece of Roman tradition. Julius Caesar moved the platform slightly to the position in which we see it now.

From the *rostra* Cicero could have looked across the open space to the great basilica named after the Aemilian family who had built it in 179 B.C. and reconstructed it on a more magnificent scale in 55 B.C. Its pillared, two-storied façade was hung with bronze shields bearing the portraits of illustrious family ancestors. Within the portico was a row of shops, and behind it the great hall used for the transaction of business and the hearing of cases. Julius Caesar was to tear down the row of shops which still stood along the south side of the Forum and build another basilica named after his own family: it may have been in the planning stages as early as 54 B.C., and was dedicated in 46. Its addition gave a certain regularity to the west end of the Forum, something much to be desired in an area where much of the building had been haphazard.

After his overthrow of the conspirators – though the question of the legality of his act was to return to haunt him – Cicero could justifiably look round at these monuments and feel himself at one with the spirit which they represented; he was identified, in his own mind and others', with the highest interests of the State. Four years later, so swiftly did the wheels of Roman politics turn, he was in grumbling, frustrated exile, elbowed aside by men with more forceful personalities and the means to have them recognized. Pompey returned from Asia amid general acclaim mixed with relief that he was still not behaving like a Sulla. He was too honest for his own good. Divesting himself of his military power and entering Rome as a private citizen, he relied on the goodwill of the senate to ratify his Asian decisions and reward his veterans with land. This goodwill was not forthcoming. The senate foolishly alienated its most powerful supporter, and Pompey was forced, for his own protection, into an alliance with other strong men, Caesar and Crassus. Cicero was invited to join them, but refused; his absence was not felt. Caesar was elected consul in 59, and in a stormy year's work carried through the legislative programme agreed upon by the triumvirate. Pompey's Asian decisions were approved and a new agrarian law passed for his men; and Rome acquired, among other doubtful blessings, its first daily newspaper. It was Caesar who benefited most from the coalition. After his year in office he was given the military proconsulship of Gaul. Pompey and Crassus were to stay in Rome.

Caesar's brilliant conquest of Gaul in the following years, including the defeat of the turbulent Belgae and two military reconnaissances into Britain, stands in marked contrast to Pompey's indecisive part in Rome's domestic policy. There was rioting and violence in the streets, much of it provoked by Publius Clodius, Caesar's man, who bore an old grudge against Cicero and used his new influence to pursue it. Clodius was a dissolute member of the venerable Claudian family who had changed his name to the vernacular spelling as one way of gaining popular sympathy. As tribune for 58, he passed a law banishing anyone who had put citizens to death without trial. This was aimed specifically at Cicero and his action on the Catiline case. The former hero, in spite of all the theatrical wiles learned from years at the bar, was hounded: 'When he realized that he was in danger of prosecution, he changed his clothes, left his hair unkempt and went through the streets begging for popular support. But everywhere he went, there was Clodius with a gang of hooligans making coarse jokes about his changed appearance, pelting him with mud and stones and keeping his entreaties from reaching the people.'[16]

His letters from his places of exile – Brundisium, Thessalonica, Dyrrachium – are sodden with misery. The rumour went round Rome that he was going mad. He claimed that the jealousy of the triumvirate had driven him out of the country.

You keep on blaming me for taking my misfortunes so badly. You ought to pity me, not blame me. You see what I am suffering; have you ever seen or heard the like before? You write about the gossip that I'm going out of my mind. No, it's still in good shape. I wish it had been this way during the recent crisis. The people I thought would have been most interested in my well-being turned out to be my deadliest enemies. When they saw me falter, they fell on me like an avalanche.[17]

I'm suffering, yes; but I'm still in possession of my faculties. And I'm suffering particularly because I can't put those faculties to work.

No opportunity, no one to talk to. You're unhappy because you've lost me. But I'm only one man. What do you think I feel? I've lost you, I've lost everybody.[18]

But by 57 Clodius had gone too far, and Cicero was recalled and compensated. He flung himself with renewed zeal into politics, under the illusion that he could still exercise his old power and profit from the dissension he suspected among the triumvirate. Events quickly proved how wrong he was. Pompey, Caesar and Crassus patched up their differences at a meeting in Luca the following year, and Cicero was ordered to come to heel. He quickly restored himself to Caesar's good graces. Crassus and Pompey were consuls for 55, after which the former led a Roman army into Syria to fight the Parthians. He was killed in 53 in a defeat that was a crushing blow to Roman pride. Pompey, as sole consul, was left to deal with a resurgent Clodius, whose brawling once again put Cicero into mortal danger near his own home: 'On 11 November as I was going down the Sacred Way, Clodius and his gang attacked me. Yells, stones, clubs, swords; it was a complete surprise. We retreated to Taetius Damio's porch, where my companions had no trouble in keeping them off. I could have had Clodius killed.'[19]

The death of Clodius gave him some peace, but he was clearly frightened of the course events were taking. The following years find him unusually silent. In 51 he was out of the country again, this time in an official position as proconsul of Cilicia.

By the time he returned, civil war was inevitable. The conference of 56 had only patched up differences between the rival politicians which were now beginning to reappear. Caesar, poised in Gaul with his legions, was anxious about his constitutional position. If he returned without troops, he had no security against prosecution. If he brought his army with him, it would be tantamount to a declaration of war. After, as he tells us, exploring every means of reconciliation, he decided on the latter course. In 49 he crossed the Rubicon with one legion and was promptly declared an outlaw by the senate, who instructed Pompey to prepare defences against him. But Pompey's forces were in Spain, and there was no time to organize any serious resistance in Italy. Withdrawing the bulk of his troops to Greece, he yielded Rome and the peninsula without a fight. After considerable hesitation, Cicero took Pompey's side, and crossed to Greece to join him in his camp. He was extremely miserable there, disliking the company he was forced to keep and being no less disliked by them. Afterwards he writes: 'I'm not sorry that I left Pompey's camp. There was so much brutality there, so much rubbing shoulders with savage, uncouth associates that whole families could have gone up on the proscription lists, not just individuals. They were all agreed; if they'd won, the property of each and every one of you would have been taken as the spoils of war.'[20]

In spite of Pompey's control of the sea, Caesar managed to ship his army across to Greece in the winter. Pompey moved to contain the invading force on the coast, and small-scale fighting occurred round Dyrrachium. Caesar's supplies were running out. In an effort to relieve the pressure on him he made a sudden move into Thessaly. This precipitated the crisis of the war. Pompey's best plan would have been to continue following him and hemming him in to prevent his getting supplies. This would have forced Caesar either to risk battle in unfavourable conditions or to make a desperate attempt to escape. But Pompey decided that the time had come to deal the *coup de grâce*, and his decision bore bitter fruit at Pharsalus with a total victory for Caesar. The surviving Pompeians fled, Pompey himself taking ship for Egypt, where he was murdered on the Pharaoh's orders.

This did not mean the end of the war. Pompey's admirals still controlled the seas. Caesar made a great sweep around the Mediterranean. In 47 he was in Egypt, where he intervened in a civil war, met Cleopatra and reorganized the country. Then back to Rome, only to leave in the winter – a crossing as risky as that which had taken him to Greece – for Africa by way of Sicily. At Thapsus he defeated the surviving Pompeians in Africa. From there he moved to Spain and crushed a local revolt. And so back to Rome again, where he moved rapidly to consolidate his position and give himself some pretence of legality.

Rome was full of Caesar. Having stunned the Roman people with his conquests, he was now to dazzle them with his triumphs, and woo them with his vaunted clemency. In a magnificent procession, he paraded the living testimony of his successes past the people in chronological order – Gaul, Egypt, Africa. He burnt the private papers of the Pompeians unread; there was to be no purge, no retribution. He strengthened his regime in more subtle ways. The senate, weakened by losses, was packed with Caesar's men. Made dictator for ten years, Caesar was given a seat of honour between the consuls. He rewarded his veterans with land, being cautious to avoid giving offence by wholesale expropriation. Care was taken to spread the veterans widely over the country, to avoid the possibility of mutiny in the future. Caesar became respectable, disowning and disbanding the revolutionary clubs which had served him so well earlier. Long associated with the popular party, he coolly disregarded its programme when in power.

Among those won over to Caesar's side was Cicero. He writes a flattering, self-congratulatory letter about his meeting with the great man:

My formidable guest has gone, and left 'not a wrack behind'. It all went off splendidly. But when he got to Philippus on the evening of the eighteenth the house was so full of soldiers that there was hardly a room left for Caesar to dine in. Two thousand men! What do you think of that? I wasn't at all easy in my mind about what would happen the next day. But Cassius Barba came to the rescue, and put a detail on escort-duty. They pitched camp in the fields and set up pickets round the house. On the nineteenth he stayed with Philippus until one o'clock, and gave orders not to be disturbed; he had Balbus with him, I think, working on the budget. Then he went for a walk along the beach. Some time after two he took a bath . . . then he performed his *toilette* and sat down to dinner. He was taking emetics under doctor's orders, and so could eat and drink what he liked. It was a grand dinner, elegantly served. Not only that, but

Well cooked, and spiced
With pleasant conversation. All went well.

Besides this, his *cercle intime* sat down to a lavish spread – three rooms full of them! – and his lower-class freedmen and slaves had nothing to complain about. I entertained the gentry in the manner to which they were accustomed. What more need I say? Just a quiet man-to-man talk. Still, he wasn't the sort of guest to whom you'd say 'Look me up when you're passing this way again.' Once is enough.[21]

There is considerable argument about the position which Caesar eventually envisaged for himself. The historical evidence is abundant, but of dubious quality. There are many indications, however, that Caesar intended to become a king of a kind that could also be recognized as a god. This was a common enough idea in antiquity, though at odds with Roman tradition. Alexander's successors, adopting the customs of the countries that they ruled, had encouraged their subjects to worship them as living deities. During the Republic a number of proconsuls in the East had been worshipped as gods or heroes, and Julius Caesar, throughout his life, had been careful to stress the divine origin of his family from Aphrodite-Venus and Anchises, whose union had produced Aeneas. In May 45 it was decreed that a statue of Caesar should be set up in the temple of Quirinus. At the beginning of 44 this process was intensified in a series of senatorial resolutions. Statues were to be erected and sacrifices made to Caesar on his birthday. Marcus Antonius (Mark Antony), Caesar's right-hand man, proposed a special quadrennial feast in his honour. Cicero snorts that, like Jupiter, Mars and Quirinus, the divine Julius has his priest now, in the shape of Antony. A temple was planned, to be dedicated to 'the clemency of Caesar'. A new college of priests bearing his name was added to the established orders.

In discussing the honours heaped on Caesar, it is important to distinguish between the extravagant and unprecedented, and what was in accordance with established republican usage. If Caesar was hailed as *parens patriae*, the father of his country, the title had already been sought by Cicero. The right to have one's image on coins was unusual but not unparalleled. What was ominous in Caesar's case was the constant and uninterrupted issue of such coins; in the past, there had only been a single commemorative minting. Divine honours were altogether unprecedented, at least in Italy, and the title of king still bore the traditional odium. Here Caesar was forced to proceed cautiously. In a couple of carefully

The founders: Father Tiber, the she-wolf, Romulus and Remus. Sculptural group from Hadrian's Villa, Tivoli

Greek influence: the thriving colony of Poseidonia (Paestum)

The fertile riverlands of the Po Valley lure invaders across the northern mountains

Etruscan country: hills near Volterra

Rome's near neighbours: Alatri, typical of the Latin hill-towns

. . . while in the museum of Tarquinia the effigies of the Etruscan dead continue their eternal conversation

Volterra: Etruscan gate by night

Roman roads: a bridge on Roman foundations lies deep beneath the modern highway at Parma . . .

. . . while modern traffic still follows the course of the Via Appia at Benevento

The religion of the household: domestic altar, Herculaneum

The religion of the farmers: carved representation of Sylvanus, from the amphitheatre at Capua

The religion of the State: bull-sacrifice, mosaic from firemen's barracks, Ostia . . .

. . . and Temple of Hercules, Ostia

Religions exotic and imported: Egyptian obelisk once belonging to the Temple of Isis, Benevento . . .

. . . and shrine of Mithra, God of Light, at Ostia

The triumph of Christianity:
the church of San Lorenzo in
Miranda rises symbolically from
the Temple of Antoninus and
Faustina, Roman Forum

The houses of the rich:
marble table in pergola,
Herculaneum

. . . trellised garden with water channel, Pompeii . . .

... and peristyle, atrium and street door, Herculaneum

Hypocaust for central heating, Fishbourne, Sussex

The houses of the workers: bakery with oven and mills, Pompeii . . .

. . . and barman's-eye view of the street, Herculaneum

Row of tenements, Ostia

Public utilities: town water cistern, Nîmes . . .

. . . and public pleasure: Nîmes, amphitheatre

Building for grandeur: staircase leading to the Temple of Jupiter, Baalbek

stage-managed scenes, he probed the public sentiment by having royal honours offered him, and loudly refusing them. He was not entirely pleased by the response, particularly from certain staunch republicans. Had he lived, he would have doubtless proceeded as Augustus was to do after him, and gradually acquired supreme power by the concentration and subversion of constitutional republican offices. But his aims were cut short by his assassination in 44 B.C., at the hands of a group of disgruntled idealists who had no constructive plans beyond the removal of the man they hated.

The spot where Caesar in all probability met his death was uncovered to modern eyes by the excavations carried out under Mussolini's auspices in the Largo Argentina. In the centre of the square are the remains of four unidentified republican temples. At one corner, visible from a pedestrian underpass, is a portion of the portico of the theatre which Pompey had erected, against strong senatorial opposition, in 55 B.C. Here Caesar died from the dagger-blows of Brutus, Cassius and the rest. His funeral took place in the Forum, a notable show in a place that had seen many well-produced displays. Suetonius records the scene:

> The bier was carried down into the Forum by past and present magistrates. There was an argument about where the cremation should take place – in the temple of Jupiter on the Capitoline, or the hall built by Pompey. It was interrupted by two men who appeared out of nowhere with swords at their sides and a brace of spears in their hands, and set fire to the bier with blazing torches. Immediately the crowd of bystanders started to pile on dry branches, benches from the courthouse, and anything else that would make a burnt offering.[22]

Plutarch expands the story, attributing to Antony the literally inflammatory speech that Shakespeare recreates from his imagination. In this account, the market-stalls were hurled into the flames, and the assassins' houses set on fire by the maddened crowd. Cicero, nearer the event, adds the detail that Caesar's body was only partly consumed, but that the house of an innocent private citizen was burnt to the ground.

Where was Cicero all this while? He had retired to the country, and to philosophy. The bulk of his philosophical writings were completed between the spring of 45 and the autumn of 44. Like the Greeks whom he inevitably imitated, his writings covered a wide range of interests He had already published several works on the history and theory of rhetoric and political philosophy. His *Republic* studies the Roman state as the basis for an ideal constitution; his *Laws*, composed as a counterpart to Plato's work of the same title, is an intellectually independent examination of how natural, sacred and magisterial law should operate in the well-run state. Once again, Cicero's theory is based on Roman practice. The rapid intensification of his interest in philosophy, which produced a continuous flow of books in the years following the Pompeian débâcle, was due, on Cicero's own admission, to two causes. He was seeking personal solace for the loss of his daughter Tullia, who died when she was about thirty-five years old. Cicero's public writings proclaim his deep affection for her, though his letters reveal surprisingly little concern for the many misfortunes of her life. She had lost one husband by death, a second by divorce, and was fretted into her own grave by the callous and irresponsible behaviour of a third. Cicero seems to treat her misadventures casually, until the last; her death was a great shock to him, and he was at least a better father than he was a husband. He had divorced his wife to marry his ward, and was plunged into the financial embarrassments we have noted as a recurrent motif in Roman comedy; before long he was to divorce his ward. An equally strong motive was his frustration at the political inactivity which had been imposed on him. Caesar's tyranny excluded him from public life, and his books, as he said, were his substitute for speaking in the senate.

Like Plato, he preferred the dialogue form, though he lacked the sense of dramatic vividness which gave spirit to Plato's discussions. His dialogues represent the talk of cultured Roman men of affairs in the library or over the dinner table. They are erudite, expansive and not a little pompous; nor are they particularly original. But Cicero saw himself as a popularizer rather than an innovator. His expressed desire was to add a new dimension to Latin literature. Philosophy had been largely neglected up to his time, and he saw the moral decline of the fading Republic as a challenge. His fellow citizens needed to be educated.

To this end, his first aim was to formulate a suitable language. Latin had not yet reached a sufficient state of development to convey the subtleties of the Greek authors, and Cicero was forced to lay down definitions, explain unfamiliar ideas in terms more meaningful to his Roman readers, and, on occasion, to coin a new vocabulary. His difficulties are seen in the opening chapters of *The Chief Good and the Chief Evil*, where he explains the necessity of using expressions and terms far removed from those of ordinary life in expounding philosophy which, like any other science, has its own technical language. In *The Nature of the Gods*, he grapples with the problem of finding Latin equivalents for Greek abstract nouns. How does one translate *eudaimonia*, the state of blessed happiness? Cicero seeks an abstract noun from the Latin *beatus*, but likes neither *beatitas* nor *beatitudo*. In other places he turns the Greek noun into a Latin phrase. He was attempting to bring Latin, in a short space of time, to a point of development that Greek had taken centuries to reach. To a large extent he was successful. His linguistic explorations won a permanent place in the Latin vocabulary, and provided a useful framework for subsequent philosophical discussion. Some critics consider this to have been Cicero's greatest service to letters.

Cicero was inclined – perhaps seriously – to belittle his philosophical works, and it is true that their influence on his contemporaries seems to have been negligible. Nevertheless, they offer a detailed survey of the principal Greek schools in vogue at his time. Cicero aptly compared his writing in this field to the Roman adaptations of Greek drama: they offered Greek ideas in Roman dress, embroidered with allusions to Roman history and tradition, and presented in a form that made them more easily assimilable. He does not commit himself wholly to any one school, though he is inclined to favour the Stoics over the Epicureans. As a practical politician, he could not countenance a system which urged the individual to withdraw from the everyday issues of society, and the austere moral code of the Stoics was in many ways highly acceptable to him. He remains, however, an eclectic, and his chief preference was for the sceptical tradition of the Academics, Plato's successors. It was the Academics' way, as he said, to oppose all schools, to maintain that nothing was known for certain, and to adopt a pragmatic approach to life. Cicero's philosophy is essentially Roman in its cautious practicality. His *Duties*, a manual of ethics dedicated to his son, shows the *paterfamilias* at his best, guiding, admonishing and creating an ideal picture of the old-fashioned Roman gentleman he would wish the boy to be. His work is Roman, too, in its contradictions. We often see the Greek tradition of high intellectual speculation at war with Roman sentiment. Cicero the Hellenist can conduct an exhaustive investigation into the nature of the gods; Cicero the orator can take the religious establishment, and the elaborate apparatus of divination that surrounded it, for granted. His works are a composite picture of contemporary upper-class Roman thought, historically valuable no less for their weaknesses than for their virtues.

Caesar's assassination had an effect on Cicero amounting almost to hysteria. The prefaces to his works and his letter to Atticus show his state of mind at the time, and his increasing suspicion of Antony.

My dear Atticus, I'm afraid we have gained nothing from the Ides of March but the pleasure of satisfying our hatred and resentment. The news I get from Rome! And the things I see here!
'*The deed was noble, but it bore no fruit.*'
You know how attached I am to the Sicilians, and how great an honour I count it to represent them. Caesar granted them many privileges, of which I am in favour, though giving them Latin rights was intolerable. However. . . . But here is Antony taking a large bribe and posting a law alleged to have been carried by the dictator in the public assembly, making the Sicilians Roman citizens! There was no mention of such a thing when Caesar was alive.[23]

He saw the confusion that followed the dictator's death as a godsent opportunity to re-enter politics and establish himself once again as the leader of the Roman people. Octavian, Caesar's appointed heir, he dismissed as a mere boy, easily manipulable; the full force of his attack was directed against Antony. On 2

September 44 he delivered the first of a series of harangues that he called the *Philippics*, in memory of Demosthenes' opposition to the king of Macedon.

My honourable friends, you mourn the slaughter of three armies of the Roman people. It was Antony who slaughtered them. You mourn the most distinguished of your citizens. It was Antony who took them too. The authority of our order has been overthrown. It was Antony who did it. All the consequences we have seen – and what evil have we not seen? – we shall place to Antony's account, if we have not taken leave of our senses. This man is a second Helen of Troy; he has brought us war, he has brought us ruin, he has brought us destruction.[24]

Once again, the coalition of more powerful forces proved too strong for him. Antony and Octavian patched up a working agreement, as a price for which the 'boy' acceded to Antony's demand that Cicero be sacrificed. On 7 December 43 he was murdered on his estate near Formiae. On the route of the old Via Appia as it descends from Itri one may still see a round tower surrounded with tall trees known locally as Cicero's tomb. His head and hands were displayed on the *rostra* from which he had spoken so many times, a reminder of the barbarities practised by Marius and Sulla, and a sufficient sign of the horrors to come before Octavian, who was to call himself Augustus, imposed a new peace and a new order on the world that Julius Caesar had divided.

Cicero survived in his writings. The language that he had formulated framed the arguments of Christian philosophers; his ghost loomed over the Renaissance. His *Tusculan Disputations* was probably the first classical work to be printed, and his influence on the later humanists was immense, though it was often seen as other than benign. Thomas Nash sees Cicero as a charlatan and poseur. He describes a séance in which the magician Cornelius Agrippa conjures up the orator's ghost to declaim his first great speech in defence of Sextus Roscius: 'At the time prefixed in entered Tully, ascending his pleading place, and declaimed verbatim the forenamed oration, but with such astonishing amazement, with such reverent exaltation of spirit, with such soul-stirring

166

gestures, that all his auditors were ready to install his guilty client for a god.'[25]

Erasmus, reacting against the acceptance of Ciceronian Latin as the only possible style, was forced to defend his right to extend the vocabulary, and to abandon the use of pagan terms for Christian subjects. As a politician, Cicero's motives have been called into question with increasing frequency. In an important modern study,[26] even the chapter headings read like an indictment: 'Greed and Unscrupulousness'; 'Unstable Family Life'; 'The Blunders of a Career that Failed'; 'The Defects of a Statesman'. But any politician who bared his private thoughts and activities as mercilessly as Cicero does in his letters – some of which must surely not have been intended for publication – would lay himself open to the same criticism. Cicero, for all his vainglory, stands revealed to us as essentially human, and the corpus of his works gives us a panorama of late republican life in all its aspects, from the most noble to the most base.

NOTES TO CHAPTER FIVE

1. Plutarch, *Cicero*, 2. 2.
2. Cicero, *De Oratore (The Orator)*, I. 157–8.
3. Suetonius, *De Grammaticis (Grammar-school Education)*, 4.
4. Cicero, *Brutus*, 90. 312.
5. Cicero, *In Defence of Sextus Roscius of Ameria*, I. 2–3.
6. Ibid. 46. 1333.
7. Cicero, *Against Verres*, I. 4. 13–14.
8. Cicero, *On Behalf of the Manilian Law*, 10. 27.
9. Sallust, *Catiline*, 5.
10. Cicero, *Letters to Atticus*, I. 2. 1.
11. Cicero, *Against Catiline*, IV. 18.
12. Cicero, *De Consulatu Suo (A Poem on his Consulship)*, III.
13. Propertius, *Elegies*, IV. I. 1–2.
14. Cicero, *De Haruspicum Responsis (The Reply from the Auspices)*, 8. 4.
15. Suetonius, *Augustus*, 72.
16. Plutarch, *Cicero*, 34.
17. Cicero, *Letters to Atticus*, III. 13. 2.
18. Ibid. III. 15. 2.
19. Cicero, *Letters to Atticus*, IV. 3. 3.

20. Ibid. XI. 6.
21. Ibid. XIII. 52.
22. Suetonius, *Caesar*, 84.
23. Cicero, *Letters to Atticus*, XIV. 12.
24. Cicero, *Philippics*, II. 22. 55.
25. Nash, *The Unfortunate Traveller*.
26. Carcopino, *Cicero: The Secrets of his Correspondence*.

Chapter Six

The Great Change

THE mystique of power exercises a continual historical fascination. Who has it, and who does not? By what means does it come?
And why are its recipients, so often, unlikely? There were many
Romans who, like Cicero, refused to believe that any real authority could ever be exerted by the grandson of an out-of-town
banker; whose family had never held any major political office;
who was only nineteen when Caesar's death was announced – the
news took nearly two weeks to reach him – and with his friends
in Greece, still pursuing his studies; whose connection with the
dictator was tenuous – his mother was Caesar's niece – even
though Caesar had officially declared him his heir. Octavius, or
Octavian, as he called himself on accepting the legacy, had other
things against him. He was not an imposing figure. Shorter than
normal, about five feet seven, he wore thick-soled shoes which
increased his stature but betrayed his sensitivity. Like certain other
world dominators, he suffered from physical infirmities. He had a
skin disease, a weakness in one leg which gave him a permanent
limp, and a dangerous susceptibility to changes of climate. All his
life he was plagued by illnesses which kept him out of battle and
which in 23 B.C. nearly provoked a constitutional crisis by
threatening his life. A born student, one would have said, rather
than a leader of men. He was well read and scholarly, with a
fondness for Greek drama, and wrote much himself; he pursued
the fashionable pastime of writing tragedies. His biographers
attributed to him somewhat puerile foibles, such as a fondness for
dice and childish games. He loved boxing-matches. And he was
cold in his personal relationships. Shakespeare's picture of him
sulking icily aboard the galley while Antony and the others have
an uproarious, drunken party must be very close to the truth.

When he died, on 19 August A.D. 14, this inconsequential weakling controlled the greater part of the known world. By a series of intricate political manipulations he had remodelled the Roman constitution; he had established a dynasty; he had exercised his authority on every aspect of Roman life, and created a system of government which was to endure for centuries, and whose repercussions we still hear. Concerned to the last with his public image, he left 'a digest of his own accomplishments, which he desired to be inscribed on tablets of bronze and affixed to the front of his tomb'.[1]

The original manuscript, deposited in the senatorial archives, has been lost to us. So has the Roman inscription. We know the document from copies erected in key cities of the Empire. One was discovered at Ancyra, the Ankara of modern Turkey, in 1555, where it had been displayed on the walls of the temple of Rome and Augustus. Fragments of another were found at Apollonia, in Greece, where the boy Octavius had gone to college, at the base of a statue erected in honour of Augustus, Tiberius and the imperial family. A third was discovered at Antioch. By comparing and collating the fragments, we are able to reconstruct a document of crucial importance in studying the transfer of power from the elected representatives of the people to the hands of an autocrat; the testament, moreover, of a consummate propagandist. We can learn much about Augustus's aims and methods by comparing his own account of his career with the information we possess from other sources.

There has been considerable argument as to when this document was first conceived, why it was written and where it was distributed. There were undoubtedly more copies; the survival of three from the same area is probably due to an accident of history. Such memorials were more likely to be left undisturbed in a remote province than in the heart of the Empire. Two of the copies are accompanied by a Greek translation, which adapts, simplifies and shortens the original, giving the impression that every effort was made to assist non-Latin speakers in mastering its complexities. Augustus was concerned that the world should see his life as he wanted it. The tone of the work is popular, and the Roman copy was clearly aimed at the plebs. It has been described as many things – a political testimony, a statement of accounts, a funerary inscription – and has some of the qualities of each. But its prime purpose was to give an appearance of legality to achievements which were, from the beginning, on shaky constitutional grounds.

For comparison, we have the accounts of Augustus's reign given by later historians and biographers. These men would have gone to the archives for the bulk of their information, and would of course have been presented with the official version. But they used other sources as well, and when they give information which is derogatory we may be fairly certain that it came from private individuals. Whatever credence we may give to such stories – and the more extravagant are obviously absurd – their very existence indicates that there was a large body of subversive opinion, which saw only illegality in the acts and deeds of Augustus. Tacitus says as much when he reports the discussions after Augustus's death. Some argued that he showed clemency in overlooking Antony's faults for the sake of avenging his father, that he organized the state without resorting to monarchy or dictatorship, that he had enriched the moral life of his people by his laws, and the city by the splendour of his buildings. Against this, it was urged that Augustus had used filial piety as a cloak, seduced the legions of a consul, usurped the symbols and powers of the praetorship by a senatorial decree, instituted savage proscriptions, betrayed Antony and achieved peace only with bloodshed.[2] We have, then, an interesting opportunity of studying the difference between the reality and the façade; and Augustus, who was to announce in a famous boast that he had found Rome built of brick and left it built of marble, was no less adept at covering the solid fabric of his achievements with the shell of constitutionality.

At the age of nineteen, on my own authority and at my own expense, I raised the army by means of which I liberated the Republic from the oppression of a tyrannical faction. In return the Senate honoured me in its decrees, and made me a member of its order in the consulship of C. Pansa and A. Hirtius . . . it ordered me as propraetor to take joint action with the consuls against any danger to the Republic. In the same year, with the death of both consuls in battle, the people made me consul, and chose me as one of the triumvirate to effect a constitutional settlement. The murderers of my father I drove into exile, avenging their crime through the courts of law as duly appointed; and afterwards, when they declared war on the Republic, I won two victories over them in the field.[3]

Concerned from the beginning to stress the legality of his position, Augustus glides swiftly over the succession of political manipulations and lucky accidents which gave him his start. After Caesar's death, Antony was the leading magistrate in a Rome where the pro-Caesarian party was still a powerful force. The murderers were obliged to leave Italy. Antony, who had taken possession of Caesar's treasure and showed himself to the people as the dictator's executor, opened hostilities against them in Gaul. Octavian's appearance was an embarrassment. He began to agitate among the soldiers, made the most of his position as Caesar's legal heir, and quarrelled violently with Antony over the inheritance. As Antony moved north, Cicero attempted to intervene. Stirred by the hope of a revived Republic, he delivered his *Philippics* and patronized Octavian, whom he saw as a useful tool. Antony was declared a public enemy, and Hirtius and Pansa were ordered to follow him and bring him to battle. Octavian accompanied them with a private army raised, as he says, at his own expense from Caesar's veterans settled round Naples. Antony was defeated and both consuls killed; Octavian promptly took over their forces. Ordered to disband his troops, he refused. Marching to Rome, he forced through his election as consul, and had the murderers declared outlaws. He says that the people made him consul. Legally, they could have done no such thing, for both consuls were dead, and without them the public assemblies had no validity. It was clearly the senate who put the measure through. Octavian had compelled it to declare itself. Since Caesar's death, the governing body had been swinging nervously between the surviving Caesarians and the 'liberators'. Now it was irretrievably committed, and Octavian had the law on his side. He was not yet, however, strong enough to oppose Antony, though skilful enough to use him. The triumvirate of which he speaks was formed in 43, with Marcus Aemilius Lepidus, a former consul and Caesar's master of horse, as its third member. One consequence of this coalition was the death of Cicero, demanded by Antony in revenge; another was the demolishing of the anti-Caesarian forces, represented by the official account as a 'tyrannical faction'. Cicero was not the only prominent man to die. A hundred and thirty senators in all perished in the proscriptions. Brutus and Cassius had taken refuge in Greece, and had concentrated their army at Philippi, in Macedonia. In the autumn of 42 they were crushed in two engagements. Both victories were largely due to the superior generalship of Antony, and the fighting quality of legions that used the superb training they had received under Caesar to avenge themselves on his murderers.

About Antony's contribution to this victory the official account is dumb. Augustus presents himself as sole conqueror, preferring to forget the assistance given to him by a man he was later to reject. Nor is there any record of the growing dissension between the two, or of Antony's misconduct abroad which gave the younger man the excuse to turn on him. Going East to invade Parthia – a campaign projected earlier by Julius Caesar – he became involved with Cleopatra. For this the Roman people would have forgiven him. But he was also foolish enough to allow himself to be treated as a Hellenistic monarch. This gave Octavian the opportunity for a sustained propaganda campaign in which Antony's reputation, before this considerably higher than his own, suffered irretrievable damage. We hear nothing of this from Augustus. Our evidence comes from the later historians and, to a certain extent, from the poets. Anti-Egyptian feeling ran high. Antony was vilified as a Roman who had disgraced his country, and who had distributed – this was the most damaging report of all – Roman land to be ruled by his and Cleopatra's children. Antony's side of the story has been lost. In all probability the conventional story of the over-ambitious general's entanglement with the Serpent of Old Nile, hallowed by Shakespeare, is only half true. Antony certainly had considerable support. Just before the final breach two hundred senators left Rome to join him in the East. In 32 Octavian forced the issue by declaring war on Cleopatra. Antony and his queen were defeated at Actium in the following year; the last of the great kingdoms created by Alexander had fallen, and the last major state was in Roman hands. But Antony's name is expunged from the official record, like that of Lepidus, always the weak man of the trio, who spent the rest of his years in retirement. With a triple triumph, Octavian celebrated the end of war.

> As I write these records, I have been consul thirteen times, and am in the thirty-seventh year of my tribunician power.... I refused to accept the dictatorship, though it was offered to me both in my absence and in person by the Senate and the people ... when offered the consulship for life, I refused to accept it ... though the Senate and the people unanimously consented to my election as superintendent of laws and public morals with supreme authority, I declined to accept any office inconsistent with our traditional constitution, and the domestic measures which the Senate requested me to carry out I effected by virtue of my tribunician power.[4]

The victory of Actium did not mark the end of Octavian's problems. He found himself the acknowledged master of a Roman world that had been ravaged by three civil wars, a world in which the old forms of government had been shattered. The old, proud families were no longer capable of providing leadership. The senate had been weakened by wartime casualties and by the influx of new and unworthy members to serve immediate political ends. There was need for a strong hand, but Octavian had to be careful how he applied it. The concentration of power in a single, decisive leader was necessary, inevitable and desirable. It had been obvious from the time of the emergence of the great generals who stalked like victorious *condottieri* over the wreckage of the constitution that the new, expansive Roman world required a new form of government, and that the needs of a world empire could no longer be met by the elective machinery devised for a small city state. Nevertheless, Octavian had Julius Caesar's fate for warning. Roman sentiment was still strong; the abhorrent manifestations of kingship were a death-warrant. His own account shows how careful he was to proceed in the republican forms. He took only those titles permitted by constitutional usage, though he retained and combined them in such a way as to give him a firm basis to act. As *imperator* (general) he had the solid backing of the armies. As consul for long periods he had the ear of the people and the deference of the senate. As tribune, he had the invaluable power of veto. As 'father of his country', a title already bestowed on Julius Caesar and listed by Augustus as his proudest achievement, he was entitled to profound respect. 'I stood before all others in dignity,' he says, 'but in terms of actual power I possessed no more than my colleagues in each magistracy that I held.'[5] Strictly speaking, this may have been true. Augustus's prestige, however, gave him the commanding position, and he increased this prestige by subtle ways. Not least impressive was his choice of name. It was related to the verb *augeo*, 'to increase', and had venerable religious connotations, being used of any particularly sacred place. By adopting it, Augustus invested himself with the aura of sanctity. It was by such means that he continued to impress his personality on the operations of the state. The legal basis of his power was slight; his real authority derived from things more intangible.

> I have been a pontifex, an augur, one of the fifteen superintendents of the sacred rites, one of the seven commissioners for religious banquets, an Arval Brother ... by new legislation I revived many ancestral traditions which were falling into disuse, and in my own person handed down many ideals worthy of imitation by posterity. . . . I built the Senate House and the adjoining shrine of Minerva, the temple of Apollo on the Palatine with porticoes, the temple of the deified Julius ... the temples of Jupiter on the Capitol, the temple of Quirinus, the temples of Minerva, Juno and Jupiter on the Aventine, the temple of the Lares at the head of the Sacred Way ... the temple of the Great Mother on the Palatine . . . .[6]

For Augustus, social, moral, political and religous reforms went hand in hand; each involved the others. The chaos of the war years he attributed as much to the decay of spirit as to inept leadership, and to this end went to work to restore a sense of the ancient virtues. For this reason the religious positions that he held were important to him. They allowed him to combine moral with political authority. He set a stern example. Although his enemies credited him with many of the vices he castigated in others, his public life was beyond reproach. To remedy the decline in public morality and the falling birthrate, he instituted stricter marriage requirements and inducements to produce large families. The scandals he uncovered in his own household were a severe blow to him. When his daughter and granddaughter, both named Iulia, were detected in unaugustan behaviour, he responded like one of the grimly pious fathers of early republican legend, and sentenced them to severe punishments. His building programme was a visible symbol of his moral reforms, as much as an attempt to unify his city architecturally. Monumental building in Rome had always been haphazard, dependent on individual whim rather then concerted planning. Cicero snorts his scorn at a Greek town-planning expert who thinks that he can give form to the city. Augustus chose his sites for their sentimental and traditional value. Those on the Palatine were particularly important, for they surrounded his house. He identified himself by association with the deities he honoured, and the poets who celebrated his architectural achievements were not slow to take the hint. Virgil writes of Augustus seated at the threshold of Apollo in his shining glory; Propertius celebrates the opening of the temple in a poem that glorifies the work of the man rather than the god.

The temple of Julius Caesar, now accorded divine honours, was the second and permanent memorial created to the dictator on the site of his cremation. The first had been 'a column of Numidian marble some twenty feet high, inscribed "TO THE FATHER OF HIS COUNTRY" '.[7] It lasted only a few months; Cicero writes happily of its overthrow. The temple stood facing the *rostra* across the open space of the Forum and contained a colossal statue of Caesar crowned with a star. Its podium was decorated with the prows of ships taken at Actium and provided another speakers' platform for major state occasions. A slight shift, but significant: the sounding-board of the Republic now confronts its simulacrum, which is part of a temple built to a dictator turned god.

> In accordance with the terms of my father's will, I paid the Roman plebs three hundred sesterces per head ... in my eleventh consulship I distributed twelve special allowances of corn paid for with my own money ... in my thirteenth consulship I gave the sum of sixty denarii to each individual among the plebs who was at that time receiving corn at the public expense; the recipients totalled slightly over two hundred thousand persons. ... I rewarded the soldiers and sent them home, ungrudgingly expending for this purpose about four hundred million sesterces ... four times I helped the treasury with my own money ....[8]

Augustus's testimony is a hymn of triumph sung to the clink of money. The above examples – there are many more – show his concern that his expenditures on the public behalf should be duly recognized. It had always been recognized that a politician needed private funds. The principal offices were honorary, and their holders were forced to reckon on a large outlay merely to keep their names in favour with the public. Augustus records his own contribution to such palliatives – gladiatorial games, athletic contests, wild-beast shows and a mock naval battle in a specially constructed lagoon near the Tiber. Such things were commonplace, though not perhaps on such a grand scale. The changing concepts of power, however, enforced new demands on the ruler. When so much depended on the goodwill of the soldiers, it was important that they be kept happy. Augustus records his rewards and donations, and stresses that he resettled the veterans at his own expense, thus avoiding the odium that dispossessions after previous wars had caused. We must add to this at least part of the cost of the elaborate building programme. When he came to power, Augustus was a wealthy man. He had already been considered rich before Julius Caesar left him sixty-six million sesterces, and had considerable other income besides. Some of this he had to spend at once for troops, but since he considered that he was serving the state in raising his first army he no doubt covered his losses from the booty at Philippi. An important item in his personal budget was the plunder from Egypt. This was enormous. Cleopatra had taken possession of all the temple treasures of the land, and confiscated the estates of her opponents. Augustus confiscated these in turn, together with those of the queen's ministers and supporters. When he died, he was by no means poor – he left his heirs a hundred and fifty million sesterces – but was certainly no richer than the magnates of the Republic. His decreasing balance bears out his claims of enormous personal expenditure. The cost of rule was high.

Augustus tells us nothing about public finances (except to indicate that the treasury had to be extricated from a budget crisis) but these were equally important to him. As we have seen, the cost of public administration under the Republic was not large. The senate controlled the purse-strings, and by this means was able to exercise some control over magistrates. The treasury in the Temple of Saturn was the official repository of moneys, and this was managed by two urban quaestors and their staff. That this office was considered relatively unimportant is seen from the fact that it was entrusted to men on the thresholds of their official careers; the quaestorship had an age qualification of twenty-five and was regarded as the stepping-stone to higher things. In theory, all money extracted from the provinces was transported to Rome, and paid out as required. In practice, a large proportion of the tax moneys was spent locally, and only the surplus of income over expenditure returned to the capital. This was the system that could so easily produce a Verres. The opportunities for graft and the falsification of accounts were virtually unlimited.

The Augustan regime required a stricter measure of control because it had to face greater demands. Under the Republic public money had been used largely for the army and navy. After Actium the latter at least would have been cheaper, but the army was improved and better paid, and the increasing complexity of administration, requiring large staffs of trained, salaried personnel, was a continuous drain on state funds. Large sums were spent on providing the city with corn and water, on the establishment of a police force, and on the erection of public buildings.

Greater efficiency was urgently needed. Augustus intervened, as usual, on the basis of powers that were not strictly legal. As supreme commander, he retained control over those provinces which he claimed still required military supervision. He was thus able to assume the ordinary duties of a provincial magistrate, collecting taxes, spending the revenue as he thought fit, and rendering a due account to the senate. To this extent, he was observing the customary practices of the Republic. The striking difference was, of course, that he was responsible for a large number of provinces, and was able to wield a greater measure of control and achieve some degree of centralization. There can be no doubt that the provinces were the better for it. The financial administrators were now responsible, not to a body, but to an individual, who was keenly interested in where the money went. Even under the worst emperors, the provincials were spared the abuses to which they had been subject under the Republic. In Rome itself, the various offices which Augustus held gave him some control over public money. He three times held a census, and, as censor, also had the duties, approved by republican usage, of determining the taxable resources of the community, letting out state contracts, and arranging the terms on which the tax-gatherers would collect the provincial revenues. Under the Republic, the censors' influence had been limited by the short duration of their appointment – eighteen months. Augustus, holding the office several times, was able to achieve some continuity.

But his main contribution seems to have been in the authority he exercised over the accounting. Under the Republic this had been at best haphazard, and under the control of young and inexperienced men. Under Augustus we see the beginnings of a treasury system. He published periodic accounts, and when, in 23 B.C., he thought he was on his death-bed, he was able to hand over to his colleague a complete documentation of the public revenue. When he actually died thirty-seven years later, he left a similar account. In finance, as in everything else, Augustus showed his power to centralize and control.

I extended the frontiers of all the Roman people, which were bordered by races not obedient to our Empire. I restored peace to all the provinces of Gaul and Spain and to Germany ... my fleet sailed along the Ocean from the mouth of the Rhine as far East as the borders of the Cimbri, where no Roman had ever gone before ... two armies were led into Ethiopia and Arabia ... I added Egypt to the empire of the Roman people.[9]

Augustus's policy on the whole was a prudent one: the Roman Empire must be kept within limits, and as far as possible use natural frontiers. There were to be no large-scale conquests. His departures from this rule were disastrous. The Arabian expedition, which carries a certain magic in the official account, was in fact inconclusive. A sally beyond the Rhine resulted in the loss of three legions, which Rome could ill afford. In the other places that Augustus mentions, the results were happier. Augustus was in Gaul from 15 to 13 B.C. and thoroughly reorganized the country. Other military occupations secured the plains of north Italy against any further threat from across the Alps. In Spain, the rebellious elements were brought down from the hills to the plain, where they could be better watched. In the East, protectorates and buffer-states cushioned the Roman provinces against invasion. Egypt was a special case. Rome had first opened diplomatic relations with Alexandria in 273, and was already intervening in Egyptian politics some seventy years later. Pompey had strong connections with the country where he was murdered. In 58 the Pharaoh Ptolemy, known as the Flute-Player, fled to Rome from the resentment of his subjects – who were grumbling about taxes – and paid a heavy price to be reinstated. Julius Caesar had intervened in the quarrel between Cleopatra and her younger brother, and established the connection which was to be fatal to Antony. Cleopatra was in Rome when he was assassinated; Egypt was at that point nominally a client kingdom, though under the protection of the Roman legions. Caesar had already recognized the prosperity of Egypt as dangerous. In the hands of an unscrupulous governor, it could finance the overthrow of the state, and it seemed for a while as though, with Antony, this threat might be realized. Immediately after Actium, Augustus set to work to remove the temptation. Egypt became a province, but with a unique administration. The centralized authority of the Ptolemies remained unchanged, but its head was a Roman governor who was appointed by, and directly responsible to, the Emperor. Its revenues went straight into the Emperor's private purse. No senators were allowed to enter the country without permission; even members of the imperial family were later to be suspect.

> The Senate decreed that vows should be offered up on behalf of my health every fifth year by the consuls and priests. In accordance with these vows games were many times celebrated during my lifetime, sometimes by the four most prestigious priestly colleges, at other times by the consuls. . . . To commemorate my return from Syria . . . the Senate consecrated an altar to Fortune . . . and ordered the pontifices and Vestal Virgins to celebrate a sacrifice there on the anniversary of my return, a day which it called the Augustalia after me.[10]

From honours paid to the gods in gratitude for the ruler, it was a short step to divine honours paid to the ruler himself. Over a large part of the Roman Empire, such practice was already condoned by long tradition. The eastern peoples had been accustomed to worshipping their rulers as divinities on earth, and the Greeks who succeeded to Alexander's empire had accepted the native custom. In Egypt, the first Ptolemy was hailed as a god, like the Pharaohs for centuries before him. When the Ptolemies were supplanted by Augustus, the practice continued unchanged. In Asia Minor, Roman governors and generals had come to accept such honours as their due. Even in Greece this ultimate form of respect was paid; Sulla had encouraged the formation of his own cult in Athens, and the people of the province of Asia had offered to build a temple to Cicero and his brother when the latter was proconsul. Augustus fell heir to a tradition which it would have been impolitic to deny. Roman discretion forbade any deliberate affront to the religious susceptibilities of the governed. Augustus was hailed as god all over the East, as the numerous surviving inscriptions testify. With his usual tact, he insisted on one proviso. His worship must be coupled with that of Roma, the personification of his city already elevated to divine status by the Greeks in the second century B.C. By combining his own cult with that of his city, Augustus was able to identify himself with the national interest in a particularly persuasive way, and to allay suspicions that he was merely seeking personal glory. Religion was used as it had long been in Rome, to secure and symbolize loyalty to the ideals of the state. Typically, Augustus gradually made such cults exclusive to himself and the members of his family. The last recorded instance of a cult established in honour of a Roman governor is in 8 B.C.

The deification of the ruler presented a more touchy problem in Italy and the West. Here there were no such precedents before the death of Caesar. The general returning victorious from the wars was hailed as a god for the duration of his triumph. As he rode through the cheering crowds, his face was rouged in imita- tion of the statue of Jupiter on the Capitoline Hill. But behind him in the chariot stood an attendant murmuring 'Remember you are but a man', and the soldiers marching in procession drew noisy attention to the human weaknesses of their leader. 'Lock up your daughters,' advised Caesar's legionaries. 'We're bringing back the bald old lecher.' The proliferation of honours paid to Caesar in the frantic months after his death marked a new, and, to many, a dangerous departure from orthodoxy. He was en- shrined among the gods of the state, with Antony as his priest. This was an advantage that Augustus quickly seized. He dared not go so far as to allow divine honours to be paid to him in his lifetime. This might have provoked the wrath of another Cicero, and given focus to the resentment that was always present behind the smooth façade of the Augustan regime. But he could, and did, allow himself to be worshipped at second hand, through his *genius*, or guardian spirit. This was acceptable to Roman practice, and particularly to the lower classes, whose religious ideas were less sophisticated. Where they had once set up altars to the *lares compitales*, the gods of the crossroads, they now erected them to the *lares Augusti*, or to his *genius*. One centre of the cult was Augustus's own house on the Palatine. It was easy for later em- perors to make the slight shift and regard themselves as gods and their palaces as temples. From Augustus's time the deification of departed emperors became commonplace. It was never, however, wholly uncritical. Even under the most tyrannical emperors, the Roman people reserved the right to refuse posthumous deification. Augustus helped to assure his place in the stars by one final, superb piece of stage-management. We are told that, when his funeral pyre was lit, an eagle rose from the flames and soared into the sky. We also know that among the documents left by Augustus on his death-bed was a list of instructions for his funeral. We can be sure that among these instructions was the command to release an eagle.

The principate of Augustus – for it was as *princeps*, chief man, that he preferred to regard himself, in lieu of more offensive titles – was essentially a practical recognition of hard facts. It gave form and order to tendencies long present, though officially ignored, in the Republic. Augustus's programme did not go without resistance. There were still many who cherished the republican dream, and several conspiracies were formed against the ruler in his lifetime. He was saved from them, and from the errors of his predecessors, by the masterly tact with which he created a despotism while preserving the illusion of the traditional liberties. His solution was accepted by most because it worked. It was not, however, complete. He bequeathed several problems to his successors, not least the difficulty of following his diplomatic example. Another was the question of the status of the provincials. Augustus had given a fair measure of unity to Rome and Italy, but this was no longer the whole world. Some positive step was necessary to reconcile the provinces with Rome, and assure their people of their rights and position. Augustus was cautious about extending Roman citizenship. His final census records about five million Roman citizens in the Empire, the great proportion being in the peninsula. His policy was not to act hastily in putting the provinces on an equal footing with Rome. The supremacy of Italy was stressed, though just government was guaranteed to all. Abuses were curbed, but the larger problem was not faced. Later emperors made tentative steps towards solving it. Claudius showed himself ready to accept cultured Gauls as members of the senate, but through the first century A.D. the exclusive Roman aristocracy still favoured the old system. The Roman world was still divided, though the divisions were on broader lines: in civic rights, between the haves and the have-nots; in language and tradition, between the Latin-speaking world of the West and the Greek-speaking world of the East. The former was to be solved by the extension by Caracalla, in A.D. 212, of Roman citizenship to the whole Empire. The latter was to deepen into a chasm that finally broke the Empire apart.

Throughout his career Augustus used every available means to bolster his position and promulgate the image that he felt to be desirable. He sought to identify himself with the most estimable and venerable Roman traditions, playing on the public sentiment no less ably than Cicero had done, and with far happier results. The frugality of his private life was intended to remind the people of the sturdy peasant origins which they praised in theory, but were increasingly reluctant to emulate in practice. He lived in a comparatively unostentatious house, and the clothes he wore were woven by his own *familia*. Yet his modest abode was linked with all the religious and historical associations of the Palatine, and stood significantly close to the hut of Romulus. He proclaimed himself as the new Romulus on his coins. And he turned particularly to the arts, realizing, like other politic despots after him, that they made powerful and palatable propaganda. He employed poets as a modern politician would use public-relations men, to create a flattering picture of himself and the state.

This is not to say that he resorted to coercion. On the contrary, the writers who supported him seem to have come willingly to his aid, shared his enthusiasm for his programmes and policies, and accepted in all sincerity their duty to adorn his regime with their genius. Augustus did not often tell the poets what to say. He discovered them largely through his friend Maecenas, who, until his fall from grace, was his unofficial minister of fine arts; he supported them; and he seems to have offered suggestions at appropriate moments, though often through intermediaries. The poets were eager to respond. We must beware of judging the

Roman situation in the light of our modern preconceptions. For us, art for art's sake has become part of our aesthetic creed; the existence of a poem is its own justification. Such a view would have been considered eccentric in antiquity. The Romans, like the Greeks before them, expected literature and art not only to be good in themselves but to be good for something, to be functional. Poetry was a means of communicating knowledge, of glorifying the city and the state, of castigating vice and upholding morality. It had a public purpose.

In Greece, poetry had been put to a practical application from the earliest times. When Aristophanes puts into the mouth of Aeschylus a defence of poetry as a teaching art, he is simply expressing, though in over-simplified form, a view that most of his audience would have taken for granted:

> *That's the proper stuff of poetry. Consider how our poets brought us*
> *good advice and blessings from the start.*
> *First came Orpheus to establish our religious celebrations and instruct*
> *us to restrain our hands from killing,*
> *Then Musaeus taught us healing and prophetic divination, and old*
> *Hesiod the arts of ploughing, tilling*
> *And of garnering our harvest. Then came Homer, the immortal: how*
> *did he acquire his honour and his name*
> *Save by teaching high accomplishments, and battle drill, and strategy,*
> *and bravery, and military fame?*[11]

The Romans shared this view; we have seen, in Lucretius, how the emphasis on the didactic could sometimes lead poets into strange paths. There was nothing shameful, then, in poetry that was politically or morally committed; our modern literature shows, perhaps, that we are coming once more to accept the Roman attitude. The possibilities of perversion of the arts, and the worst abuses of censorship, were, of course, evident. It is to Augustus's credit that he did not unduly foster them. The worst abuses were left to his successors. The poets responded frankly and warmly to the new Romulus, and the voice that cried loudest in his favour was that of Virgil.

Publius Vergilius Maro was born in 70 B.C., in Andes, a village near Mantua. Its exact location has been disputed, as has his parental background. His name is an unusual one, and, as often in the case of great men, the fame of his later years clouded his origins. It has been suggested that he had Etruscan, Celtic, Greek or Jewish blood in his veins; the associations of his mother's name, Magia, contributed to the legend, which snowballed in the Middle Ages, that he had supernatural powers. If the whole earth, as Pericles claimed, is the sepulchre of famous men, there is also considerable competition to have a share in their birth. He went to school at Cremona, and then at Rome, going on in the customary manner to plead in the courts, though without distinction. He seems to have avoided military service, though not the hardships of the aftermath of war. His early poems, pastorals written in imitation of the Greek of Theocritus, suggest that he lost his land to a returning veteran in the confiscations of the post-war years, and was forced to seek the assistance of powerful friends.

His contacts brought him under the influence of Maecenas, for whom he wrote a poetic manual of farming, the *Georgics* (from the Greek *georgos*, farmer). He indicates that the subject was neither of his own choosing nor entirely agreeable to him. It may have been suggested by Augustus through his aide to encourage the back-to-the-land policy which formed part of the ruler's return to the traditional ways. The length of time that Virgil took to complete it may reflect his distaste – seven years for four books, an average of less than a line a day; though his biographer noted him as a slow worker whose practice was to write a few lines and then spend infinite care putting the first draft into shape. For all this, the *Georgics* offers fine poetry as well as sound practical instruction. Scholars with a practical bent have followed Virgil's advice in the appropriate terrain, and found that it works. Virgil took a broad enough view of his topic to launch out into a panegyric in praise of Italy which must have been highly acceptable to the regime. The *Georgics* also reveals, if the tradition is to be trusted, a notable example of governmental interference. As originally conceived, the work contained a poetic tribute to Gallus, the viceroy of Augustus in Egypt. This, as we have seen, was a peculiarly sensitive position. Gallus was a poet in his own right, and an old friend of Virgil; it may have been he who saved his farm from confiscation. But something went wrong in Egypt. We do not know exactly what. A surviving inscription suggests that Gallus conducted himself with too much self-importance. He was removed from office, and committed suicide; and Virgil filled the necessary lacuna in his poem with a description of bee-keeping.

From 30 B.C. to the time of his death he was occupied with a work of vastly different scope and character, the twelve books of the *Aeneid*, unfinished and published posthumously against his will by his friends. Hesiod's Greek farming poetry had suggested a model for the *Georgics*; it was Homer's work, both the *Iliad* and the *Odyssey*, that Virgil emulated in his masterpiece. Yet though the themes and incidents are similar – the workings of a divine purpose in shaping the doings of mankind, the military triumphs of a hero, adventures by sea – Virgil's work differs in one important aspect from that of his predecessor. The *Iliad* had roots deep in the Greek folk-tradition. It was spun from the minstrelsy of generations of wandering bards, assembled and ordered by a master hand. The *Aeneid* is the work of a single creative poet, the product of conscious art. For his subject, Virgil had few native precedents to draw upon. Ennius had composed his epic treatment of Roman history, and Naevius seems to have introduced the Dido and Aeneas story into his poem on the Carthaginian wars. But Virgil was, for the most part, breaking new ground. Why did he choose to treat the Aeneas story? He had long contemplated writing a patriotic poem, and such a work would be warmly welcomed by the new administration. But contemporary history offered no convenient point of focus (as Lucan was to discover later, when he wrote his epic on the Civil War) and no real unifying figure. The story of Aeneas must have suggested itself as a natural possibility. By glorifying the first founder, Virgil could pay tribute to his city, and the boasted descent of the

Caesars from Venus offered an opportunity of linking the mythic past with the living present.

Virgil's purpose, then, was to glorify the Roman state, and to provide an account, part history, part allegory, of his city's illustrious lineage. The Aeneas story, as we have seen, had been seized upon with delight by the earlier mythographers. Great Rome shone in the reflected glory of great Troy. Virgil presents his hero as a man of destiny, and the original founder as one who walked with the gods, and over whom the heavens fought. Although unfinished, the work must have been close to completion at the time of Virgil's death. It occasionally appears diffuse, for its author was a man of many interests; he will pause in his narrative to examine some fact of antiquarian interest, to suggest etymologies, or to discuss the historical origins of some point of Roman ceremonial. In reality, however, the work is very tightly structured; an increasing amount of modern criticism has been devoted to the way in which its various episodes interlock and balance each other to illuminate the central theme. What would Virgil have added if he had lived? We do not know; we are only told of his dissatisfaction, and his request that the poem should be burned. Part had already been read to Augustus and his empress. Their response typified the reaction of the cultivated Roman world when Virgil's executors defied their orders.

Homer had begun with the customary invocation to the Muse. Virgil announces his theme at once.

> *I sing of war and a hero, driven by*
> *His destiny to exile and the shores*
> *Of Italy, and of the sufferings*
> *Of this, the first adventurer, by sea*
> *And land, impelled by heaven's will*
> *And Juno's long resentment, through the blood*
> *And tears of battle, to establish here*
> *A city and a haven for his gods.*[12]

We immediately see Juno's wrath in action. She calls up a storm which turns the ships from their course and drives them towards

Carthage. While Aeneas seeks safety the gods argue over his head. His mother Venus reminds Jupiter of his promise that Aeneas should found a new Trojan dynasty:

> Then tell me, how have my Aeneas or
> His Trojans so offended, that the men
> Who lived through war now find the world barred to them
> To stop their reaching Italy? You promised
> That in fullness of time the Romans would be born
> From them, to rule, to summon back to life
> The Trojan bloodline, to impose their will
> On every land and ocean.[13]

Jupiter comforts her, and assures her that Rome will be founded by Aeneas' descendants:

> Then Romulus, the leader of his race,
> Shall raise towers sacred to the God of War
> And call his people Romans after him.
> I set no end or limit to their power;
> A boundless empire has been given them. . .
> And from this noble line there shall be born
> A Trojan Caesar, whose domain shall know
> No limits but earth's end, whose glory shall
> Be bounded only by the stars. His name
> Shall be called Julius, in memory
> Of great Aeneas' son; and there shall come
> A happy day when you will welcome him,
> Bowed under eastern spoils, into the gates
> Of heaven. Men shall offer prayer to him
> As to Aeneas. Then the wars shall cease,
> And Faith, and Vesta, and Quirinus with
> His brother Remus come again to judgement,
> And so the great, grim, iron-bound gate of War
> Shall close.[14]

It is, of course, not the dictator but Augustus – after his adoption Gaius Julius Caesar Octavianus – of whom Jupiter speaks. Virgil represents him as the embodiment of the divine will, and deliberately underlines the main points of his programme: the eastern conquests, the restoration of the traditional religion, the closing of the gates of Janus to mark a new era of peace, and the attribution to the *princeps* of divine honours.

Aeneas finds hospitality in Carthage. Book Two is a flashback, relating the destruction of Troy and the hero's flight; his exit was attended by the epiphany of Venus and a thunderbolt from Jupiter. Book Three, which has been called 'the dullest book in the *Aeneid*' continues Aeneas' narrative of his past adventures. Its keynote is fatigue. The dispirited Trojans, exhausted by the war through which they have passed and uncertain of their future, limp across the sea to Delos, the home of Apollo. Perhaps Virgil, in his desire to create a mythic parallel for the contemporary Roman situation, intends this *ennui* to represent the spiritual exhaustion that followed the civil wars. Aeneas, like Augustus, is to revitalize his shattered people. On Delos the Trojans receive a new divine admonition. They consult the oracle, and interpret the answer – Apollo was traditionally ambiguous – as an instruction to found their new city in Crete. But their settlement is blighted by a plague, and Aeneas' gods appear to him in a dream to reveal Apollo's true meaning:

> But change your seat, for this was not the land
> Apollo meant. You must not stay in Crete.
> There is a place the Greeks call Hesperia,
> With ancient pride in arms, and fruitful soil.
> The Oenotrians farmed it once, and their descendants
> Have called it Italy, from their leader's name.
> This is our true home, the birthright of Dardanus
> And old Iasus, in whom our race began.[15]

Once again the foundation of Rome is established as a god-given design, and the colonization of Italy is represented as a return home. Leaving Crete the Trojans fight, as heroes must, with monsters. The winged Harpies attack them and, though driven

·off, predict struggle and purgation before the wanderers reach the promised land.

In Book Four we return to the immediate action, and the growing love of Dido for Aeneas. He is tempted to remain, but chastized by the heavenly messenger, Mercury:

> *What, do you build*
> *The towers of Carthage and construct a city*
> *To tease a woman's fancy, when your own*
> *Awaits you? Has your kingdom been forgotten?*
> *Out of the pure Olympian skies I come,*
> *Sent by the king of all, who holds the earth*
> *And heaven in his compass: at his orders*
> *This message comes to you upon the wind.*
> *What are you doing? What temptation holds you*
> *Idle in Libya? If the promised glory*
> *Does not inspire you, then remember this.*
> *You have a son, who looks to his succession.*
> *The day will come when he must be the lord*
> *Of Rome and Italy.*[16]

Aeneas, obedient to his destiny, leaves Dido, whose curses foreshadow the historical conflict between Carthage and Rome. On the eve of death, she is gifted with prophetic power:

> *And you, my Tyrians, pursue his progeny*
> *For ever with your hatred; gratify*
> *My grave with this. Let there exist no love*
> *Between our peoples, no alliances.*
> *Out of my ashes some avenger come*
> *To hound the Trojans and the land they hold*
> *With fire and sword, both now and for all time,*
> *Whenever strength is granted us. Our land*
> *Shall be their curse, our waters war with theirs,*
> *Our armies fight them and their children's children.*[17]

Virgil wraps every major episode of Roman history in mystic significance. Dido looks forward to Hannibal; the Carthaginian

Wars are presented not as a simple trade-war but as part of the predestined pattern.

In Book Six the Trojans have finally reached Italy, where Aeneas visits the Sibyl. He descends to Hades and consults with the ghosts, in a passage reminiscent of a similar conjuration in the *Odyssey*. Virgil surrounds him with the traditional apparatus of the Greek underworld. Ferried across the river by Charon, he talks with those whom he knew in life, the most recently dead first. He sees Dido again, and the ghosts of his companions who fell at Troy. Then, like Macbeth in the witches' cave – though under happier auspices – he is offered a panorama of the future, a parade of the generations of Roman rulers to come. It is led by the kings who traditionally filled the gap between Aeneas and Romulus; then comes Romulus himself, and, in significant association with him, Augustus Caesar.

> *Now turn your eyes this way, and see the race*
> *Of Romans that is yours. Here Caesar waits*
> *His hour of destiny, and with him all*
> *The Julian line. And see, here stands the man*
> *Whose promised coming you have heard not once*
> *But many times: Augustus, born of god,*
> *Who will revive the Golden Age, a Saturn*
> *Come again to Latium. His domain will reach*
> *To India, and where the Garamantes*
> *Have their homes; the land beyond the stars*
> *Is his, beyond our clime, where sun has never*
> *Shown its face, where Atlas scrapes the skies*
> *And bears the pole of heaven on his shoulder,*
> *Stuck with bright stars. For so the gods have spoken,*
> *And the Caspian lands and Lake Maiotis shiver*
> *In expectation of his coming, while*
> *The seven mouths of Nile run mad in fear.*[18]

Augustus is compared to Hercules and Bacchus, both of whom represent heroic virtue devoted to the service of mankind and rewarded with divine honours. The final tribute is a paean of praise to the young Marcellus, Augustus's son and destined heir, whose premature death was to threaten the continuation of the dynasty.

The central book of the *Aeneid* is also, psychologically, the turning-point for its hero. Up to and including the descent into Hades, both the poem and its protagonist have been primarily concerned with the past, and regret for the fall of Troy; there has been a tendency to linger, first in Crete and then in Carthage. But when the ghosts of the dead Trojans are driven from Aeneas' attention by the pageant of Rome to come, his mood changes. From this point there is a mood of excitement, of urgency; Aeneas needs no other admonition. Travelling north, he lands near the future site of Rome, and the remaining books tell his struggles in the Homeric manner. Aeneas is welcomed by some and viewed with jealousy and suspicion by others. The battlelines are joined and the combatants enumerated in the style of the Catalogue of Ships in the *Iliad*. Venus persuades Vulcan to make her son a suit of armour, just as Thetis commissioned the shield of Achilles. And so, amid the appropriate portents, the promised land is gained by force of arms, and the Julian line implanted in Latium.

Virgil stood head and shoulders above the other poets of his time, but there were other voices that sounded the same note. His friend Horace was a man who owed much to the Augustan regime, and paid appropriate thanks in song. His father was a freedman turned tax-gatherer who scraped together enough to buy a small farm for himself and a Roman education for his son. In Greece for further study when Brutus was assembling his army, Horace enlisted in a flush of republican enthusiasm, but was quickly disillusioned by Philippi. Returning to Rome, he found his father dead and the estate confiscated, and was forced to work as a secretary. Through Virgil, with whom he had much in common, he was introduced to the circle of Maecenas, and profited handsomely from the official policy of forgiveness towards former republicans; this he was later to celebrate in an ode. He was given a farm, which he loved, and the leisure to write. A certain captiousness in his earlier poems disappears, and his work becomes mellow, serene and urbane; in the turmoil of the transition years there was at least one thoroughly contented man. Like Virgil, he could be sincere in his admiration of Augustus, for he had everything to thank him for. Among the mass of writing which Horace has provoked – increasing sharply with the bimillennium of his birth in 1935 – not the least interesting is an article which appeared in *The American Journal of Psychiatry* describing Horace as a type of the perfectly integrated personality.

Though Horace occasionally puts on the seer's robe, he speaks with a quieter voice than Virgil. His Muse, as he tells us himself, was not suited to martial or patriotic verse, and his poems usually concern themselves with everyday matters, giving us a running commentary on the daily life of his times. His early work, collected and published at the insistence of Maecenas, shows the trepidation with which the Romans looked forward to another civil war. One poem strikes a note of utter hopelessness; the only thing to do, Horace says, is to leave Italy and emigrate to a happy land elsewhere, where life is like the Golden Age described in Virgil's Fourth Eclogue. We hear of Maecenas leaving for the front, and of the victory at Actium.

Thereafter the mood changes. The next poems breathe the air of good living. They are full of food and wine, of journeys with good friends, of chance encounters in the streets. By the time he began the *Odes*, in the same year that Virgil had started on the *Aeneid*, he had grown a little more solemn, and more conscious of the dignity of his position as an official poet. In this capacity he recommends the traditional Roman virtues, moderation, justice, patriotism, a sense of responsibility, respect for tradition; he parallels Virgil's *Georgics* in his description of the decay of the countryside through selfishness and urban luxury. Book Four of the *Odes* contains poems said to have been composed at Augustus's request, celebrating the ruler's return from Gaul and Germany in 13 B.C. and the military successes of various members of Augustus's family.

Not all writers accepted the Augustan regime with whole-hearted joy. There were dissentient voices among the poets, just as there were grumbles among the politicians. Witness Propertius, who is clearly more happy when handling personal themes; although he can turn out the expected verses on the completion of the temple to Apollo, Augustus's journey to the East, or Rome's legendary history, his individual concerns are closer to his mind. When Propertius writes of Actium, he is more interested in Antony's fatal passion for Cleopatra, and compares it to the dominance his own mistress exercises over him. Witness particularly Ovid, who strikes a note of defiant frivolity in a period that, officially at least, was growing increasingly moral and austere. Born in the year when the death of the two consuls so conveniently gave Octavian an army, Ovid emerged as a witty, garrulous, well-educated Roman playboy, the poet of the *dolce vita*. The vaunted Augustan clemency did not extend to him. In A.D. 8 he was banished to Tomi, on the Black Sea, the modern Constanza. It is a popular seaside resort now, in approximately the same latitude as the French Riviera. From Ovid's lachrymose complaints one would think he had been sent to Siberia. And for all practical purposes he had; cut off from the brilliant, sophisticated life he loved, he had nothing to do but learn the native language and send home pathetic poems and letters begging for release. The exact circumstances of his banishment are not clear. Ovid says it was because of a poem and a mistake. From hints dropped elsewhere, it has been assumed that he was involved, as a member of the smart set, in the scandal caused by Augustus's grand-daughter Julia, which the Emperor, to keep face, was bound to punish with the utmost severity. The poem was certainly Ovid's *Ars Amatoria*, *The Art of Love*, or, as it has been called, *The Plain Man's Guide to Seduction*.

Take her to the Circus. Opportunities abound.
You can use your racing licence, as the horses gallop round.
No need to correspond with her by nod and furtive touch;
You can sit right down beside her — no one else will bother much —

> *And cuddle close; you have to, if the lady likes or not,*
> *For the seats are packed together, it's a very crowded spot.*
> *Then start a conversation. Fit for any ear at first.*
> *Ask the names of all the runners. And of course it wouldn't hurt*
> *If you backed the horse she fancies. When the celebrations start*
> *And they carry in the statues of the gods, you'll win her heart*
> *With some loud applause for Venus. If a speck of dust should fall*
> *On your lady's lap, reach over – it can happen to us all –*
> *And flick it off. But if her lap is clean of any dust*
> *Then flick it anyway. Let your imagination serve your lust.*[19]

And so, from the gaiety at the heart of the Empire, Ovid passed to the bleakness of its inhospitable fringes:

> *The snow is like a mantle on the ground;*
> *Nor sun nor rain can melt its icy face.*
> *The north wind blows, and freezes all around;*
> *There is no way to move it from its place,*
> *A new snow comes before the old has fled*
> *And lies there often for a year or two.*
> *The storms wreak havoc, and the people dread*
> *What tower or hamlet will be next to go.*
> *The men wear skins, hides, breeches, anything,*
> *Against the cold, with but the face left bare.*
> *Their beards are frosted; as they walk, they ring*
> *With icicles that gather in their hair.*[20]

Severe treatment, perhaps, for a poet whose only real vice was flippancy. But an age of moral rearmament had no place for such a man.

NOTES TO CHAPTER SIX

1. Suetonius, *Augustus*, 101. 6.
2. A free translation of Tacitus, *Annals*, I. 9–10.
3. *Res Gestae Divi Augusti* (*The Life and Achievements of the Divine Augustus*), I. 1–12 (excerpted).
4. Ibid. I. 28–39; 3. 11–21 (excerpted).

5. Ibid. 6. 21–3.
6. Ibid. 1. 45–6; 2. 12–14; 4. 1–8 (excerpted).
7. Suetonius, *Caesar*, 84. 2.
8. *Res Gestae*, 3. 7–8, 11–12, 19–21, 28–34.
9. Ibid. 5. 9–24 (excerpted).
10. Ibid. 2. 15–18, 29–33 (excerpted).
11. Aristophanes, *The Frogs*, 1032–6.
12. Virgil, *Aeneid*, I. 1–6.
13. Ibid. I. 231–7.
14. Ibid. I. 276–9, 286–94.
15. Ibid. III. 161–8.
16. Ibid. IV. 265–76.
17. Ibid. IV. 622–9.
18. Ibid. VI. 788–800.
19. Ovid, *Ars Amatoria* (*The Art of Love*), I. 135–52.
20. Ovid, *Tristia* (*Melancholy Poems*), III. 10. 13–27.

Chapter Seven

The Rome of Seneca

IN Chapter Five we considered Cicero as a man of his time, whose multifarious activities show the pattern of life in the closing years of the Republic. To counterbalance him, on the other side of the Augustan principate, we may look at Lucius Annaeus Seneca, whose life was like Cicero's in many ways. He too was poet, philosopher, politician; he too knew the degradation of exile and the delights of power; he too paid for his involvement with a premature death. But the lives of those two men, so similar in their facts, could not be more different in their environment. Seneca lived in a Rome that had changed more than Cicero, at his most gloomily prophetic, could have dreamed, and the change was directly attributable to the work of Augustus.

In assuming virtually total control of the State, either through the combination of legally constituted offices or by the tacit consent of the governed, Augustus had created a precedent which his successors were bound to follow. No one could deny that the new centralized administration worked more smoothly. The senate had come by imperceptible degrees to regard itself as serving in an advisory capacity to the Emperor, rather than as an independent legislative assembly. Not the least effective of Augustus's devices was his habit, in his later years, of calling senate meetings at his own house, making illness his excuse, rather than in the proper building. When Augustus died there was still a Republic, in theory. The forms persisted, and the dream endured: years later, when Caligula was assassinated, the senate could sit down and solemnly debate the restoration of the Republic. In practice, Rome assumed that Augustus would appoint his own successor. This he did, after much heartsearching. It was a brutal disappointment to him that a series of promising candidates, including his own son, had been eliminated by death. *Faute de mieux*, he settled on Tiberius, his wife's son by a previous marriage. Augustus's successor was too old for the job, and too embittered by having been relegated to minor positions for so long. He made a half-hearted attempt, but alienated the senate from the beginning by his lack of finesse. At their first meeting after Augustus's death, the senators, realistically accepting their situation, offered Tiberius the supreme power. Grasping, perhaps, at the precedents offered by Julius Caesar and Augustus, he went through the motions of refusing. But what had once been seen as tact was now considered hypocrisy. The senators jeeringly advised him to face the facts, as they had done. It was a bad start, which led to worse. Increasingly alienated from the people he was supposed to rule, his bitterness augmented by a series of personal disappointments, Tiberius finally withdrew into gloomy isolation on Capri. The Roman writers, faithful to the time-honoured tradition of heaping every sort of scurrilous abuse on unpopular figures, let their imaginations run riot, and depicted him as turning his island paradise into a centre for unmentionable vices. Tiberius let power slip into the hands of his ministers, and only aroused himself from his inertia to suppress a potential *coup d'état* and initiate a savage purge of supposed traitors which set an unfortunate example for the years to come.

History has not dealt kindly with the dynasty that Augustus established. Tiberius is portrayed as a senile lecher, Caligula as an ogre, Claudius as a drooling idiot, Nero as a paranoiac sadist. To a large extent, this bad press is due to the literary conditions of the time. Emperors unsure of their positions saw everything that was not outright flattery as a veiled attack. To write about the Republic might imply unfavourable comparisons; even Claudius, before he ascended the throne, had to be dissuaded from writing a republican history because it was politically undesirable. Censorship became increasingly rigid. Under more enlightened reigns came the inevitable reaction. Writers poured out the venom they had previously been forced to suppress, and the new permissiveness became licence. Even Tacitus, who claims to be writing a sober and impartial account of the early emperors, hardly allows them a single honourable motive. We must remember that he is speaking comparatively. If we could still read, for example, the lost diaries of Nero's mother, Tacitus would probably seem objective indeed. Much of the surviving folklore derives from these sources. Visitors to Capri are still shown the pool where Tiberius fed slaves to the fish; guides in the Roman Forum point out the tower from which Nero serenaded the fire of Rome (in defiance of the fact that the tower in question is medieval); Nero's ghost is still said to walk in the street where he was buried with his ancestors.

It must be emphasized, though, that the preoccupation of these ancient biographers with the personalities of the emperors, sensational though their writings were, stems from a recognition of the hard facts of the Roman situation: that the well-being of the city, and of a good proportion of its inhabitants, was now dependent on the whims of one man. In the provinces, the caprices of an emperor were cushioned by distance. The subject peoples, on the whole, felt only the more benign aspects of the change. When Nero died several adventurers outside the capital promptly claimed to be the emperor and found a following. But at the centre of power all depended on the temperament of the ruler. Attempts to find social and economic causes for the troubles of the early Empire, and for the Year of the Four Emperors, the period of anarchy which followed Nero's death, are misguided. In almost every case, the responsibility must be ascribed to the man in charge, and his distorted conception of his own position.

It must be emphasized, also, that the efforts of modern historians to rehabilitate the Julio-Claudians are often as far from the truth as the calumny of their ancient predecessors. There was a streak of unbalance, if not insanity, running through the whole line, accentuated by inbreeding and given scope by power. One of Augustus's grandsons was undoubtedly insane. Caligula may never actually have made his race-horse consul and ordered his army to pick up shells, but many of his acts, well-attested by serious authorities, were hardly those of a rational man. Perhaps the difference between Augustus and Nero was only that impalpably fine line dividing genius from lunacy. Certainly the forcing-house of palace politics, with one branch of the family pitted against another, heirs made and unmade by those extraordinary, dominating women whom the Julio-Claudians produced or married, and the nagging insecurity which beset all those close to the throne, was no healthy atmosphere in which to grow up. Caligula and Nero, who both began well, were corrupted by it; Claudius, who had many admirable qualities, was stifled by it. In the end, Rome could only purge herself by a year of struggle and a change of dynasty.

Rome showed the change in her architecture. The Forum continued to sprout monuments which transformed the old urban centre into an alfresco Hall of Fame, and individual emperors, following Julius Caesar's example, added other fora nearby. But this period is best characterized by the activity on the Palatine. On this hill, once occupied by temples and by the houses of the rich and famous, Augustus had lived in comparative simplicity. But his house, like its neighbours, was rapidly overshadowed and overbuilt by the architectural extravagances of his successors, the palimpsest of palaces that they scrawled upon the Palatine's three peaks. The showplace of one reign became the foundations for that of the next. Spreading like a brick fungus over the hill, the palaces, patios and gardens did not even stop when the available surface was exhausted. New substructures were thrown out to make a larger area available. Spilling into the Forum on one side and down towards the Circus Maximus on the other, the palaces finally crumbled into a complex of ruins so interlaced that the baffled people of the Middle Ages saw them as one enormous whole, the *palazzo maggiore*.

Archaeologists, often equally baffled by the problems of disentanglement, have engaged in heated controversies over the dates and purposes of the various layers uncovered. The salient facts, however, are clear. The grandiose constructions began with Tiberius. His palace lies behind the substructures visible from the Forum. Most of the rooms are under the Farnese Gardens, first laid out in the sixteenth century as one of the sights of Rome, used for vegetables by the nineteenth, and gradually encroached upon in our time to make excavation possible. The ruins suggest a central, pillared courtyard surrounded by a network of small rooms and service stairs; there is a fishpond, perhaps designed to serve the imperial table. Caligula enlarged Tiberius's work, pushing further towards the Forum in an expansion which involved the Temple of Castor and Pollux. Suetonius tells us that Caligula saw this as an appropriate vestibule to his own residence. Using existing buildings as stepping-stones, he threw a bridge across the valley to the Capitol. As an architectural project, this was not in itself offensive. Its symbolic value was more dangerous. The Emperor was reaching out to annexe the ancient seat of the most sacred Roman deities to his private house. One interesting relic of Caligula's design is a chapel dedicated to the worship of the goddess Isis, its walls appropriately decorated with Egyptian motifs.

Nero's projects for the Palatine, which involved the levelling of republican houses to spread the palace system still further, were frustrated by the fire of 64. He took advantage of the massive rebuilding programme which this entailed to move off the hill and appropriate some 125 acres in the heart of Rome for his own use, an action which infuriated a city where the devastation had already caused an acute housing shortage. Here he laid out an estate, with landscaped grounds, game-parks, follies and palaces; this was his Golden House, linked to the Palatine by a corridor running along the side of Tiberius's palace, and half underground. Hyperbolic descriptions survive from those who admired or resented it – which means, in effect, whether they served under Nero or his successors. Its chief marvel was a revolving dining-room. We do not know how it worked, though the feat was technically within the Romans' grasp. (There are equally tantalizing hints, elsewhere in Rome, of two theatres, set back to back, that could be revolved, audience and all, to form a single amphitheatre.) It has been speculatively located in the octagonal room surviving in the ruins, which also boasts an indoor waterfall. The ruins are difficult of access, and unrewarding. Closed for unreasonably long periods of time by the authorities, they present a blank and disappointing exterior, mainly a curved façade pierced regularly with doors. Inside, these doors give access to long rooms and corridors which once led to the sumptuous centre where Nero declared he would at last begin to live like a human being. The Golden House suffered with its builder's memory. Anxious to obliterate the infamy of the reign, later and more liberal emperors turned the site to public purposes. Trajan took advantage of the fire to build his baths above. The area is still a public park, where boys play ball amid the ruins of Trajan's monument, and over the roof of Nero's.

At a later period, when the Julio-Claudians were no more, Domitian returned to the Palatine, moving to another part of the hill to build a palace more than twice as large as that of Tiberius. It had two colonnaded courts, a throne room with niches for colossal statues, its own bath-house and a banqueting-hall with walls of coloured marble, a forest of columns and a golden vault for a ceiling, perhaps topped with a representation of Domitian as Jupiter, by whose attributes the poets address him. Our information comes from awestruck writers who sought, and were occasionally granted, an invitation to dinner. Towards the Circus Maximus lay Domitian's so-called stadium – in fact a private garden for recreation – with an imperial box from which the host could stare down on his family and guests.

It is not surprising that the Palatine soon acquired a bad atmosphere. Later Roman writers see the palaces as sinister labyrinths, honeycombs of dark rooms where victims of imperial displeasure meet furtive death, corridors where Caligula comes face to face with his assassins, curving walls that appeal to the picturesquely minded as architectural embodiments of the deviousness of their builders, courtyards faced with reflecting stone through which stalks a nervous Domitian, peeping for the daggers of his enemies. Out of this miasma more medieval legends were born: where the Palatine meets the Forum, a popular tradition located one of the entrances of Hell. Trajan tried to purge the place by turning parts of it into a museum, and displaying the imperial treasures to the public. The Palatine retained its prestige as a monument. Septimius Severus frilled it with its last great work, the *septizonium*, a huge façade to welcome travellers entering Rome, which did not disappear till 1589. But even when one has admitted the grandeur and discounted the legends, one sinister aspect remains: the business of governing Rome, once transacted in the open Forum, was now brought behind closed doors into arcana impenetrable except by the select few. The history of the Palatine shows how decisively the ruling families divorced themselves from a people happy to be left in peace. The ruins today, even though the marble has peeled off and only a few columns, in a mass of brickwork, tell of vanished glories, show the obedience these families could command; the auxiliary buildings, like the pages' school still visible on the Circus side, show what a vast staff was now necessary for the conduct of government, and for the maintenance of the emperors on an increasing scale of luxury. It was this sort of world into which Seneca was born.

His father, Marcus Annaeus, was a Spaniard, dividing his time between his own country and Rome, where he was a professor of rhetoric. Nothing more conclusively shows the change in the Roman condition than the way in which rhetoric had suddenly lost its importance. It remained one of the fundamentals of a Roman education, and was to continue to be so for centuries. But it no longer had any practical outlet. In Cicero's time, as we have seen, rhetoric was the key to public advancement. But, with the senate reduced to a crowd of yes-men, the proletariat kept in a state of mindless euphoria by corn-doles and free shows, and all effective decisions made by the emperor and his ministers, the art had lost its significance. No longer could pupils cut their teeth on issues currently being debated: it was no longer politic to debate current issues. Deprived of its utility, the art of rhetoric became increasingly academic, and more inclined to feed upon itself. Restricted in subject matter, the professors concentrated on form, and on the adornment of hackneyed themes with epigrammatic brilliance and erudite illustration. Students were asked to speak

on topics safely remote from actuality: should Hannibal march
on Rome? Juvenal comments on the dreariness of such exercises:

> It takes iron guts to teach rhetoric now
> And hear a whole class on the theme of tyrannicide,
> Rising in turn to intone the same clichés
> They culled from their textbooks the minute before,
> With about as much meat as there is in a cabbage.
> Professors could die on a diet like that . . . .
> Give me credit for knowing whereof I speak.
> Come down from your ivory towers, rhetoricians.
> Stop beating your brains out for less than you'd get
> On public relief. Find another profession.[1]

Or the students would be asked to debate imaginary cases involving improbable problems. A young man seduces two girls
in a single night. One demands his death, another marriage, as
each is entitled to do by Roman law. Discuss. Or, a young man is
captured by pirates, and refused ransom by his father. The pirate
chief's daughter falls in love with him and helps him to escape.
In gratitude he marries her. When he takes his bride home, his
father orders him to divorce her and marry a rich heiress. By
which obligation should the son be bound – his duty to the
paterfamilias, or his debt of gratitude and honour? Pirates figure
prominently in such controversies. They remove the problems to
an acceptable world of fantasy. The students debate academic
questions.

The elder Seneca composed a number of volumes of such cases.
Time, with unusual discretion, has removed some of them.
Enough survive to show how tedious the pursuit of rhetoric had
become. This art for art's sake was cultivated by the professors
no less than by the students. The custom arose of holding private
recitals in the schools. A professor might declaim for the instruction of his pupils, or invite his colleagues for a competitive display. Each tried to outdo the other in his parade of learning. This
was the environment in which Lucius grew up. It left an indelible
mark on his own work, particularly on the style of his tragedies.

The elder Seneca had three sons. Gallio, the eldest, entered public service, and eventually became proconsul in Achaia. He is, almost certainly, the same Gallio before whom St Paul appeared after the riot he provoked there. The youngest, Mela, preferred a quiet life. Lucius Annaeus, the second son, followed the traditional course of Roman education by studying under different philosophers. He worked for a while under Sotion the Pythagorean, and was greatly influenced by the principles of this school, particularly by the insistence on respect for life in all its forms, which led him for a while to abstain from meat. He returned to normal eating habits at the request of his father. There was, apparently, some fear that he would be suspected of Jewish sympathies, and minority groups were at that time unpopular in Rome. Seneca also studied with Attalus the Stoic, who again insisted on the avoidance of self-indulgence. In Attalus's case such avoidance was inevitable. He had been stripped of his property by Tiberius's chief minister. But Seneca, on paper at least, kept faith with Attalus all his life.

His studies behind him, Seneca began his career in the traditional way by practising at the bar. He was a gifted speaker, whose epigrammatic brilliance was well suited to the taste of the times. Displaying his talents under Caligula, he was almost too good for his own safety. The emperor, no mean speaker himself, was jealous, and nearly had Seneca put to death. He was saved, as he tells us, by his own failing health; it was pointed out that he would die so soon that he was not worth killing. Seneca ruminates that a disease which had killed others had saved his life. He survived where many did not. Caligula's reign, which had begun happily, ended in a bloodbath, brought to an end only by the emperor's assassination.

Subsequent events show how clearly the power-structure had changed. As the senate debated the restoration of the Republic, the soldiers chose their own emperor and the senate could do nothing but accept their choice. It was an uneasy foreshadowing of the years to come, when armies in different parts of the Empire would select their own candidates and battle out the issue between them. In this case, the choice was not entirely unhappy. Claudius, thrust to power against his will, was a scholar by nature. He had written widely on historical subjects and, among other interests, conceived the project of adding new letters to the Latin alphabet. Like several of the Julio-Claudians, he was not physically prepossessing. We are told of his obesity, the involuntary shaking of his head, and his disastrous stammer. But he had a keen interest in litigation (which his biographers, typically, make into a reproach) and his legislation shows that he had more insight, in some ways, than Augustus, particularly as regards the relation of Rome to her subject peoples.

Under Claudius we see the increasing centralization of Roman government and the creation of a civil service. Augustus, in coping with the mass of administrative business, had been compelled to employ secretaries. Claudius created a permanent staff, drawn not from the ranks of the hereditary aristocracy but from self-made men, freedmen who had risen in the Roman jungle by their abilities alone. The influence of these men was enormous – too great for Claudius, who found himself the victim of the system he had created; the victim, too, of his wives, for he was putty in the hands of anyone with a stronger will. The secret of surviving at court was to join whichever faction had the strongest influence on the emperor at the time. Seneca gambled on this, and lost; caught on the losing side in an intramural dispute, he was sent to bitter exile in Corsica.

From his banishment he wrote a document which shows clearly where the real power now lay. Polybius, the emperor's literary secretary, had lost a brother; Seneca addresses to him a letter of consolation which is, in reality, an appeal. Couched in terms of the most obsequious flattery it asks, without ever actually saying so, for Polybius to use his influence on Seneca's behalf.

> Caesar's affection and your own literary pursuits have long since elevated you to high places. Not for you the vulgar or commonplace. But is anything so lacking in dignity and manliness as extravagance of sorrow? You share your brothers' grief, but not their liberty in expressing it. You have a moral and a literary reputation

to maintain: there are many things you must deny yourself. People ask a great deal of you. They expect much. If you wanted to do as you please, you should not have attracted all eyes towards you. You are committed now, and must fulfil your obligations.[2]

Historians have traditionally affected to find Seneca's behaviour distasteful, and out of harmony with his avowed philosophical principles. Some have even attempted to save Seneca's face by arguing that the document is not his, but a bad imitation of his style. It is difficult, however, to see what else Seneca could have done. Compromise is the soul of politics, and in a system where personal influence was all-important a man fallen from grace had no other recourse. Seneca was eventually recalled, but not through the agency of Polybius. The court saw a new power-shuffle. Claudius, always a complaisant husband, had been shame-fully abused by his wife Messalina. This lady, credited by her biographer with voracious sexual appetites, had ventured to go through a form of marriage with one of her lovers while Claudius was away at Ostia. Stung at last to activity, the emperor punished savagely and swiftly. With Messalina removed, there was room for a new wife, a new influence, and the freedmen-ministers entered into competition to provide their own candidates.

The winner was Agrippina, Claudius's niece. Such a match was considered incestuous, but the emperor was too infatuated to care. Agrippina brought with her a son by a previous marriage, Nero, and once in power used all her influence to ensure that the succession devolved upon him. It was Agrippina who, for reasons of her own, became Seneca's saviour:

> Agrippina, anxious that people should have at least one good thing to say about her, had Seneca pardoned, brought back from exile and appointed to a praetorship. She thought that a well-known literary figure would be good for public relations. Nero would profit from such tutelage, and Seneca would be useful in planning the bid for power. His gratitude towards Agrippina, and his resentment of Claudius for an injustice which still smarted, would place him firmly on her side.[3]

Restored to court, Seneca became once more a potential instrument for good. In this he was joined by Burrus, commander of the praetorian guard – the picked troops detailed for duty in the capital, and originally quartered in barracks throughout the city; the early Empire saw them brought together in one place and transformed into the palace bodyguard, a source of protection and at the same time a great danger, for the praetorians might at any time swing their affections to the candidate most likely to reward them. In Burrus, at least, they had an honourable and conscientious commander. He and Seneca became the chief formative influences on the young Nero, continuing to advise him after he rose to power.

Agrippina saw one stumbling-block, the prince Britannicus, Claudius's own son and presumptive heir. Using all her influence on her husband, she secured unusual honours for Nero. He was always in the public eye, while Britannicus was systematically degraded. Nero made another bid for the popular affection when he married, in 53, the young and beautiful Octavia. It was a good choice. Britannicus, however, still had his sympathizers. As long as he was alive he was a constant threat to Nero's success. The year after Nero's marriage, Claudius died. Later historians are convinced that he was murdered, and report in detail a plot involving Agrippina, a notorious poisoner, and the emperor's own physician. Claudius, they say, was fed poisoned mushrooms at a banquet. When he vomited them up and seemed likely to recover, his doctor, pretending to assist, inserted a poisoned feather down his throat. Agrippina, acting swiftly, took advantage of the confusion and the support of the praetorian guard to have Nero proclaimed emperor over Britannicus's head.

In spite of this gloomy beginning, Nero's reign seemed at first to be a triumphant success. With his mother's influence in the background and Seneca and Burrus to advise him, the young emperor introduced a programme of popular legislation which, combined with his own highly personable qualities, won the people's hearts. Seneca now had a new function as imperial ghostwriter, composing, among other speeches, the eulogy delivered by Nero at Claudius's funeral. It was remarked that Nero was the first emperor not to write his own orations. In his tract

On Clemency, written about this time, Seneca puts into Nero's mouth a soliloquy representing the emperor as Destiny personified, with the pious hope that he will use this power for good:

Am I then the chosen one, deemed worthy out of all mankind to act as regent of the gods on earth? I am the arbiter of life and death for nations; each man's destiny and station in life is in my hands; whatever Fortune wishes to bestow on mortals, I am her spokesman; cities and nations take joy from my answers; no part of the world flourishes except by my good will; swords by the thousand, kept in durance by my peace, will leap from their scabbards if I nod my head; whole populations may be wiped from the face of the earth, or shipped abroad, be granted liberty or lose it; kings are made, or made slaves; cities may rise and cities may fall; all this is done by my decree alone. And though my will is law I have never been impelled by anger, by youthful impetousity, by the refractory behaviour of those whose stubbornness would provoke the mildest temper, or by that fearful ambition which all too often leads great kings to make their power evident in the terror they inspire to punish men beyond their just deserts. My sword lies buried in its sheath, bound there by my chariness of spending even the vilest blood. Let a man be never so devoid of favour, he is a man still, and for this reason pleasing in my sight.[4]

All the hopes and aspirations of the State are now identified with its leading man. Seneca shows a vision of what Rome could be, if its despot were truly benevolent. But it is a far cry from Augustus's statement that he had no more power than any other man.

Seneca's tribute was probably sincere. Rome had by this time accepted power-politics as the natural order of things. What mattered was how the power was used; and Nero's first five years showed golden promise.

This happy state of affairs was not to last. New influences arose which revealed Nero's essential weakness. Increasingly restive under Agrippina's domination, the emperor began to assert himself. Agrippina retaliated by various impolitic demonstrations. With mother and son divided, the basis of Nero's power was no longer secure. Nor was his marriage happy. Nero was attracted by other women, first by the slave Acte, and then by Poppaea, who skilfully used her fascination to establish herself in Octavia's place. We have a curious document illustrating this rivalry in the form of a play. Tradition ascribes it to Seneca himself, who appears as a character in it, but this is hardly likely. One episode shows the philosopher-tutor reasoning with his infatuated imperial protégé:

SENECA: *A wife should be chaste, honest, virtuous, loyal,*
Careful of honour. All the rest will pass,
But these are treasures of the mind and spirit,
While beauty fades a little every day.

NERO: *God has joined all perfections in one woman.*
She was made for me. The gods have so decreed.

SENECA: *Fight this infatuation. It will pass.*

NERO: *Fight Love, the king of heaven, that the Thunderer*
Himself could not deny? Fight Love, that flies
Through storm and sea into the realm of Death?
Fight Love, that levels human and divine?

SENECA: *That is how men paint Love. A flying scourge,*
A god with bows and arrows, with a torch
To fire our hearts, whose father was Volcanus,
Whose mother, Venus. They are wrong. This love
Is but a passion, kindled in the mind,
Born of youth, and nourished on indulgence
For those whose ample fortune gives them leisure.
Starve it of sustenance, and love will soon
Drop from exhaustion, wither up and die.

NERO: *For me, love is the principle of life*
And source of pleasure. Love can never die.
For mankind could not recreate itself
Without love's aid, that soothes the savage breast.
Kindle the marriage torches, God of Love,
And light Poppaea's way into my bed![5]

Britannicus, still alive and in the palace, was another threat. The first clear manifestation of the new Nero was his removal. In spite of the tasters who, by now, were the indispensable accessories to any feast, Britannicus was poisoned at a banquet. Racine, who sixteen centuries later based a tragedy on the event, shows Burrus looking gloomily into the future and wishing that this crime could be Nero's last.

It was not. Nero's reign rapidly exhibited the worst features of tyranny, compelling subservience from all around him. Seneca, now at the height of his power, was not immune. We see him humouring his emperor with a viciously funny satire on his predecessor. In a sardonic reference to the Roman custom of deifying their dead rulers it is called, not *Apotheosis*, but *Apocolocyntosis Claudii, The Great Gourd Claudius*. Robert Graves has seen in the title an allusion to the method of Claudius's removal by poisonous fungi, but such a memory would hardly have been palatable to Nero. The title surely refers to the content of the satire, where Claudius, with all his physical oddities cruelly caricatured, is seen almost as a living vegetable, seeking admittance at the gates of Olympus:

> Report to Jupitei: unknown party at the door, height above average, hair grey, chronic head-tremor, limp in right foot. Asked for country of origin, gave unclear reply. Speech defects make answer unintelligible. Language unknown. Not Greek, not Latin; some hitherto unheard-of tongue. So Jupiter told Hercules, who had been all over the world on safari, to go and find out where this fellow came from. Hercules took one look and nearly went out of his mind. He'd never met the monster that could scare him. But when he looked at this unidentified object which moved by a mode of progression unknown to man, and made noises like no animal on earth but rather like the bellowing of a whale, he thought his thirteenth labour had come. Then he looked more closely and discovered it was human. So he went up and asked a question out of Homer (which came naturally, Hercules being a Greek boy):
> *What people do you come from? From what land and parents?* Claudius was delighted to find himself among booklovers. He hoped they'd have a place for a historian.[6]

The gods argue, in a parody of a senate meeting, what to do with him. Augustus, making his maiden speech, proposes that he be sent to Hell. Mercury takes Claudius down by way of Rome. When Claudius sees the dancing in the streets and hears the brass bands playing, he realizes he must be dead. Arriving in Hell he meets all his old friends and is put on trial for the crimes of his reign. Aeacus, the Judge, condemns him to play an eternal dice-game with a bottomless box. But an even worse fate awaits him:

> All at once Caligula arrived on the scene, and asked for Claudius to be handed over to him as a slave. He produced eyewitness testimony of how he had slapped, kicked and beaten Claudius in his lifetime. So Claudius was awarded to Caligula; and Caligula made a present of him to Aeacus; and Aeacus passed him on to his own freedman Menander, and made him clerk of the court.[7]

This savage denigration of a dead ruler for the amusement of the living is typical of the literary temper of the times. Gossip had been elevated to the status of a fine art. As in the case of the *Consolation to Polybius*, scholars who prefer to think of Seneca as nobler than he was claim that the *Apocolocyntosis* was not written by him. But other writers did as much. The poet Lucan, Seneca's nephew, wrote an epic on the war between Caesar and Pompey, the first book of which contains a paean of praise to Nero.

> *So when your earthly watch is done*
> *There will be joy in heaven as you seek*
> *Your place in the stars. Jove's sceptre shall be yours.*
> *Or Phoebus' fiery chariot shall bear you*
> *Around a world for whom this change of sun*
> *Will hold no terrors. Every deity*
> *Will yield to you, and yours will be the choice*
> *To be what god you will, and where to reign.*
> *But do not choose the North for your abode,*
> *Nor yet the South, beneath the shelving skies*
> *Scorched by siroccos. Then your light would fall*
> *Aslant on Rome. Whatever part of space*
> *You set your weight upon will tilt the pole*
> *Of heaven. Take the central place, maintain*
> *The balance of the spheres.*[8]

In Lucan's case, at least, we are allowed to see the other side of the picture. He had the presumption to differ with Nero on literary matters. On one occasion the Emperor walked out of one

of his recitals. The later books of the *Pharsalia* contain an attack
on the imperial government, with Caesar's victory at Pharsalus
seen as the death-blow to liberty.

> *And every nation, every age would bear*
> *The scars of this day's battle. More was lost*
> *Than human life. The future had surrendered*
> *And pledged its sons for perpetuity.*[9]

Nero was now rapidly casting aside his old advisors. Angered
by his mother's claims, he engineered her death. The boat which
took her from Baiae to Capri was rigged to collapse and sink in
mid-crossing. Agrippina miraculously escaped, only to meet her
death at the hands of an assassin. Octavia died also, and Seneca
was the next to be discarded. Seeing that his time was over, he
removed himself from politics and went into semi-retirement.
At Nomentum, near the capital, he cultivated his model farm,
and like Cicero sought a new vocation in philosophy. Nero did
not let him go completely. Seneca was consul in 62 – one of
several, for the office had become largely honorific. It was in this
year too that Burrus died. If Seneca had hoped to remove himself from notice, he was disappointed. But he found time to write
widely on philosophical matters. His letters show a marked dis-
content with the Rome of his time and a longing for a new
scheme of society which has certain Christian affinities. He shows,
for example, a humane attitude to the problem of slavery which
could never have existed under the Republic: a slave, he argues,
is a man like others, and deserves to be treated as such. Seneca's
thought here shows, perhaps, the changing social attitudes of his
own time, when former slaves could rise to be equal or superior
to their masters:

> I am happy to learn from your emissaries that you treat your
> slaves as members of the family. And so you should. You are a
> sensible, well-educated man. 'They're slaves.' Yes, but still human.
> 'They're slaves.' Perhaps, but comrades too. 'They're slaves.' No,
> friends, denied advancement. 'They're slaves.' Then so are we, if
> one reflects that slave and free alike are subject to the caprice of
> fortune.[10]

For Seneca the things of this earth were of comparatively little account. In spite of the training of his early days, he was no ascetic – the familiar double bust which couples him with Socrates shows a man who obviously enjoys the good things of life – but he made a clear distinction between the mind and the body:

> Let us form the habit of forswearing ostentation, and judge things by their usefulness, not their outward show. Let us eat to satisfy our hunger and drink to quench our thirst. Let us indulge our bodily appetites at need. Let us keep our bodies fit for use, and adapt our way of living to the traditions of our forefathers, not to current fashions. Let us teach ourselves greater self-control, and less indulgence, greater humility and less anger. Let us view poverty for what it is, no more, and cultivate a frugal disposition.[11]

The Christian tone of Seneca's work has led some to suggest that he was influenced by the new sect. This is almost certainly untrue. The similarity does suggest, however, why Christianity achieved such rapid popularity and why it was able, as no other imported religion had been, ultimately to subvert the Roman system. It was speaking to the converted. A humane Stoic like Seneca, or the friend Lucilius to whom he writes, if he practised the ideas of moral responsibility and social obligation that he preached, would be fulfilling most of the Christian dictates without having heard of the Bible.

The year 64 brought the fire of Rome, for which tradition has unhesitatingly blamed Nero, and in its wake the Christian persecutions. The next year an attempt was made on the emperor's life, led by Piso, a disaffected patrician. It failed because of criminal stupidity. The conspirators seem to have dropped hints, issued veiled warnings and dramatized their goings-on in a way which positively shouted their intentions. They were all arrested and the familiar purge followed, including all those who could conceivably be suspected of the remotest connection with the crime or the criminals, and many who could not; it was a convenient opportunity to dispose of anyone who was unpopular. Conspirators were prosecuted under the charge of *maiestas*, which, in the Republic, had meant an offence against the State. Now, with the State personified in the emperor, any personal attack on him could be so construed. *Maiestas* became a blanket term for any behaviour of which the emperor disapproved. The more prudent emperors had let the charge lapse, but Nero had revived it. It was on these grounds that the supposed associates of Piso were condemned, and Seneca was one of them.

We do not know whether he was guilty or not. It did not matter. On Nero's instructions, Seneca committed suicide in the approved aristocratic manner, by slitting his veins. Tacitus describes his death, which seems to have been modelled, probably consciously, on that of Socrates:

When he saw his friends weeping he told them, mildly at first, and then more firmly in a tone of rebuke, not to show such weakness. What, he asked, had happened to their Stoic principles? Their years of philosophical study designed to strengthen them against adversity? Nero's brutality was notorious. He had already murdered both mother and brother. Now, to make his crimes complete, he killed the guide and mentor of his youth.[12]

Seneca also wrote plays. It is as well to consider them separately, as they belong to a different category from the rest of his work. Neither he nor his contemporaries mention them: we have to take on trust their attribution to him by the manuscripts and by later authors. The plays were tragedies, and in writing such pieces Seneca was merely following the taste of his times. As we have seen, tragedy was not popular at Rome, at least so far as performance was concerned. It is interesting to speculate why. Like the comedies, the tragedies were adapted from Greek sources, and surviving fragments suggest that the Roman versions were rather heavy-handed. Another reason may be the same as that which has been given for the avoidance of drama in later Byzantium: in a society which already had so much pomp and spectacle, the theatre was largely redundant. And, in the last analysis, Roman audiences were not really interested. They had lost the sense of community participation in the drama that had made the Greek theatre so vitally exciting, and though they accepted tragedies at first it seems to have been the novelty of the performances that appealed to them. Familiarity bred, if not contempt, at least dislike. The Roman public wanted to be amused, and the tragic writers tried to spice their versions with metrical invention and added musical effects. They failed. Even plays based on Roman history soon palled, and one may notice a steady shift towards comedy on the part of the early writers. Livius Andronicus wrote both tragedy and comedy, Plautus comedy only.

Tragedy survived as a diversion for the élite. It was as fashionable for cultivated Romans to compose tragedies in the Greek manner as for modern dons to write detective stories. Julius Caesar wrote some while campaigning in Gaul. Augustus was a noted amateur. Nero, who had a weakness for the theatrical arts, was a writer as well as a performer. Such plays rarely reached the stage. They were literary diversions, nothing more, and often dealt with the same themes used for oratorical exercises.

It is against this background that we must see Seneca's plays. The argument about whether they were written to be staged is an old one. We do not know. They have been staged a number of times since, but that is another story. Most probably Seneca intended them only for closet performance – for reading, perhaps, in the same sort of literary circle that attended the recitals at the rhetorical schools. Seneca goes to the Greeks for his sources, and particularly to Euripides, but his style is a product of his Roman education. One can almost see Seneca's father beaming in approval, for the son has learnt his lessons well. All the tricks of the rhetorical schools are here. We see the shallow brilliance of the dialogue, the epigrams reeking of midnight oil:

COURTIER: *But are you not afraid*
Of public outcry?

ATREUS: *That is monarchy's*
Supreme advantage: power to enforce
Obedience and love.

COURTIER: *Fear may command*
Approval, but it still makes enemies.

>   *Sincere applause comes only from the heart.*
>   *Lip-service will not give you lasting glory.*
> ATREUS: *Truth is for commoners to enjoy. A king*
>   *Hears only flattery. Let them curb their will.*
> COURTIER: *If the monarch's will is just, who can deny him?*
> ATREUS: *If you will set that limit on a king*
>   *He rules on sufferance.*
> COURTIER: *A kingdom without law*
>   *Or fear of heaven, or respect for man,*
>   *Is built on sand.*
> ATREUS: *Law, fear, respect! Such things*
>   *Bind private men. A king goes where he pleases.*[13]

We see, too, the painstaking display of erudition, the allusions gleaned from the obscurer byways of mythology. Seneca hates to say anything simply. He rarely names the deities directly, but refers to them obliquely, by their functions: the onus is on the listener, whose level of comprehension proves his right to participate. Every statement is elaborated with a relentless parade of learning. Here is a description of Medea preparing her poison:

>   *When she had called this serpent progeny*
>   *She blended juices culled from poisoned herbs:*
>   *Those that grow upon the precipice*
>   *Of Eryx, or the inaccessible*
>   *And snow-bound heights of Caucasus, watered by*
>   *Prometheus' blood; the herbs rich Arabs take*
>   *To tip their arrows, that Parthian or Mede*
>   *Use for their running battles with the bow;*
>   *Herbs plucked by Suebians under winter skies,*
>   *Walking fearless through the Hyrcan forest . . . .*
>   *These poisons on Thessalian Athos grew,*
>   *These high on Pindus; these the tender leaves*
>   *Medea severed with her bloody scythe*
>   *On the summit of Pangaeus. These were fed*
>   *In Tigris' deep and turbid waters, these*
>   *By Danube, these upon the sunbaked shore*

> *Washed by the warm Hydaspes, with its freight*
> *Of precious stones, or Baetis, which has given*
> *Its title to the land whose sluggish waters*
> *Beat the Hesperian sea.*[14]

Euripides, it may be noted, makes the same point in two lines.

And we catch a whiff of the textbooks that Juvenal satirizes, from which the student culled his examples. Every speaker had his collection of commonplaces, his repertoire of set speeches on popular themes which could be inserted on appropriate occasions:

> *Where but in the country could you lead*
> *A life so blameless, so devoid of care,*
> *So faithful to the precepts of our fathers?*
> *Not in the town. The itch of acquisition*
> *Devours us there. But on the mountain tops*
> *The hermit lives serene, untouched by fear*
> *Or passing favour, by prestige that sells*
> *Its honour cheaply, by the scourge of malice*
> *Or fickle fame. He waits upon no tyrant*
> *Or gapes to be one, chasing empty titles*
> *Or the mirage of wealth. Free from desire*
> *And fear alike, he does not feel the tooth*
> *Of envy, that has left its shameful brand*
> *On other men. The iniquities begotten*
> *On crowded streets he does not know, nor shrinks*
> *In terror at each footfall, framing words*
> *To hide his heart. He does not boast his wealth*
> *With columns planted thick around his home*
> *Or beams that sneer beneath encrusted gold.*
> *His altars are not flooded with the blood*
> *Of snow-white oxen slaughtered by the hundred.*
> *He has the fields to roam in at his pleasure,*
> *Pure in heart beneath the open sky.*
> *This is the only cunning that he knows:*
> *To build a trap for beasts, and wash the dust*
> *Of labour from his body in the stream.*[15]

Through these plays stalk characters who are greater than life size, who remind us, in their booming preoccupation with their own emotions, of the *dramatis personae* of Italian opera at its most florid. It is a dark world that they inhabit, full of violence and corruption. Seneca favours Euripides because of the latter's concern with the gloomier side of human nature. The Latin tragedies are case-books of perverse psychology, where we explore the ramifications of warped and twisted minds. The Greek models are violent, their imitations doubly so. In Euripides' play Medea kills her children out of sight, and our imaginations work upon the deed of horror done behind closed doors. In Seneca's version the violence is more patent: Medea kills one child before our eyes, and the other, after an agonizing protraction, on the roof from which she taunts Jason. In Euripides' *Hippolytus*, the young prince is carried on at the end of the play to die; in Seneca's *Phaedra* (the title is significantly changed, for it is in a mind gone bad that the author is most interested) Hippolytus is torn to pieces and his father and the chorus work with the remnants as a ghastly jigsaw puzzle:

CHORUS: *Gather the parts of your dismembered son*
And lay them in their places, where each piece
Should be. See, this is where his right hand goes,
And here the left, that could control the reins
So well: I know the marks on his left side.
Oh, let us weep for what is wanting still!
Hands, do not tremble at your gruesome work.
Hold back, you tears, and do not flood my face
Till all is ordered, and the father makes
The fragments whole.

THESEUS: *What shapeless blasphemy,*
What rent and bloody thing is here? I know
It is some part of you, but more than this
I cannot tell. Here is an empty space.
Here lay it down. It does as well as any.[16]

For us the violence is so exaggerated that in Seneca, as in the Renaissance imitations of his style (*Titus Andronicus*, for example, or *The Spanish Tragedy*) it becomes grotesque and laughable. But we have to remember that in both cases the plays were composed in an environment where violence was casual and commonplace. Seneca writes for an audience used to the bloodbath of the arena, which he condemns (an attitude for which he was praised by an anonymous but apparently well-read gladiator from Pompeii, in a scribble on a wall). Apart from the regular bouts, the Roman public enjoyed the slaughter of condemned criminals thrown into the amphitheatre to fight battles they were doomed to lose:

> Nothing is so ruinous to the character as time wasted at the public games. Vice is more insinuating when it comes as pleasure. You see what I mean? I come home more greedy, more discontented with my lot, more self-indulgent – more of a beast, in fact – from being with my fellow-men. I happened to drop in at the lunch-time show, expecting to see some comic turns, a little light relief from the spectacle of human blood. Quite the contrary. The previous combats were merciful by comparison. Now they got down to business. It was pure, unadulterated murder. The men have no way to protect themselves. They leave their bodies wide open, and every blow tells. Many people prefer this to the regular bouts and request matches. Why shouldn't they? There's no helmet or shield to interfere with the swordplay. Who needs armour? Who needs skill? Such things only postpone the moment of death. In the morning they throw men to the lions and bears, at noon they throw them to the crowd. Kill, then be killed, that's the rule; win one bout, be slaughtered in the next. Every fight is to the death, and the means are fire and sword.[17]

It was difficult to shock audiences for whom this was the daily fare. Seneca is forced to raise the level of his violence one notch higher.

Yet the violence is not exploited for its own sake, any more than it was in Euripides. Seneca is faithful to the Greek tradition of using familiar myths to illustrate contemporary problems. He shows us a world of brooding suspicion, peopled by tyrants for whom there is no rule unless by force, and who are haunted by the nightmares of their own creation. Sophocles' Oedipus at the beginning of the play is a serene and kindly monarch, the father of his people. Seneca's character writhes from the start in the penumbra of half-recognized guilt:

> Now night has fled. The fitful sun returns
> To raise its wan disc in the shrouded sky
> And cast its mourning lantern on the houses
> Gutted to feed the hunger of the plague.
> Night's carnage shows by day.
>   Can any king
> Be happy in his lot? How fair of face
> Is royalty; what joys it promises.
> What woes it brings. As mountains bare their heads
> To the tempest's fury: as the jutting cape
> Is buffeted by breakers even when
> The sea lies calm; so those who wear the crown
> Are fortune's playthings.[18]

We are reminded of the biographers' portraits of Nero wandering through the labyrinth of his palace, fearing an assassin round every corner and tormented by a guilt-ridden conscience.

Seneca's plays deal with power-politics at its worst, and their application to his age is evident. A good reason, perhaps, why he never refers to them, and for their never having been performed in his lifetime. One final point of comparison with the Greeks must be made. Sophocles and Euripides wrote in a democracy where citizens could still speak their minds, and mastered the art of rhetoric to be able to do so most forcibly. The tragedies betray this preoccupation. Hecuba, pleading with Agamemnon, prays for her whole body to become a tongue. Jason summons up all the resources of oratory to answer his indignant wife.

In Seneca, though the plays are embellished with every known trick of the speaker's art, the power of rhetoric is never mentioned. It is for entertainment only. The characters, like Seneca's audience, have lost sight of their ability to move the powers-that-be by oratory. They can only protest hopelessly against the force that moves inexorably against them; they die elegantly, with an epigram.

Seneca's tragedies, though studied for their historical and rhetorical interest, have generally been dismissed as unstageworthy. It is true that there is much in them to tax the patience of a modern audience. Yet the playwrights of the Renaissance idolized him. That was partly out of necessity: he was their principal classical model, for the universities came late to the study of Greek, and the tragedies were popularized through their Latin imitations. All the same, these playwrights were practical men of the theatre, writing to please a difficult and noisily critical audience, and the fact that they found Seneca such a prolific source of ideas suggests that we ought to be less contemptuous of him. He gave his imitators themes, characters, language, plots; the device of the interior monologue, which shows its full power in *Hamlet*, is essentially derived from the soul-searching soliloquies of Seneca, who develops this mode of expression from concepts present in the Greek, but makes it peculiarly his own.

Since the Renaissance, however, it cannot be denied that Seneca's reputation as a dramatist has slumped. In part, this low esteem has been self-perpetuating. Once dismissed as second-rate, Seneca attracted only second-rate translators, and the available English versions are far below the calibre of the current translations of Greek plays. In fact, Seneca, for all his love of the florid and ornate, is a master of language, and deserves better. It has been objected, too, that his plays are not really suitable for the stage. Entrances and exits are often unmotivated; it is sometimes doubtful who is speaking to whom; when approached with naturalistic preconceptions, the plays present alarming technical difficulties; and the Chorus, a device which Seneca inherits from the Greeks, seems curiously aloof, with no clear connection with the action. But the critics who make these points are usually comparing Seneca with Euripides, and finding him wanting. This is unfair. The borrowings from the Greek are obvious, but misleading. Seneca is formulating his own kind of drama, which has more affinities with *Under Milk Wood* than with *Hamlet*. His plays present a poetic continuum in which the normal laws of space, time and logical continuity are blurred. Borne on the rhetorical torrent of his language – whose very artificiality suggests a dream world in which normality has abdicated – his tortured characters swim into the light to make their individual statements, then disappear; his Chorus works not so much with characters as in counterpoint to them. Seneca would make – has, in fact, made – excellent radio material. And there are signs of his theatrical reinstatement. Vittorio Gassman has been playing *Thyestes* in Italy for years. At the Avignon Festival in 1967 Jorge Lavelli offered a production of Seneca's *Medea* in which the characters, glistening in metallic costumes and with their faces made up in abstract patterns, chanted Seneca's lines to an insidious musical accompaniment. A year later came Peter Brook's notorious London production of *Oedipus*, which borrowed its conventions from the Japanese *noh* play and presented the action to the audience, frankly, as a ritual. A theatre which is currently vitally concerned with ritual as a mode of dramatic expression can easily countenance Seneca. A generation influenced by the Theatre of Cruelty, which proposes to stun its audiences by a progression of emotional shocks, finds him natural material. *Marat-Sade* and *Thyestes* belong in the same world. Disquieting though it may be, Seneca, who portrays the hapless struggles of the individual against inexorable forces, may well be the dramatist of our times. Our age has provided an emotional climate and a theatrical grammar in which these long-neglected tragedies are once more meaningful.

NOTES TO CHAPTER SEVEN

1. Juvenal, *Satires*, 7. 150–4, 172–5.
2. Seneca, *De Consolatione ad Polybium (Consolation to Polybius)*, 6. 2–3.
3. Tacitus, *Annals*, XII. 8.
4. Seneca, *De Clementia (On Clemency)*, 2–3.
5. Seneca, *Octavia*, 547–71.
6. Seneca, *Apocolocyntosis*, 5.
7. Ibid. 15.
8. Lucan, *Pharsalia*, 1. 45–59.

224

9. Ibid. VII. 638–41.

10. Seneca, *Letters*, 47. 1.

11. Seneca, *De Tranquillitate Animi* (*The Tranquillity of the Soul*), 9. 2.

12. Tacitus, *Annals*, XV. 63.

13. Seneca, *Thyestes*, 204–18.

14. Seneca, *Medea*, 705–13, 720–7.

15. Seneca, *Phaedra*, 483–509.

16. Ibid. 1256–68.

17. Seneca, *Letters*, 7. 2–4.

18. Seneca, *Oedipus*, 1–11.

Chapter Eight

Imperial Places

THE PORT OF ROME

OF all the ancient sites, Ostia is the most easily accessible from Rome. A half-hour's drive along the road by which we first entered the capital, or by electric train, it rests in a countryside surprisingly unspoilt. A few steps from the quadruple highway are sleeping fields and tiny villages. The ancient city has become a sanctum, a triumphant demonstration of how much the archaeologist's spade can recover from the soil; a city virtually complete with its public and private places, a vanished sea-port awakened to a new half-life.

It is from the sea, perhaps, that we should enter it, at least in imagination, for this is where its importance lay. Holiday resort as well as harbour, it attracted trippers from Rome just as the modern Lido di Ostia does today, a mile or two beyond the ancient coastline pursuing the receding sea. We may imagine the beaches then much as they are now, though the shipping has moved north to Civitavecchia. Packed in summer, restful out of season, the seashore provided a welcome relief from the heat and congestion of the capital.

A Christian writer of the second century A.D. has left us a charming description of this aspect of the town:

> We thought it would be pleasant to take a trip to Ostia, an extremely agreeable resort, as I was feeling rather under the weather and regular dips in the sea would set me up without too much exertion. It was the grape season, holiday time, when the courts were out of session. The summer solstice had come and gone and the milder days of autumn were upon us.
> After breakfast we strolled out to the beach, to get the benefit of the fresh sea breeze and enjoy the feeling of the sand between our

toes.. Caecilius noticed an image of Serapis and blew it a kiss – a vulgar supersitition. . . .

Our conversation brought us halfway from the town to the open beach. At the water's edge, the ripples had caressed the sand into a sort of promenade. Even on calm days the sea is in constant agitation, no waves, no surf, just the ripples, over and under, back and forth. We amused ourselves by trying to chase them, paddling along the water's edge: the waves advanced and licked our feet, then slid back and withdrew upon themselves again. So we strolled along without a care in the world, skirting the gentle curve of the shoreline and telling stories to pass the time. Octavius talked of his adventures at sea.[1]

The friends pass some boats hauled up on the beach, watch boys playing ducks and drakes, and sit down to talk of Christianity.

Ostia also drew the wealthy. Pliny, the ubiquitous and tireless correspondent, who had a villa nearby, tells of its attractions:

You're surprised that I'm so pleased with my villa . . . you won't be, once I've described it. It's a charming place, a delightful location, miles of beach. It's about seventeen miles from Rome, just the right distance, so that after a hard day at the office there's still time to come down for the night. There are several ways to get there. Take the Laurentine or Ostian highway . . . in either case, turn off onto a byroad, sand part of the way, heavy going for wheeled traffic but a good surface if you're on horseback. The scenery's constantly changing. At one point the road is almost crowded out by trees. And then the country opens up into pastureland. Plenty of sheep, horses and cattle, taking their winter holiday from the mountains to enjoy the grass and spring-like temperature.[2]

The Christian Octavius, from his own maritime experiences, would have been interested in the harbour. We saw in Chapter Two how the military post at Ostia marked Rome's first move to the sea. From that time on it had been intimately connected with Rome's naval adventures: the growth of Ostia parallels the expansion of Rome's power throughout Italy and the world. Used as a naval base in the wars with Pyrrhus and Hannibal, it had taken longer to develop as a commercial port. Other coastal cities were preferred. Under the Republic, however, Ostia was already offering competition, and assuming a new role as the entry point for imports to feed Rome's swelling population. It was not until the early Empire that it had its own harbour. Before this, the larger freighters were moored off-shore and serviced by lighters, while smaller craft, sometimes even warships, could make their own way up river. Claudius began work on the harbour in A.D. 42, opening an artificial basin on the right bank of the Tiber. He did not live to finish the project. Nero celebrated the completion of the harbour in 54 with a commemorative coinage. Trajan enlarged his predecessors' work and constructed a new hexagonal basin.

An impressive feat in its own right, the harbour had connections with other monumental projects of the time. Caligula had had a huge obelisk shipped from Egypt, in a vessel described by Pliny as nearly as long as the left side of the port of Ostia. The obelisk itself was erected in one of Nero's racecourses, in the Vatican district. In 1586, when it was moved to its present site in front of St Peter's, it took nine hundred men and a hundred and forty horses to raise it. The ship that had made the perilous journey from Alexandria was sunk to form the foundation for a mole. On this was erected Ostia's famous lighthouse, two hundred feet high, the shape of which we know from a scratched outline on an Ostian wall, and from its appearance in a decorative mosaic.

Once in service, the harbour changed the pattern of commerce. It now became the practice to transfer cargoes to smaller river-vessels which worked their way to the capital by a combination of oar and sail. Sometimes, particularly in the later Empire, they were towed by oxen. The harbours are lost to us now, though part of their outline has been traced by aerial photography. It is interesting that the ancient harbour and the modern airport share the same territory, Fiumicino: though the mode of transport differs, the point of entry is the same.

The city itself we now see largely as a ground plan – or rather two, one superimposed upon the other. The Republican foundation soon expanded beyond the limits of the original *castrum*, and was ringed by new walls. The imperial city overlaid its predecessor within the same limits. Thus at various points – particularly in the street of tombs outside the gate that points to

Rome – one may still observe the two layers of construction. Substantially, however, it is the imperial city that we see. Serious excavations began at the end of the nineteenth century and are still in progress. They were given new stimulus by the Fascist government with a view to impressing the world at the projected Exposition of 1942. War cancelled the Exposition, but the work was not wasted. Ostia remains our most complete example of a Roman city brought to light. Nearly half of the ancient extent is still not uncovered, but there is enough to permit an accurate impression of what life must have been like there, and to allow us to make inferences about contemporary Rome. In the capital, only the monuments have been spared, and those selectively. The houses of the people have almost completely vanished, or exist in fragments as an underground city, buried beneath the new. A five-storied apartment house at the foot of the Capitol is today buried up to its second floor. Bits and pieces of the old foundations exist all over Rome in crypts and cellars. Ostia gives us a more complete idea of how these buildings must have looked in their prime. And the Roman writers, describing, often bitterly, the places in which they lived, allow us to clothe the bones of Ostia in flesh.

We see in Ostia a city which held, at its greatest development, some fifty thousand people. We see their houses and shops, their places of worship, entertainment and employment. Most of the buildings are truncated, cut off at their lower storeys. When the city suffered its economic slump and was abandoned, the tall houses began to crumble: Roman brick-building technique was often insecure. The low walls that remain, firmed and cemented by the excavators, give a curious impression, from a distance, of the pueblo villages of the American south-west. But the mosaics remain also, crumpled like quilts by time and the subsidence of earth, and help to illustrate the daily life of the population. Inscriptions, found in plenty, allow us to piece together the administrative and commercial workings of the city. They permit us also to penetrate into more personal matters, such as the gloomy statistic that over eighty per cent of recorded deaths occurred below the age of thirty. Even allowing for the high incidence of infant mortality and the fact that only upper-class burials tended to carry epitaphs (it has recently been argued that the Roman aristocracy was unknowingly poisoning itself from the lead in water-pipes and drinking-vessels) the figures corroborate what we may guess from other sources, that the average Roman could not anticipate a long life-span. But while they lived the Ostians were busy.

It is their commercial activity that chiefly concerns us here. Its extent is recorded in mosaic, in the Square of the Corporations behind the theatre. This was originally surrounded by a double colonnade, and the mosaics, of various dates, were laid down by the representatives and agents of overseas shippers, who advertized themselves underfoot. So close a grouping of traders in one place suggests imperial control from an early period. The mosaics depict, in picture or symbol, the various enterprises in which Ostia engaged. Dealers in ivory are represented, together with rope-sellers, timber-merchants and, perhaps, suppliers of animals for the amphitheatre. This favourite attraction seems, curiously enough, not to have been enjoyed at Ostia itself. No amphitheatre has yet been discovered, and as most of the public quarters have been brought to light it is reasonable to assume that none existed. The beasts must have gone on to meet their spectacular deaths inland. We know from inscriptions of a guild of wine-merchants, importing in bulk: there was perhaps also a guild of auctioneers.

Ostia's function as a clearing-house may be seen from a merchantman discovered in 1962 by underwater archaeologists diving off the coast of Ibiza in the Balearic Islands. One of its anchor-stocks is stamped with what appears to be the name of the port of Rome, and a tentative appraisal of the contents suggests that it sailed from Ostia with a large cargo of oil lamps for sale around the Mediterranean. From there it crawled, under its single sail, down the coast and across to Alexandria, where it picked up new cargo and particularly a shipment of art works, including a bronze Hercules, another bronze statue of a dancing faun which is a coarser cousin of the famous figure from Pompeii, and a silver pouring-jar. Quantities of Greek vases had also been picked up on the voyage, copies or forgeries of antique originals. The ship may have been specially commissioned for this purpose, with the more normal cargo carried as a side-venture. It is armed with a catapult, which could fire the round stones shipped as ballast in case of attack. This defence, unusual for a merchantman, may have been dictated by the precious nature of its freight. The vessel seems to have sailed in the reign of Nero, who was, like other emperors, a notable and indiscriminate collector of fine art. From Alexandria, it is conjectured, the ship sailed for Carthage and Spain, where it picked up nearly two thousand amphorae of wine. Some of the contents, black and foul-tasting, were still liquid in the sealed and stoppered jars. Also in the cargo were lead ingots and murex shells for making the well-known purple dye. Beating back from Spain to Massilia before the winter set in, the ship came to destruction on the reef. This reconstruction, though still conjectural, is a vivid illustration of the complexities of imperial commerce in which Ostia played such an important part. Ships went out to all parts of the Roman world. It was a three weeks' voyage to Alexandria, six months to India. Strabo tells us that in one year 120 ships had reached the latter country alone. China was accessible by Hadrian's time. The wreck also illustrates the frightening dangers on which Ostia's commercial prosperity was based. Every voyage was a gamble. If successful, it could make its financer a rich man. If it failed, it could ruin him. The floor of the Mediterranean is dotted with the failures, and their gradual rediscovery is one of the most exciting aspects of contemporary archaeology.[3]

In the centre of the Square of the Corporations stands a temple to Demeter, an appropriate goddess to preside over the most important commercial activity of the city. Ostia's greatest concern was corn, and this mainly from Africa. We have already seen something of the agricultural decline in Italy, and of Rome's increasing difficulty in feeding her population. Italy could not grow enough, or did not care to. The introduction of a corn-dole under the Republic increased the problem, and the control of the markets became an important official responsibility. Pompey held this position in 57 B.C., and Julius Caesar appointed two new magistrates to make it their sole concern. Africa, Numidia and Sicily came to be relied on to fill the national need. Augustus stimulated growth in Egypt and appointed a permanent commissioner to charter shipping, store supplies and control monopolies. In his time five million bushels of grain were imported annually from Egypt. Under Nero, we are told that African grain fed Rome for eight months and Egyptian grain for four months. The man who controlled Egypt had a hand on Rome's throat; this is why the emperors were so cautious in their appointments. The flow of imported grain caused a drop in local prices, and the Emperor Nerva's increased distributions made the question of supply even more vital.

Ostia became, pre-eminently, the granary of Rome. As one walks the city from end to end, one sees the storehouses on every side. The earliest are republican, the most impressive imperial. A good example of the latter is the granary of Epagathus and Epaphroditus, presumably two freedmen partners in a safe investment. It has sixteen large rooms on the ground floor alone. Such a granary would have been fit to receive the cargo of the Egyptian merchantman described by Lucian, the contents of whose holds would have fed all Attica for a year. It has been suggested that these enormous commercial structures provided the architectural model for the later Italian *palazzi*.

The unloading and storage of the grain, and its transfer to river boats, was carried out under careful official scrutiny. Administration of the corn supply was in the hands of a quaestor appointed from Rome. Tiberius, before he came to the throne, had held this office. Under Claudius the quaestor was replaced by officials directly responsible to the *praefectus annonae*, Minister of Supply, in the capital. It was important work, and a serious responsibility.

Ostia, then, gives us a kitchen-door view of the realities of Roman economics. What of the Ostians themselves? How did they live and amuse themselves? The inscriptions are revealing. Like any great port, Ostia had a mixed population. There were immigrants from Africa, Spain, and the Greek-speaking East; from Egypt and Syria; from Corsica and Sardinia; from Thrace. The majority were housed in tall apartment blocks called *insulae*, islands, because they stood out above the sea of surrounding buildings. Large areas of these buildings survive, and we may see from them how Rome must have looked at this time. Most of the Romans lived in such tenements. Only a few traces survive in the capital: on the Caelian Hill, for example, where the walls of an ancient *insula* have been built into the fabric of the Church of Saints John and Paul. Literary evidence is ample. Building-space was at a premium, and Rome, like New York, was forced to grow up rather than out. Tenements reached precarious heights. Augustus tried to impose a seventy-foot limit, which Trajan reduced to sixty. In practice this meant four storeys and a low fifth. Even this, given the slapdash methods of contruction and the reluctance of landlords to spend a penny more on upkeep than they had to, was precarious. Cicero is appalled by the sum required to repair one of his properties, and would rather do anything than lay it out. To judge from the writers, the tenements were noisy, crowded, insanitary and uncomfortable. We have both the dry testimony of architects and the complaints of indignant inhabitants. In Italy, it is not difficult to recreate the environment. Go out to Tivoli, not far from Rome, and walk through the medieval quarter that classicists normally shun. Examine the web of dark, congested, ill-paved streets. Add, in your imagination, a few extra storeys to the buildings that crowd upon them. Call up a picture of tottering tenements almost touching, and you will feel the force of Martial's complaint:

> *I can reach out of my apartment window*
> *And shake my neighbour Novius by the hand.*[4]

Martial lived, as he tells us, 'three flights up. And long flights, too.'[5] This was dangerous. Seneca mentions 'the incredible feat of engineering that shores up apartment blocks beginning to crack at street-level'.[6] Juvenal testifies to the constant danger, both from the urgent traffic and the menace overhead:

> *What horrors can a desert island hold*
> *Worse than this city, where each second brings*
> *New risk to life and limb – a house on fire,*
> *A wall collapsing? . . .*
> *Consider Rome by night. Death comes in strange*
> *And diverse ways. They toss their broken china*
> *Out of the penthouse windows, fit to crack*
> *My skull, or the pavement. Going out to dinner?*
> *Made your will, I hope? No? You're an idiot,*
> *Or else an optimist. Every open window*
> *Is a death-trap, when you walk the streets at night.*[7]

This was the Rome that most people knew – not the monumental city so piously resurrected, in all its shining splendour, by film-makers, but with all the worst features of pre-Haussmann Paris. And yet the people came pouring in. The lawbooks of the period show the profiteering that went on, and the frantic demand for accommodation. Tenants faced with crippling rents were often forced to sublet, increasing the noise and inconvenience.

The surviving buildings at Ostia seem less grim than the writers make out. Some features, it is true, smack of jerry-building, such as the balconies that hang along a wall without windows to give access to them. Nevertheless, they seem to have been relatively spacious, in some cases almost lavish. Access to each apartment was from a common entryway. Some of the blocks involve small courtyards or arcades, with the central well as the most prominent feature. Reconstructions show them to be no more unpleasant than such housing developments have to be, and certainly, when the balconies were full of flowers, more attractive than the faceless enormities built by Mussolini for his EUR.

But the well reminds us that space was not the only considera-tion. When one looks at the shells of the buildings, it is easy to forget the everyday necessities of heat, plumbing and water. This is where the hardships began. For the upper floors at least there was no possibility of central heating. Plumbing was equally difficult. The tenants either used the large public latrines, or poured their slops from the windows after dark. Any water supply above the ground floor was virtually impossible. The Romans had no difficulty in bringing water into a city. In Rome itself, the imperial period saw the completion of an elaborate system of aqueducts, crossing, interlocking, tapping the sources in the surrounding hills. Once arrived in the city cisterns the water was piped off at ground level. Without hydraulic machinery, the engineers could not conduct the water to the top of a building. Most of it therefore went to the public fountains, which combined a decorative and a practical function. By the end of the third century A.D. there were 1,352 such fountains in Rome, and the modern city has continued the tradition: there are 2,300 now. Many of them are original Roman constructions restored and embellished by Renaissance and baroque sculptors: the Fontana di Trevi, which every visitor to Rome knows, has a history going back to Augustus's time, when water was brought into Rome from springs to the east. A peasant girl pointed them out to the military engineers, and the aqueduct was named, in her honour, the *Aqua Virgo*. In Ostia and Pompeii the fountains are still evident. They were the inhabitants' chief source of supply, and the surplus continued on its course to flush out the city's drainage system. So in theory there was plenty of water, even though one might have to go some distance to get it. In practice, things were often different. The barely satisfactory water pressure was often reduced to incapacity by the inroads of private citizens, who tapped the pipes – usually illegally – and drew off supplies for their own use. How great this problem eventually became we know from a man who was Water Commissioner for Rome in A.D. 70. He comments on the alarming losses between intake and output, and explains:

This is attributable to dishonesty among the employees of the Catchment Board; my investigations show that they have been diverting water from public conduits for private use. There is also a significant number of landowners tapping the conduits that by-pass their property. As a result, the public supply is brought to a standstill by private citizens, just to water their gardens. . . . I have found irrigated fields, shops, garrets even, and every house of ill repute in Rome, with fixtures to ensure constant running water.[8]

The combination of poor water supply and urban congestion indicates another recurrent problem, the danger of fire. In Rome it was frequent. Livy tells us that all buildings between the Aventine and the Capitoline were burnt down in 213 B.C. We have already noted the consequences of Caesar's cremation. Under the Republic firefighting was organized haphazardly under private enterprise. Unscrupulous capitalists acquired huge fortunes by purchasing blazing property for ridiculous sums from the desperate owners, and then sending in their firemen to extinguish the blaze. In the Empire things were better arranged, but fires could still spread with terrifying rapidity. Considerable sections of the city had been burnt in 27 and 36; Tacitus reports the best-publicized fire of all, under Nero in 64:

> The fire started in the Circus Maximus where it touches the Palatine and Caelian hills, and fed on the shops full of inflammable merchandise. Fanned by the wind, it became a holocaust in a few seconds. The whole perimeter of the Circus was blazing. There were no walled houses or temples standing in their own grounds to provide a fire-break. The fire roared over the low ground first, then up the hillside and down again, devastating everything in its way. It spread so rapidly that there was no time to take precautions. And the city lay open to the menace – the old Rome of tortuous alleys and enormous blocks of houses[9].

Although this catastrophe was never repeated on a like scale, there were other great fires in Rome under Titus in 80, Commodus in 191 and Carinus in 283.

Ostia shows the same concern. One of the largest buildings in the city is the firemen's barracks. Claudius had detached urban troops to Ostia for this service, and Hadrian replaced them with trained firefighters. Their quarters are impressive. The barracks consists of a large open courtyard surrounded by a portico, off which open eighteen rooms; the upper storeys, now destroyed, presumably followed the same plan. One room has been identified as a latrine, and others may have been the officers' quarters.

At one end of the courtyard stands a large trough, presumably used by the men for their ablutions. There was also a chapel for emperor-worship, and an elaborate mosaic floor. Bars in the street outside catered for the men's off-duty hours.

Ostia is laid out according to the conventional Roman plan, with a principal street running the length of the city intersected by others which divide the buildings into symmetrical blocks. Towards the sea the main road forks, one branch leading down to the Marine Gate, which now looks out on the *autostrada*. A traveller entering this way in antiquity would have found the gate considerably more impressive than it is now. A few scattered columns and marble basins hint at the former dignity. Once inside the walls, our traveller would have found a city used to the needs of sailors. Near the gate stands a public bathhouse and further along the road is a large tavern where stone basins still rest on the mosaic floor. Up a nearby side-street are shops surprising in their modernity, with large display-windows like our own, but glassless. The road leads past the headquarters of the great commercial guilds to the forum, built on the site of the original *castrum* and enclosed by the principal temples, another public bath and the basilica. The forum was, as everywhere, the centre of local government, and Ostia's constitution was that of the capital in miniature. There were two chief magistrates who, as in Rome, gave their name to their year of office, a council of a hundred members to assist and advise, and *aediles* to supervise the public works with the help of town-owned slaves. Inscriptions give us interesting sidelights on how Roman politics could influence local affairs. During the party crisis following Caesar's crossing of the Rubicon, no magistrates were appointed at all. Under the Empire, members of the imperial family were often offered magistracies as a compliment.

If the traveller was pious, or superstitious, and wished to render thanks for a safe voyage, he could find almost every deity represented. The divine triad of Jupiter, Juno and Minerva presided over one end of the forum, while the temple to Rome and Augustus stood at the other. This was standard practice. But the religious affections of the Ostians went chiefly to Vulcan. There is also a temple to Castor and Pollux and one to Hercules, whose worship Augustus encouraged as an analogue to himself. Caecilius, in the account which began this chapter, provoked Christian scorn by acknowledging a statue of Serapis. He would have found many such in Ostia, which imported exotic deities as readily as grain. The temple of Serapis was appropriately decorated with Nilotic scenes. Anubis, another Egyptian god, was also worshipped, as was Cybele, the Great Mother. This profusion of foreign cults in Ostia testifies to the state of contemporary religion in Italy generally. Most popular of all was Mithra, the eastern god beloved of the military, whose worship will be discussed elsewhere; it is sufficient to say here that fifteen of his shrines have already been discovered in Ostia and more will undoubtedly follow.

Leaving the city for Rome, the traveller would pass other impressive public buildings. On his left he could see the theatre, where ancient plays are still performed on summer evenings, and the huge Baths of Neptune with their aquatic mosaics nearby. Then in front of him would be the Roman Gate and the city walls, and, outside, the street of tombs, memorials to the prosperous dead forbidden by law to be buried within the city limits. Here the rich preserved in death the unity which had bound the *familia* in life. In the *columbaria*, or dovecot tombs, so called from the rows of niches in which the funerary urns were placed, the ashes of the freedmen occupy the lower tiers, recalling their ties with their patron in lifetime.

There is a peculiar wistfulness about Ostia which one does not feel about Pompeii, and certainly not about the monuments of classical Rome, for all the spectacular demise of the one and the enduring grandeur of the other. The workaday nature of Ostia commands affection. It was a city for use rather than for show. It had its grand buildings, but in red brick rather than gleaming marble; it died a slow natural death when its usefulness was done. Ostia began to decline in the fourth century A.D., affected by competition from a newer harbour nearby. The monuments began to crumble, and no one bothered to repair them; the marble facings lay where they fell until private citizens carried them off. Traffic on the Tiber dwindled. Later commentaries show us a river empty of boats, and a highway overgrown with weeds. Ostia lay on the coast like a disused and rusting tool, desolate, silted, malarious and forgotten until the archaeologist called it back to life.

THE CITIES OF THE SOUTH

The road to Campania is a familiar one to classical travellers. Or rather, two roads; one may either plunge from Rome straight to Naples by the *autostrada*, or go from Ostia by the more leisurely route which winds along the coast. The latter is, as usual, more interesting. It passes through regions sanctified by Greek and Roman myth to the pleasure belt, the resort towns of the ancients. First comes Anzio, site of the Allied beach-head in the Second World War. This was the ancient Antium, a city of legendary origins and, in the fourth century B.C., a centre of local resistance to Rome. Once subdued, it was developed as a seaside resort with splendid temples. Horace invokes Fortune as the goddess of Antium, an appropriate deity for a sea-port, while Appian mentions the city as a grainstore during the Marian wars and as a rich source of temple treasures later.[10] A favourite dallying-place for Cicero, it still attracts bathers today. Then to the village of Sperlonga, where in 1957 archaeologists found a cave lavishly decorated with statuary, presumably built as a seaside dining-room for the Emperor Tiberius, and after his death turned into a museum. Further down the coast lies Cicero's Formiae on the magnificent sweep of the bay. The road comes within sight of Ischia, where the Greeks made their first settlement, and passes through the cluster of Hellenic cities round the Bay of Naples, a far better natural harbour than Rome had to offer. A side road leads to Cumae, the home of the Sibyl. The main highway, following the course of the Via Domitiana that we saw Statius celebrating in Chapter Two, passes by Lake Avernus, a gloomy enough place, once regarded as the entrance to the underworld. On a grey day it may still seem so; tall trees ring water which seems infinitely deep. Augustus turned it to more utilitarian purposes, digging a canal to the sea to make a naval harbour. Around this mythical *memento mori* the Greek towns stand close together. We pass through Pozzuoli, founded by islanders from Samos about 521 as Dikaearchia and renamed Puteoli by the Romans in 318. This was the chief port of entry for shipping from Egypt. Even after Ostia grew to prominence it continued to supply the luxury market with elephants, and the urban proletariat with corn. The city sprawl soon chokes the road, but a few nuggets of antiquity remain: an amphitheatre which was the third largest in Italy, with a capacity of forty thousand people, and the foundations of an Augustan temple on which the Duomo di San Procolo now stands. A few columns remain from the ancient market hall.

Nearby is another watering-place, Baiae, celebrated by Martial, who in our day would have been a gossip columnist. The occasional poet of the smart set, he went everywhere that was fashionable, and recorded what he saw. Like the reporter in *La Dolce Vita*, he preferred the haunts of the rich to his own humble garret.

> *Baiae, blessed Venus's* côte d'or:
> *Nature in her pride could give no more.*
> *A thousand cantos, Flaccus, could not tell*
> *The praise of Baiae, that deserves so well.*[11]

We are now in Virgil country. Baiae was reputedly named after Baios, a companion of Aeneas, just as Cape Misenum, the northern headland of the Bay of Naples, is said to bear the name of the hero's trumpeter who was buried there. In the late Republic Cicero was already describing the site as malarial, but this did not prevent several emperors from building villas. It was from Baiae that Agrippina, Nero's mother, embarked on the voyage that, by her son's instructions, was to end in her death.

Then comes Naples itself, colonized by Rhodians, according to a doubtful tradition, in the eighth century B.C., as Parthenope, by

Cumeans a century later as Palaeopolis, 'Old Town', and later still as Neapolis, 'New Town'. It prospered from alliance with Rome and attracted many visitors from the capital. Virgil is supposed to have died there; Publius Vedius Pollio, a self-made man who had risen to be Augustus's friend, had a villa there called Pausilypon, 'Begone, Dull Care.'

And finally, on the far side of Naples, Pompeii. It was of a class with most of the towns through which we have passed – though not itself a Greek foundation, a city in which the Greek influence was strong; a place, like the others, which offered an attractive climate, good land, and the opportunity for gentlemen of leisure to pass their time amid comfortable Hellenic surroundings. In the background loomed the dormant volcano of Vesuvius. This bothered no one. At some distant, unrecorded time, the volcano had erupted, spewing forth the ridge of lava on which Pompeii was built. But no one dreamed that such a thing could happen again. The location was considered a good and healthy one. A few miles away was Stabiae, now Castellamare, with health-giving springs and baths. Even now, the local mineral waters bear quotations from Virgil and Columella in their praise. Good wine came from grapes grown on the mountain, as it still does. Lacrimae Christi and Vesuvio have the distinctive quality of grapes grown in volcanic soil.

Pompeii was an old foundation of the Oscan people, a Campanian tribe. The derivation of its name is obscure. One theory suggests that it came from *pompe*, the Oscan word for fire. If this is true, the sinister implications were ignored. Inscriptions show that the Oscan language was retained for certain titles whose sound suggests their Roman counterparts; *kvaisstur*, for instance, is the equivalent of the Latin *quaestor*. But the Greek domination of the sea-coast and the surrounding countryside gave the city its culture. In the fourth century B.C. Pompeii accepted the inevitable and succumbed to Roman rule, while still retaining much of its individuality. This happy position was jeopardized when Pompeii took the wrong side in the civil wars, but by the time of the Empire amity had been restored. Pompeii became a thoroughly

Romanized city, at least on the surface, but there remained a substratum of aboriginal independence, and a distinctly Greek coloration. Pompeii spoke three languages, Oscan, Greek and Latin.

In February A.D. 63 Pompeii and adjacent cities were shaken by an earthquake. Several temples and other public buildings were demolished. The banker Caecilius Jucundus, who saw his home destroyed, erected a plaque to celebrate his own escape, on which he portrayed the buildings of the forum crumbling as the shock-waves reached them. No one connected the disaster with Vesuvius. When the tremors ceased, the people returned to the city and set about repairing the damage. Some private houses, particularly on the outskirts, had to be abandoned, but work started on restoring the temples. Financial aid was sought from Rome and private donors. The priests canvassed with the same zeal that the popes were later to show in selling cardinals' hats to finance their enterprises. A boy of six was elected to the senate because of his father's contributions to the restoration of the Temple of Isis. There was another earthquake the following year, but this was felt mostly in Naples: it shook the theatre where Nero happened to be performing, but the emperor, with admirable aplomb, finished his song. In Pompeii, the work of restoration continued, and served as the excuse for a wholesale programme of rebuilding and modernization. The city adopted the latest building fashions, becoming even more attractive to the wealthy who were looking for a place to rusticate. And so life went on for fifteen years.

On 24 August A.D. 79, after a few preliminary rumblings, Vesuvius erupted. The previous earthquakes had been caused by the pent-up fury of the volcano unable to find an outlet. Its force was now great enough to blow the top off the mountain. The effect on the nearby towns was catastrophic. Stabiae was covered with volcanic ash. Pompeii was inundated with lapilli, puff-balls of pumice which piled up in the streets and on the roofs. The effect must have been, as Goethe was to say later, like a snow-bound village; roofs began to collapse, and statues were torn from their pedestals under the accumulated weight of the deposits. Herculaneum, nearer the volcano, was most decisively hit. It had already suffered from the previous earthquakes; now a river of volcanic mud came pouring down upon it, filling the streets and houses. Seeing that their town was doomed, the inhabitants evacuated at once, most of them escaping with their lives. In Pompeii, the citizens were not so fortunate. The shower of lapilli did not seem immediately fatal, and many took refuge in cellars and under arcades, or waited to gather their precious belongings. By the time they realized what was happening, it was too late. They were trapped by falling walls or caught in the streets as they ran. The rain of pumice covered the roofs. To the north-west of the city, where the excavations come to an abrupt halt, one can walk round the perimeter and see how deep this covering of pumice was. The city was choked. When the excavators came, they were able to recreate the shapes of the human and animal bodies caught by the avalanche, by pouring plaster into the cavities left around the skeletons. The body of a dog, straining at his leash and gasping for breath, is thus preserved in the museum, together with two women, mother and daughter, huddled together for protection. Two men captured in their last agony lie in the Forum Baths.

We have an eye-witness account of the disaster. Tacitus, seeking material for his history, asked for help from Pliny, who had been there. The relevant portion of Tacitus's work has not survived, but we still have Pliny's letters recording his observations and, from a distance, the fate of his uncle, admiral of the fleet at Cape Misenum at the time, whose scientific curiosity took him to his death.

There was a cloud rising from one of the mountains. We couldn't tell which, at the time; it turned out to be Vesuvius. It looked like a tree, an umbrella-pine — that's the best way I can describe it; a tall, thin trunk mushrooming out into branches at the top. . . . We decided to leave the house. A dumbstruck mob formed up behind us, only too anxious for someone else to take the initiative (as always, panic's substitute for prudence) treading on our heels, breathing down our necks. Once outside the built-up area we halted. On every side some strange, awesome phenomenon. The wagons we'd ordered were rocking back and forth, though the ground was as flat as you could wish. When we ballasted them with stones we still couldn't hold them straight. And another thing: the sea was receding, as if the land had shrugged it off. No doubt of it, the coastline was high and dry, with marine life stranded all along the beach. The opposite shore was covered with a dense, formidable cloud, split by long zigzag tongues of fire, like lightning, only bigger. . . . And then it was night. Not just an overcast, moonless night, but like the darkness of a closed room with all the lights out. You could hear women screaming, children crying, men shouting, calling for their parents, their children, their wives, trying to recognize them by their voices. . . . Stories kept coming in from Misenum. Such and such a house was down, another was on fire: false rumours, but we believed them at the time. . . . At last it was really daylight. The sun was shining, but with the wan light of an eclipse. What a transformation we saw, when we plucked up courage to look. The place looked as if it had been hit by a blizzard. There were ashes, inches thick, over everything.[12]

The smoke of the eruption could be seen as far as Rome. Stoics thought it was the promised doomsday, the end of one cycle and the beginning of a new. Others attributed the disaster to divine interference – as did at least one inhabitant of Pompeii, a Jew who paused to scrawl 'Sodom and Gomorrah' on his wall. A Jewish interpolation in the Sibylline Books regards the eruption as an act of God's vengeance against the persecutors of Christianity. The poets noted the calamity in their various ways. Statius invokes a Naples smothered in dust and speaks of how

> *The Father wrenched the mountain from its seat*
> *And hurled it down from heaven on the cities*
> *That grovelled helpless on the earth beneath.*[13]

So too Martial:

> *This is Vesuvius, that yesterday*
> *Lay under the green shadow of the vine;*
> *Where vats were running over with the wine*
> *Of princely grapes. The satyrs' roundelay*
> *Rang from this hillside, as they danced away*

> The hours. It was to Bacchus more benign
> Than his homeland, Nysa. Venus set her sign
> Of favour on the mountain, and chose to stay
> Here, not in Lacedaemon. With the grace
> Of Hercules and his resplendent name
> This land was sanctified. Upon its face
> It wears a veil of ashes, for the flame
> Has taken all. It is a blasted place,
> And guilty heaven hangs its head in shame.[14]

When Vesuvius was quiet, the survivors crept back to rescue what belongings they could. In Pompeii it was not too hard. Shafts could be dug in the soft lapilli and furniture and valuables carried up from the buried houses. There was not much furniture: the rich differed from the poor in the quality, not the quantity of their possessions. Almost everything portable was removed. But the public buildings, the monuments, the statuary had to be given up as lost. Assistance was sought from Rome, and the Emperor declared Campania a disaster area, but the capital was soon distracted by her own troubles; a fire broke out in 80. In any case, little could be done. In Herculaneum, the position was virtually hopeless. The volcanic mud had solidified into an impenetrable carapace over the city. After sinking a few abortive shafts, the survivors gave up and went away.

So Pompeii and Herculaneum were abandoned and gradually forgotten. Vesuvius continued to smoulder over their buried remains. Cassius Dio records its appearance in the third century A.D. when it had settled down to a sullen grumbling, and the vines, now untended, had crept back up the slopes, comparing it to a giant incense-burner. Vesuvius is quiet now. Even the thin plume of smoke, long pointed out with nervous pride by Neapolitans, has vanished from its summit. But in a sudden thunderstorm, when the sky turns leaden, the clouds mass over the mountains and the rain pelts down streets empty but for a scattering of tourists running for shelter, one may still remember that terrible day in August 79.

Even the names vanished, except from certain old maps. In dim recollection of the former city, the few peasants who risked the volcano to grow their vines knew the site as Civita. Fresh eruptions over the centuries continued to change the terrain, and sealed Herculaneum even more firmly under a layer of lava.

In the Renaissance, with the rediscovery of classical learning, the sites began to be remembered. About 1592, a Roman architect tunnelling a canal through the hill of Civita turned up a few coins and marble tablets. Other chance discoveries followed, and scholars began to speculate on what lay buried beneath the soil. In 1735 the Prince of Elbœuf, searching for a site for his house, was led by the discoveries of a peasant to suspect the presence of antiquity. Excavations recovered a statue of Hercules, and other relics began to come to light. The interests of amateur archaeologists were aroused. Digging was carried out under private, sometimes royal auspices, for Naples was ruled by a succession of powers and some of its kings were keen historians. Many famous names were involved – Casanova's brother, Sir William Hamilton (who had to run to escape a new outburst from Vesuvius), and the Bonapartes. The theory that this was the site of Pompeii was first enunciated in 1748. Little by little, clumsily at first but with increasing exactitude, the city was uncovered. The history of Pompeii is, in a sense, the history of archaeology as a science, beginning with dilettante excavations by treasure-hunters, attracting quasi-mythical speculations about the origin of the place, and finally involving the full resources of scholarship and technology. It was not until 1860 that methodical investigation of the city began, quarter by quarter. In 1895 a number of the more important houses were discovered. The first half of the present century saw important excavations in the heart of the city and its outskirts. In the late summer of 1968 a film production unit took over the site, and restored several areas of the city to the appearance they must have had when the major excavations were in full swing. It was strangely exciting, a double re-creation of the past, to walk among the extras, costumed for pre-First World War days and see replicas of the ancient statuary, now scattered among the world's museums, littered about the streets and piled on barrows as they were originally discovered, to see the theatre replanted with grass, a re-creation of a faded archaeological photograph. In 1943 much of the work was undone by a bizarre accident. Allied bombers, flying overhead, thought that they saw enemy tanks in the ruins, and bombed them. Once again, however, Pompeii repaired her damage. More than half the city is now uncovered, and the work continues. Pompeii shows us a Roman city preserved in time by a freak of nature, an archaeological fossil cut off in its prime.

Pompeii takes the form of an irregular oval, rather less than a mile long, less than half a mile wide. It is heavily walled. The Porta Marina, the old sea gate, is now the principal entrance to the excavations. To the north-east other gates look towards Herculaneum and Vesuvius. To the north-west stands the Nola Gate, at the end of a street where excavators have barely scratched the surface, contriving to look like a living Piranesi engraving. There are four others.

The streets are laid out on the usual grid-plan, with the two main thoroughfares crossing at right-angles. The city's brothel is appropriately enough on one of the few crooked streets. Public buildings are grouped in two principal areas. The forum holds a balance between the sacred and secular. It was small, and closed to wheeled traffic. At the north end stands the enormous Temple of Jupiter, and at the south the offices of city government – the council chamber, the office of works, the election hall. To the west stands a building more impressive in its present appearance than the temples – the basilica, used as in Rome for the hearing of commercial cases. In a town as engrossed with financial affairs as Pompeii, it was a principal centre of community activity. Adjacent to the basilica stands the Temple of Apollo, with a statue of the god and a bust of his sister Diana. Its fractured columns are dominated by the cone of Mount Vesuvius in the distance.

Proceeding along the west side we find ourselves concerned again with the secular. The weights and measures office is set into a niche in the temple wall. Here were displayed the standards against which the measures of private dealers were set. Next is a large storehouse, probably a granary, whose hollow shell now serves to hold the detritus of the excavations – small things crafted of stone, tiles, pedestals, fragments of marble figures stacked and ordered, the teeth and bones of a dead city. Then, at the end of the west side, a public lavatory and two underground chambers which perhaps held the treasury for the Temple of Jupiter.

Opposite, on the east side, is the *macellum*, or covered market. It was elegant in its time, with a marble colonnade looking out onto the forum. There were shops all round and, on the inside, small taverns along the south wall; in the centre of the hall stood a shrine with niches holding busts of the imperial family. Next door, the city *lararium*, erected after the earlier earthquake to circumvent the horrible portent; next to this again, the Temple of Vespasian, and finally, another building where commerce and worship met and joined hands, an elaborate construction dedicated by the priestess Eumachia, patroness of the Fullers' Guild, to the worship of the imperial cult. The fuller was the equivalent of our laundryman. He collected the soiled woollen garments that were everyday wear, and cleaned and restored them. A number of such establishments have been discovered at Pompeii, one with much of the equipment intact. The cloth was first immersed in urine, which the fullers collected from the public lavatories for its ammoniac content. It was then squeezed out in bronze basins, much as one squeezes grapes, purified with sulphur and hung on racks to await the client.

The importance of such a guild, attested both by the magnificence of its headquarters and the part it played in the municipal elections, is a pointer to the changing shape of the Roman economy. The days of the individual, independent craftsman were waning. Instead we have group activity, fostered both by the craftsmen's desire to unify and by the growth of huge capitalistic organizations using skilled workmen for supervision and slaves trained in various specialities for mass production. Such *collegia*, or associations of artisans, began as social or burial clubs. It was only later that they began to evolve into something equivalent to the modern trade union, with rules and protective practices; to exercise, too, an undoubted political influence which the emperors tried in vain to curb. Under the busts of Romulus and Aeneas with which Eumachia had adorned her hall, the fullers made collective decisions which affected the conduct of their city. Such associations, under the Byzantine Empire, evolved into approximations to the medieval guilds. Eumachia's building may even have been used for the storage and selling of stuffs, a Roman equivalent of the 'cloth hall' of the Middle Ages.

In the forum one is always conscious of the presence of emperors – not only in the arches which they built at the north end, but in the shrines and temples erected to them. It was no longer necessary, as Augustus had done, to couple the worship of the emperor with that of Rome, for fear of giving offence, or to worship the ruler indirectly through his *genius*. The later emperors were only too pleased to be regarded as gods, and to have temples erected to them in their lifetime. Gaius Caligula had conceived the insane project of erecting a giant statue to himself in the temple at Jerusalem; fortunately he died before the plan could be carried out, for his misjudgement would surely have precipitated a major uprising. In Italy, the people were now more tolerant, or subservient, and divine honours to living emperors proliferated.

The second group of public buildings lies near the small triangular forum to the south. This was the earliest forum of the city, which had gradually fallen into disuse. Around it were built the places of public entertainment. Pompeii had two theatres. The larger dates from the second century B.C., and held five thousand people. The Greek influence on the city is clearly revealed in the construction of so impressive a building for the performance of plays, so early: Rome, as we have seen, did not have its first permanent theatre till the time of Pompey. It has the usual form, with a semi-circular auditorium, a high stage and an elaborate scenic façade, now collapsed but once rich with statues. There are dressing-rooms and arrangements for complicated stage machinery, much of which remains incomprehensible to us. There were also facilities for the water-displays that the public loved. The smaller theatre nearby is more properly an *odeum*, or covered recital-hall, for more intimate musical performances.

Behind the larger theatre is a huge square enclosed by a colonnade. Originally intended as a meeting-place for the spectators it was turned, during Nero's reign, into a gladiatorial barracks. Enough has remained to show a forbidding place, sombre in its austerity. The gladiators lived in cell-like rooms on two floors – the wooden balcony has been restored in one corner – and ate in a common mess kitchen; the entrances, significantly, are narrow and easily guarded. There were gladiators in residence at the time of the eruption. Two were in the stocks for punishment. Forgotten in the panic, their bodies remained for the excavators to find. There were also elaborate ceremonial helmets, greaves and shoulder protectors.

From the barracks the gladiators marched for their brief moment of glory past the public exercise ground to the amphitheatre at the other end of town. It was built about 80 B.C., under the auspices of the same magistrates who had constructed the little theatre, and was one of the first Pompeiian buildings uncovered in the eighteenth century. It was designed to hold sixteen thousand people – more than the town's population at the time, showing that the games attracted many visitors. In its general outline it follows the familiar pattern, though the builders seem to have been cramped for space and, perhaps, short of funds: some of the stairways lead up outside the building, instead of within the walls as in larger arenas, nor is there provision for rooms or passageways below ground level. Nevertheless the Pompeiians were proud of their amphitheatre and followed the games with the passionate interest that the Italians now reserve for soccer, and sometimes with the same violent animosity. In the time of Augustus, one man sponsored forty pairs of gladiators in a day. In A.D. 59 there was a major riot between the Pompeiians and visitors from Nuceria over a disputed decision. The battle overflowed the amphitheatre, and many were killed. Nero forbade any further gladiatorial fights for ten years. It seems, however, that the prohibition was soon disregarded.

There were other places where a naturally gregarious people might meet on safer ground – notably the public baths, of which Pompeii had three. Frequent bathing was a habit the Romans took some time to acquire. In the early Republic, once a week was enough. There was little incentive for more, since private bathrooms were primitive, containing only a sunken wooden barrel for hot water. Seneca, visiting the house of Scipio Africanus, describes the bathroom as a dingy cell lit only by a grating, hardly fit for a slave. The earliest public baths were not much better. They were run for profit, and gave the client little in the way of creature comfort. Agrippa, Augustus's friend and aide, built the first free baths in Rome, and started a new trend. Under the Empire all cities had them. They were not merely bathing-places but social centres. You could transact business, meet your friends, and spend the best part of the day there, if you were so inclined. In the evening of the Roman Empire, when the barbarians were at the gates, one of the bitterest complaints was that the enemy had cut the aqueducts, so that the public baths were no longer in service. Built on an increasingly magnificent scale, they were taken by the awestruck people of the Middle Ages for ruined palaces. In Rome, the Baths of Caracalla have become an opera house, and the cavernous halls of the Baths of Diocletian a museum. There are several baths in Ostia, one of which contains a shrine of Mithra, and still preserves the network of underground passages along which the slaves ran with food and clothing for their masters. But the baths are best preserved in Pompeii, and we may conveniently study them here.

Pompeii had its great bath-houses sooner than Rome – another mark of Greek influence. The earliest were the Stabian Baths, named from the road which led to the nearby city. The Forum Baths were added later. Both were out of commission after the earthquake of 63, when the water supply had to be cut off to repair damage to the pipes. A third establishment, even more luxurious, was still under construction when the city was destroyed. We may look at the Forum Baths, which now have the greatest air of life. They abut today on a restaurant, so that the buzz of conversation, an echo of ancient gaiety, is still heard along the corridors. The baths were built with shops along two sides, and duplicate facilities for men and women. The men's section is the larger and better preserved. One can follow the course of a patron as he moved from the disrobing-room through a series of larger rooms with increasing temperatures, each with its own pool. The warm room was heated by a large bronze brazier, and the hot room by air circulating between the double walls and under the floor. Here there is also a circular hole in the dome for ventilation. Vitruvius tells us how the amount of fresh air entering could be regulated by a bronze baffle suspended on chains. Seneca, who lived above such a bath in Rome, has left us a vivid pen-sketch of the activity:

> My lodgings are right over the public baths. Imagine all the different noises I have to listen to – loud enough to make me hate my own ears! For instance, when the muscle-man is exercising with the barbells, either working hard or putting on a good act, I can hear every grunt, and the asthmatic panting when he lets his breath out. Then there's the idler who drops in for a massage at popular prices. I can hear the slap of the masseur's hand on his shoulders; I can even tell from the sound whether the hand's cupped or flat! And then the resident pro shouting the latest score of the ball-game; that's all I needed. On top of this, some drunk or pickpocket being hauled off by the police; the man who likes to sing in his bath; the bathers who hit the water with an almighty splash . . . and then the cries of 'Cakes for sale!' (several varieties); 'Hot sausages!' 'Get your candy here!' Every kind of vendor you can think of, hawking his wares with his own distinctive sing-song.[15]

Or the Pompeiian could meet his friends in the temples. We have already seen those around the forum. There were others, of which the most important belonged to a more exotic cult, that of the Egyptian Isis. Made familiar in the Mediterranean world by the Hellenistic monarchs, Isis was one of the most popular of Rome's divine importations. Her worship took the form of a mystery cult in which the initiate participated in a series of ritual acts (in some cases, with a passion play celebrating the death and resurrection of her husband Osiris) to attain a state of exaltation

Apuleius describes the carnival procession, with masked representations of the deities, that accompanied such rites:

First came a company of women vested in white, with laughing faces, attired for the ceremony with garlands in their hair. They carried posies in the folds of their robes to spread along the route of the sacred procession ... there followed a crowd of both sexes with lamps, candles, torches and other illuminations in honour of the Daughter of the Stars of Heaven. Then an orchestra, a dulcet harmony of pipes and flutes. Then a handpicked choir of boys dressed for the occasion in white surplices ... then the crowd of initiates, of every manner and station in life ... the women with veils over their anointed hair, the men with shaven heads that twinkled in the sun like fallen stars ... and in due course the gods themselves, condescending to walk like ordinary mortals: especially Anubis, the go-between of heaven and hell, with one half of his face black, the other gold, his dog's head held high, a wand in his left hand, a green palm-branch in his right. And at his heels a cow walking upright, in likeness of the goddess who is mother of us all.[16]

We do not know what form the rites at Pompeii took, or if they were as strenuous as these. Certainly the local cult was long-established. A temple had stood before the earthquake of 63, and its damage was immediately repaired. It was a gaudy building, approached through a portico covered with painted stucco. The walls of the outer courtyard were decorated with scenes of naval life, for Isis was a protectress of navigation. Inside the temple were niches, presumably for the statues of other Egyptian deities, who were also painted elsewhere on the walls. The principal altar may still be seen as well as an underground basin for Nile water. Various items of furniture have been uncovered, including a small brazier, presumably to heat water for the ritual ablutions, and some of the temple treasures. When the volcano erupted, one of the priests gathered up what precious things he could and ran for safety: he had reached the main street before he succumbed. Another was trapped inside the temple by falling masonry. He cut through two walls, but died before he could penetrate the third.

The cult of Isis, like other orgiastic religions, attracted many for the wrong reasons. Suspicious of its licentious practices, the senate had forbidden it soon after its first appearance in Rome. Its strength in Pompeii shows the increasing permissiveness of the times. If Juvenal's satire is based on fact, the cult covered many vices: he writes of a married woman who met her lover nightly on the pretext of keeping vigil at the temple of Isis. Similarly the Dionysiac rites, officially frowned upon in republican Rome, seem to have enjoyed a resurgence in Pompeii. Outside the city walls stands a house known from its decorations as the Villa of the Mysteries. The walls portray the reading of the ritual, scenes from the Dionysus myths, the offering of the sacrifice and what appears to be an act of ritual flagellation. It was this sort of ceremony which the senate of earlier days had sought so sternly to repress.

But as Paul MacKendrick has remarked in his admirable archaeological survey, 'the real god of Pompeii – as of most other cities, ancient and modern – was the God of Gain'. To catch the religious temper of the times we may look at a poet who, though not of Pompeii – he was born in Etruscan country, in Volterra – captures the contemporary cynicism in a verse whose curious limping metre is a series of verbal shrugs:

This is a day to number in life's register,
Macrinus, in black ink, and let it stand to credit
When the Great Accounting comes. Go toast
Your guardian angel. You were never niggardly
In prayers, or wanted things that you dared only
Ask for on the quiet. But the greater part
Of our distinguished citizens pray out of
The corners of their mouths. It isn't every
Tom, Dick or Harry that can tear himself away
From muttering and whispering inside the temple
Walls, and bring his prayers out in the daylight.
'God give me honour and discretion and
Good standing with my fellow men.' ... That's how he prays
Out loud, so any passer-by can hear him. But
Under his breath the voice of his subconscious

> *Mutters 'I wish my uncle would pop off.*
> *Now that would be a funeral.' And 'If only*
> *I had the luck to turn up buried treasure*
> *When I was ploughing!' 'If I could get rid of,*
> *That kid – I'm next in line for the inheritance.'*[17]

Pompeii was an unashamedly frivolous city. As the buildings were uncovered, it was remarked that the frescoes seemed to prefer to portray the less admirable exploits of the gods: the amours of Jupiter are copiously represented. This is a fair indication of the general mood. Pompeii had its business interests, but it was a playground too. On his way home from bath or temple, the Pompeiian might stop at any of the numerous bars which seem to occupy every street corner. Some of them are in a remarkable state of preservation, with their marble counters, sunken containers for hot food and wine, and jars still stacked in a corner. On the wall of one, a dissatisfied toper has scrawled 'You serve coloured water to us, and drink the good stuff yourself!' Graffiti elsewhere, full of endearments, suggest that the barmaids had a second line of business. If abstemious, the citizen could take a drink from the fountains that punctuated the main streets: like Rome, Pompeii was lavish with its running water. The streets were well laid out, and even in wet weather the pedestrian could keep his feet dry. Stepping-stones were set at the intersections, spaced widely enough to permit the passage of high-axled carriages. One can still sense the busyness of the place – in the baker's shop with its great oven and hand-turned millstones worked with much grumbling by slaves; in the shop that sold *garum*, a sauce made from rotting fish and a recognized Pompeiian delicacy: in the restored oil-press; the druggist's shop; and in the bordello with its lurid paintings, now closed most of the year by an Italian government lately come to morality and apparently ignorant of the fact that the paintings have been available in published form for years.

Arriving home, our Pompeiian could usually withdraw himself completely from the outside world. The houses reveal the desire for privacy that was the rich man's prerogative. Small tradesmen slept in a single room behind their shops, but the houses of the affluent are on a grand scale. Pompeii, like other cities, suffered from congestion, and one can see how the commercial premises were beginning to encroach on residential zones, driving the wealthy outside the city walls; but the development was cut short at a time when the single-family residence was still standard. The apartment blocks of Rome and Ostia have no place here. Typically, the Pompeiian house was entered by a narrow passage-way in a blank façade, or between shopfronts where space was at a premium. From this the house unfolded into a sequence of large rooms or courts. Opening off the entrance-way was the *atrium*, or central hall, roofed, with a rectangular opening to let smoke out and sunlight in, and a pool beneath to catch the rainwater. Around this were grouped the smaller private rooms and store-chambers. To this extent the house recalls the type used by Romans from early times: *atrium* means literally 'black room', with the walls and beams discoloured by smoke from the central fire. Walking along the dusty, sunburnt streets of Pompeii one may look through the vestibules and see the *atria* set deep within as islands of coolness and quiet. It is as well to remember, how-ever, that the citizen paid for his seclusion with loss of comfort. The *atria*, richly decorated though they might be, were claustro-phobic, airless and dark. The roof opening was the chief source of light. Windows were rare, for glass was expensive and mica an inadequate substitute. Some houses show small round windows shaped like portholes. Others had straw mats to fill the empty frames. One may get some impression of this today, as the canvas hangings over the wall-paintings and graffiti along the street, flapping gently in the breeze, recall a past Pompeii at siesta time.

Little wonder then that those who could afford it threw out an open, colonnaded patio – the peristyle – at the rear of the house. Here, far from the street noise, the householder could withdraw himself completely and still get the benefit of the sun – or rather observe the sunlight from a shady arbour: the Romans believed that exposure was unhealthy, and justified the narrowness of the streets on these grounds. In the richer houses there might be more than one peristyle, set out with baths, fountains and running water. And within this area the owner could tame nature, as the Romans preferred to do, by planting an elegant formal garden. Some of these have been restored by tracing the line of the original bedding-trenches, to show the care with which the Pompeiians, like the Japanese, brought nature within walls and trained it into a work of art, combining natural beauty with marble basins, columns and statues. One house recently excavated in the quarter near the amphitheatre has a long canal in its garden, and trellises over which fruit trees are trained.

The inside walls of the house were richly painted, sometimes in architectural and abstract shapes, sometimes, as in the house of Augustus on the Palatine, with vistas to open up the rooms and give an illusion of space. Often several types of decoration meet and clash in the same house, one heavy and cloying, another light and graceful – the husband's taste, perhaps, conflicting with the wife's. And everywhere there is marble, the use of which still indicated the wealth of the owner; marble fountains in gaudy colours, marble furniture and facings, and mosaics which sometimes spill out through the house into the street beyond. One house has HAVE, welcome, set into the threshold like a stone mat; another, less hospitable, has the representation of a chained dog and CAVE CANEM. It is interesting to note how modern Italy has completely reversed this pattern of taste. With the disappearance of the woodlands and the opening up of new quarries, many householders are now forced to use marble floors where they would much prefer wood: the luxury of the ancient world has become the economy of this.

It is as well, too, amid this profusion of splendour, to remember how the other half lived. If the owner's rooms were dark, the slaves' were darker. In one palatial establishment on the east side, one may walk past the rich frescoes of the atrium, through a peristyle with a magnificent marble – and then, stooping, down a cramped flight of stairs into a subterranean kitchen, lit by a single window at street level. Most of the space is taken up by a sprawling stone oven, where the slaves must have roasted themselves as well as the food. From such dismal quarters came Trimalchio's feast.

It is difficult now to see Pompeii whole. The statuary and furniture are mostly gone, some removed by the inhabitants themselves, others deposited in museums. In 1967 an attractive travelling exhibition set a number of the more famous artifacts against blown-up photographs of their original locations; for many it was the first opportunity to see these works in context. Normally the traveller needs a memory capable of creative montage to allow him to superimpose the contents of the Naples Museum on the shells of the Pompeiian buildings; or, perhaps, to infuse a little of the spirit of modern Pompeii, the tourist town that has grown up round its ancestor, where the modern shops are little bigger than the ancient, where children play hopscotch in the *piazza*, as they once did in the forum, and where the chief aim is still to cater to the leisured.

It is a help to go to Herculaneum. If Pompeii is a showplace, its neighbour is a garden. Encased in tufa, it presented immeasurably greater difficulties to the excavator but for this very reason offers the visitor richer rewards. Only about thirty people died at Herculaneum, as compared to the two thousand at Pompeii, but the majority who escaped left their belongings behind. The city is less grandiose than Pompeii and less agreeably situated, so closely embedded in the modern town of Resina that, from a distance, the modern houses on the hill seem to blend with the Roman structures beneath without any perceptible break, and the inevitable laundry fluttering from the balconies might belong to either. The excavations are full of dead ends, for Herculaneum has been won back by inches. Tunnels dive into the hillside and stop where the funds ran out. Only one edge of the great *palaestra*, or exercise ground, has been excavated; the rest, including most of the cruciform bathing-pool with its fountain of bronze serpents, lies beneath the overpass which carries cars into the site.

But the past seems closer here. The visitor has the feeling of assisting in the rebirth, for the work goes on all round him. A workman props his ladder against a wall and freshens the sunset colours of a fresco. In another of the grand houses, students labour with infinite care to replace tiny squares into a mosaic pattern. And the human detail of the past is evident. The archaeologists have been adroit with flowers and foliage. Trees shadow a garden on the hill, looking out over the public baths. A marble table set within a pergola gives a view of the trees and massed flowers beyond. A simple garden shrine is dappled with leaves. In many cases, more of the fabric of the houses survives than in Pompeii. Looking up the intersecting streets, one may see the restored elevations with their overhanging balconies. In some of the buildings, the folding wooden doors that separated one room from another have been carbonized but preserved. Herculaneum is Pompeii with an upstairs.

Even the shops have been left better provided. One of them contains the skeleton of one of the few inhabitants who failed to get out in time, stretched out on his bed beside his loom. In the grain shop nearby are the carbonized remains of its stock-in-trade. In a baker's establishment, holes in the stonework show where the store-room was, and how the owner reached it by a narrow ladder. The forum has not been excavated, but the road leading to it has. As in Pompeii, it was barred to wheeled traffic: it also had its fountain (in this case decorated in honour of Hercules) and its great arch.

What sort of people lived in these places? We know much about them from the objects with which they surrounded themselves, and from the writings they left on the walls – election slogans, declarations of love, agnostic pronouncements, the common content of graffiti anywhere. The inhabitants belonged to a period when the rigid stratifications of the old Roman society were disappearing. Some were aristocrats of the old school, transplanted from Rome. But the social revolution made it possible for new men to enter their company, if they had brains, endurance and luck – even if they were descended from slaves. The fictional *curriculum vitae* put by Petronius into the mouth

of a self-made man in a town that must have been very like
Pompeii would have summarized the lives of many of its inhabitants:

I used to be just like you. It was strength of character that got me
where I am. It takes guts to make something of yourself. All the rest
is hogwash . . . well, as I was saying, I took care of the pennies and
the millions took care of themselves. When I got here from Asia I
was no higher than that candlestick. Do you know, I used to measure
myself against it every day, and grease my lip with lamp-oil to grow
hair on my snout quicker. Well, by the will of heaven I became
master in the house. Took after the boss, see? He named me in his
will, along with Caesar. So there I was, rich as any of the nobs. . . .
Well, I don't want to bore you. I built five ships, loaded 'em with
wine – money in the bank in those days – and sent 'em off to Rome.
And then – anybody would think I'd planned it that way – a ship-
wreck. Lost the lot. Honest. No kidding. Three hundred thousand
down old Neptune's mouth in one day. Did I give in? Not me, by
god. Just a fleabite. I carried on like nothing had happened. Built
more ships – bigger and better, luckier, too. Nobody wasn't going
to call me chicken. Anyway, 'Hearts of oak are our ships . . .'. Loaded
'em with wine again; bacon, beans, perfume, slaves. And you know
what Fortunata did, bless 'er? Sold her jewellery, clothes, the lot,
and put a hundred gold pieces in my hand. And that's what made
the money-tree start sprouting. Things happen quick when they're
heaven-sent. I scooped up a hundred thousand on that one voyage.
First thing off, I bought up my old master's farms. Built a house,
started to invest in livestock. Everything I touched grew like honey
in the hive. When I had more money than all the folks back home
put together, the party's over, I told myself. Got out of business.
Went into the money-lending racket. . . . Built this house. It was a
shack when I started. It's a temple now. Four banquet halls, twenty
bedrooms, two marble porticoes, an upstairs dining-room, master
bedroom (that's for me), a boudoir for the snake-in-the-grass I
married, and a damn good porter's lodge.[18]

A PROVINCIAL CENTRE

The town of Nîmes lies in the very south of France, not many
miles from the Gulf of Lions, near where the River Gard joins the
Rhône to run down to the sea. It is in the part of Gaul that the
Romans called Narbonesis, after its capital Narbo, the modern

Narbonne, where they founded a military colony in 118 B.C. This was an area highly susceptible to Roman influence. Aix-en-Provence, not far away, was once a vast Roman encampment, and the scene of one of Marius's most striking victories; if the Romans could see it now they would feel very much at home, for the water (*aquae*) which gave Aix its name is still in evidence, with fountains on virtually every corner. Arles and Avignon boast their Roman theatres, still in use, and turn history to commercial advantage in the Hôtel Jules César. Nîmes has monuments no less impressive. Now the capital of the *département* of Gard, with a population of ninety thousand and the noisiest railway station in France, it is a favourite stopping-place for tourists. The crowds pour south in the annual exodus from the Parisian August, and eat their way through the *menu touristique* in the shadow of the amphitheatre. It is a good place to examine, for the surviving antiquities show clearly the various stages by which Rome made its acquisitions simulacra of itself.

Phase one: the conquest. The site had been busy long before the Romans came, or even before the Greeks arrived to colonize Marseilles. It was originally Ligurian country, overrun, about 300 B.C., by the Volcae Aricomici, who made it their capital. It was called Nemausus, after the local deity. Then Rome began to make its presence felt across the Alps. The oldest monument of Nîmes, and of all Roman Gaul, a tower whose enigmatic ruins perch on the Mont Cavallier, may date from these exploratory marches. Gnaeus Domitius Ahenobarbus first carried Roman arms through the country in about 120 B.C. He was a good though unscrupulous soldier – his major coup was the seizure of a prominent Gallic chieftain at a conference – and a shrewd administrator; following the accepted pattern of linking new conquests with good roads, he founded the Via Domitiana, running from Provence to the Pyrenees. He was also a great tower-builder – one of his monuments may be seen at St Rémy – and the Tour Magne at Nîmes may be his, erected to commemorate a victory. Or it may have been part of a defence work, or a signal tower. An affectionate commentator has called it 'yet another conundrum posed by ancient Gaul to tease the sagacity of historians'. Its crumbling hexagonal structure may still be climbed, for a splendid view of the country over which the legions campaigned: the range of the Cévennes cutting off the north, the coastal plain sloping away to the south, and all around the low pebbled hills covered with olives and vines, over which the French.army still holds manœuvres.

Phase two: settlement and indoctrination. Tacitus describes the process. His illustration is taken from the work of a governor in Britain, but can equally well apply to Gaul:

> A population scattered, uncivilized and for that reason prone to war had to be accustomed to the pleasures of a quiet, settled life. He therefore gave his personal encouragement and official support to the building of temples, fora and houses, commending initiative and reprimanding slackness. Thus, by encouraging the people to compete for distinction, he achieved what another man would have done by force. The chieftains' sons were educated in the liberal arts . . . and sought proficiency in the hitherto despised Latin tongue. Roman dress was à la mode, and the toga appeared everywhere.[19]

Gallia Narbonensis, early pacified, remained more or less tranquil. It was left for Julius Caesar, in his campaigns from 58 to 51, to subdue the wilder tribes further north. Eventually all transalpine Gaul was annexed: the newer acquisitions were called Gallia Comata, 'Long-haired Gaul', and with typical ingenuity subdivided into administrative districts that dissipated any lingering nationalism by cutting across existing tribal boundaries. In the event, Gaul was surprisingly quiet, and the Romans saw no need to keep a standing army there. The legions on the Rhine, a constant danger-point, could swing south in time of need, and the only force of any size in the country was the police detachment guarding the mint at Lugdunum (Lyons).

Narbonensis, always more Italian in character, was particularly responsive to Romanization. The conquerors worked, as in other provinces, through local influence. Schools set up for the sons of Gallic chieftains instructed them in Roman ways. At Nîmes, new buildings began to rise in the familiar pattern of the Italian town.

The Gauls saw growing up around them (or, rather, were encouraged to build for themselves – French historians are particularly emphatic that most of the work was done at local expense) structures that embodied the Roman way of life.

About 16 B.C. the town was laid out with walls enclosing some 550 acres, as a military *colonia*. Coins found on the site with pictures of crocodiles suggest that some of the first colonists were soldiers returning from the East, perhaps Antony's veterans. But there are stronger links with Antony's conqueror at Actium. The second stage in the Roman history of Nîmes is inseparably connected with Augustus, and its chief monument is the Maison Carrée. The familiar modern name, which means simply 'the rectangular building', first appears in 1560; the building in question was constructed as a temple, and resembles several contemporaneous buildings erected elsewhere. Built of local stone brought in from quarries all around, it is set on a podium approached by broad steps; the sanctuary is set back within a portico, and receives light through the great front door alone.

Why was it built, and by whom? It took a long while to provide even tentative answers to these questions. The story is worth summarizing here, if only to illustrate the difficulties that archaeologists face in identifying buildings even of this size and grandeur. In the Middle Ages, it was generally known as 'the capitol', though there was an old tradition that it had been used as a Christian church. The local court sat in it at the end of the ninth century. Then it became the town hall; in the sixteenth century it lost dignity when houses were built into its walls, and was turned into stables. The Augustins rented and redeemed it, and the Bourbons laid out money to restore it. After a brief period as a granary it was returned to official use as the prefecture in 1802. Finally, it was declared a historical monument and opened to the public.

There had long been speculation as to its origins. The bronze letters forming the dedicatory inscriptions had been removed, presumably in the metal-hungry days of the barbarian invasions. As early as 1605, a French antiquary formed the project of restoring them from marks left in the stonework, but the first serious attempt was not made until the late eighteenth century. Scaffolds were erected and tracings made of the faint impressions of the letters and their fixing-points. In the succeeding controversy these marks were examined in minute detail, and it eventually became clear that there had been two inscriptions, one preceding the other. It is now generally accepted that the first was erected by Agrippa, Augustus's aide and son-in-law, who presented the building to the town, either as a capitol or as the temple of Rome and Augustus. It was later rededicated to Gaius and Lucius, the grandsons that Augustus adopted as his heirs. They disappointed him by dying, Lucius at Marseilles in A.D. 2, Gaius two years later.

The Maison Carrée is thus significant in the study of provincial politics. It was built, after approved Roman models, to impress the populace with the presence of Rome in their midst. It still has an uncompromisingly official look, of which even a modern French departmental administration might be proud. At an appropriate moment its dedication was changed to show a new insistence on the ruler-cult, which was one of Augustus's chief ways of securing loyalty in the provinces. Gaul was particularly susceptible to this treatment: in 12 B.C. the emperor had established at Lyons a great altar to Rome and himself, a focal point for the sympathies of Gallia Comata. Further investigations, conducted with difficulty because of later building on the site, have revealed that the temple was part of the forum complex, surrounded by colonnades and balanced by another, similar building, probably the *curia*. Nîmes had been given the stamp of Romanization in the shape of the public meeting-place. In the forum stood an outdoor altar, with a water channel to remove the blood from the sacrifices.

Other Augustan relics can be seen in the two surviving Roman gates. The larger, known locally as the Porte d'Arles, was constructed for defence and strict control of traffic. Originally flanked by two towers and protected by a rampart, it has two large archways for vehicles and smaller entries on each side for pedestrians. Nearby, among the debris of statuary and a milage-marker like that in the Roman Forum, stands the image of Augustus raising his hand in benediction.

Phase three: the amenities. Closely following the organization came the agreeable frills of Roman life. Nîmes has its great amphitheatre, Les Arènes, the best preserved in France. It stands seventy feet high, and was built to hold twenty-four thousand people; as usual in such structures, they were protected from the sun by great awnings stretched across the top, the rope-holes for which can still be seen. The arena was large enough for a separate quarter of the town, with its own church, to grow up inside it in the Middle Ages. The houses were cleared in 1809, and since then the amphitheatre has reverted to something like its original purpose, being regularly used for bullfights. Nearby, in the delightful Jardin de la Fontaine, are the relics of another familiar amenity, the baths. Stairs, hypocaust and colonnades may still be seen, half submerged beneath the eighteenth-century garden. At one side stands the so-called Temple of Diana, a puzzling misnomer, for the building is clearly a nymphaeum dedicated to the eponymous deity Nemausus. As we have seen, the Romans encouraged the worship of existing gods, providing they did not conflict with their own. The old worship and the new luxury flourished side by side.

Nîmes rejoiced in its water supply. One of the most famous Roman aqueducts, the Pont du Gard, was built in A.D. 14 to carry water across the valley of the Gardon from Uzès: A masterpiece of engineering and a work of art, it is built in three tiers. The lowest, which supports the modern motor road without apparent damage to the fabric, has six arches, buttressed against the force of the current. There are ten arches in the second tier; the third, which can now be walked across, originally carried the water. After traversing the river, the watercourse bored through a hill to descend into the city, depositing its burden in large cisterns, some of which are still extant. The population doubtless rejoiced in the blessings that subjection had brought them. But the feeling was not unanimous. Tacitus comments caustically on the softening of once vigorous races once they have experienced Roman luxury: 'And so people gradually succumbed to the blandishments of decadence – arcades, public baths, elegant dining; what the unsophisticated called culture was in reality part of their slavery.'[20]

Pro-Roman feeling was followed by a desire for equal rights and participation in government. The Emperor Claudius took the first step by admitting Gauls to the senate. In a speech recorded at Lyons, he defended his action by citing Roman precedent:

> In the period of the monarchy, the succession of power was not a domestic monopoly. Non-citizens and even foreigners held office; Numa, for example, who succeeded Romulus, came from Sabine stock – a close neighbour, certainly, but at that time still a foreigner. And Tarquinius Priscus succeeded Ancus Martius . . . .
> My uncle on my mother's side, Augustus, now among the gods, and on my father's, Tiberius Caesar, expressed the desire that the finest products of the colonies and municipalities, men of good repute and financial standing, should take their places in this senate. What? Better an Italian senator than a provincial? When I come to that part of my programme, I'll have something to say on that matter. But I don't think we should even eliminate the provincials, provided they can contribute something of value to this body.[21]

It seems to be a typical Claudian speech, erudite, garrulous and clumsily phrased. But there was sense in it, even if it took the Romans a long time to see it. Later emperors showed increasing favour to the Gauls, as we see at Nîmes. Nero gave it a theatre and circus, Hadrian a basilica; Antoninus Pius, Hadrian's successor, was himself from Nîmes stock. The town came to be one of the richest in a province increasingly allied with Roman interests. Perhaps by the second century A.D. it was the capital of Gallia Narbonensis. And by the fourth Gauls were holding important offices in almost every branch of the imperial administration.

A HARBOUR AND A TEMPLE

About 16 B.C., in the same resettlement programme that saw the Augustan building at Nîmes, another colony, to house the veterans of two legions, was established in Syria. In Gaul, the Romans were able to bring civilization where none had existed. In the East, they settled in lands whose history went back to remote antiquity. They respected the traditions, and allowed themselves to be influenced by them in important ways.

Syria, as a satrapy of the old Persian Empire, had been conquered by Alexander the Great. Hellenized by his successors, the Seleucids, it passed to the Romans after Pompey's adventures in the East, and under the Empire became an important military command. Four legions were stationed there until A.D. 70, when one was removed to occupy Judaea. It was always important as a recruiting-ground, both for legionaries and the native auxiliaries. There were many Syrians in the Roman army; some served in the occupation forces in Britain. Neither the Greeks nor the Romans did much to change the face of the country. It was still predominantly rural, with small villages serving as administrative centres. The larger towns, where Roman influence chiefly made itself felt, were on the coast. Berytus, now Beirut, is now so over-built that serious excavation is impossible. But, seventeen miles north, the little harbour of Byblos shows the metamorphosis of the coastland under a succession of masters.

Byblos – the Gebal of the Bible, the Gibelet of the crusaders, and the modern Jebeil – has the distinction of being, probably, the oldest continuously inhabited town in the world. Occupied as early as the Neolithic Age, it was flourishing by the Bronze Age; in the trade of the early Mediterranean it developed important connections with Egypt, which left its mark on the site, and became the centre of the papyrus market. This valuable commodity received its Greek name, *byblos* (which gives us 'Bible', the papyrus book) from that of the harbour which exported it to the Aegean. After the collapse of the Egyptian Empire in the twelfth century B.C. Byblos became the principal city-state of Phoenicia, until it was in turn dominated by the growing power of Tyre and Sidon to the south. The Romans set their stamp on it. A row of columns now crowns the hill overlooking the bay and the ancient harbourworks: Rome had at last dominated the civilization that begat Carthage. There is evidence of mercantile activity – a large stone basin for an oil press – and the inevitable sign of Roman occupation, a small theatre, which the excavators carefully removed, stone by stone, to a point nearer the coast, to permit access to the earlier ruins underneath. But the Roman works, in their turn, succumbed. The town was captured by the Crusaders in 1103, and Roman columns were built into the walls of the new castle. Some of them, half cut through, are still lying round the site.

Byblos lay at the end of one of the great caravan-routes. Camels brought their merchandise from Babylonia and the Far East to the cities of Palmyra, Damascus and Petra, and from there to the coastal ports. It was along one of these routes that the Romans established their military colony. One may still follow it from Beirut, up into the hills where the inhabitants take refuge from the summer heat, along a road which grows continually more precipitous, where the mists close in early and camel-trains still make their way beside the sparse modern traffic. Baalbek is a high green patch in a grey-brown landscape, 3,850 feet above sea level. Arab tradition associated it with the Creation; Adam was said to live here, and his descendants before the deluge. According to another story of a familiar type, the site was settled by Cain, the first town-builder, and the race of giants he created: the early peoples could find no other way of accounting for the enormous buildings they saw there, and evolved an explanation similar to that which the later Greeks found for the massive walls of Mycenae. Abraham was said to have passed this way, and Solomon to have built a temple here.

The name of Baalbek has been the source of much controversy. Its obvious derivation – from the god Baal – may not be the correct one; another theory takes it from Ba al Beka, 'Lord of the Beka', or surrounding plain. But nothing has been found on the site which antedates the Greek conquest of Syria, and the Greeks themselves called the place Heliopolis, unquestioningly associating it with the sun god. In 36 B.C. it formed part of the Syrian territory given by Antony to Cleopatra; then, after the civil wars, came the colonial settlement, and soon after that the first monumental buildings. It used to be believed that the construction belonged to the reign of Antoninus Pius, but continuing excavations have forced the date further and further back. It is now clear that Nero built there. The site was particularly attractive to the megalomaniac emperors. Septimius Severus gave its inhabitants Italian rights; Caracalla engaged in new building and restored the old; Heliogabalus had himself named high priest. There were private donors too. We know from an inscription that Aurelius Antonius Longinus, an important official, gave the capitols that grace the propylaea.

The acropolis of Baalbek, all that has been excavated, consists principally of two enormous temples. They are approached from the east, through the propylaea, or monumental gateway, flanked by two square towers. The orientation is Egyptian, the columns Greek, the decoration oriental: in this remote place, Rome was more easily susceptible to foreign traditions. Inside the portico is a hexagonal courtyard, and, beyond this again, the great court of the Temple of Jupiter. As one enters this court now, it is the towering ruins of the temple itself that automatically draw the eye. In antiquity, this was not so. When the excavators began serious work on the site, they found the court occupied by a Christian basilica, with three naves, built perhaps in the fourth century, certainly not later than the sixth. With some reluctance they tore it down – archaeology is full of such painful decisions – to find the pagan remains underneath. It was clear that the Christian structure had been built over an earlier altar, a monumental work whose plan the French scholars have painstakingly reconstructed. Pierced by corridors, ascended by a system of staircases, it towered towards the sky, masking the façade of the temple. On the far side stood another, smaller altar; their precise purpose is still a matter of dispute. It is held by some that the great altar was used for sacrifices, faithful to the Eastern principle (of which Abraham's attempted sacrifice of Isaac is an early example) of making the offerings on high places. Others argue that the limited area would make it impossible for crowds to participate and that the smaller altar was used for sacrifices, with the larger reserved for the ritual communion. At either side of the altar stood long basins for ritual lustrations. Here, the decoration is more familiarly Roman: Tritons blowing on their shells, Nereids, and Medusa with her snaky hair: this well-known monster probably took her origin from distorted tales of octopuses, and so has a rightful place among the water-creatures. The walls of the surrounding court contain twelve apses – the number of the Olympian gods – now empty. They were protected by a colonnade roofed with cedarwood. Some scholars have seen further Eastern influence in this segregation of the Holy of Holies. The worshipper has to walk some distance, through other rooms, before he reaches the sacred place; this gives time for contemplation.

Behind the altars, on an artificial podium forty-two feet above ground at its highest point, stand the two great temples. The larger, six of whose original fifty-four columns remain, was dedicated to the triad of Jupiter, identified with Hadad, the Syrian thundergod; Venus, identified with Astarte or the Syrian Atargetis, as the spirit of fertility; and a young vegetation god associated by the Greeks with Hermes and the Romans with Mercury. It is a persuasive example of the ability of the Roman religion to compromise, and to amalgamate with local cults whenever these were appropriate. We have a description of the ceremonies, written not long before Christian influence began to close the temples down:

> Jupiter is here identified with the Sun, distinguished by the same ritual and the same regalia. His gold, beardless statue presides over the temple, holding a whip, charioteer-fashion, in his upraised right hand, and a thunderbolt and ears of corn in his left, the visible tokens of Jupiter and the associated power of the Sun. This temple is also cultivated for its oracular associations – an attribute of Apollo, who is also identified with the Sun. The image of the god of Heliopolis is carried on a palanquin, like the divine effigies at the circus processions, usually on the shoulders of the leading men of the province. Their heads shaved, and purified by a long period of chastity, they progress as the divine spirit moves them, going not where they wish but where the god forces them to carry him.[22]

The description of Jupiter-Hadad is supported by a mutilated relief found in the hexagonal court with the same attributes – the whip seems to indicate the chariot of the sun, or perhaps its tortuous course –, and flanked by two bulls, animals associated with Hadad. The oracular reputation of the temple is given force by the story of Trajan's visit. He sent in wax tablets to the shrine, following the customary procedure for submitting questions to the oracle; but, to test its skill, the tablets were sealed, and blank. Blank tablets were returned to him. Impressed, he asked a question about his own campaign; the oracle cryptically prophesied his death.

Adjacent to the Temple of Jupiter is a smaller temple – though still larger than the Parthenon – usually attributed to Bacchus. It is almost Gothic in the flamboyance of its decoration, and the intricacy of its carved ceilings, with reliefs of familiar deities and of Cleopatra succumbing to the asp. A conjectural reconstruction shows a great hall, glowing in subdued golden light, with the statues of the deities looking down from their niches, and the columns bursting into stone foliage above their heads. At a little distance from the acropolis is another temple, to Venus, small, round and almost perfectly preserved, reminiscent of the circular structures of an earlier Rome. The whole complex is a witness to the extravagance of the Roman Empire at its zenith. It is an architectural, as well as a geographical, oasis, an efflorescence on the barren plain, framed by the low lines of the mountains. The labour that went into its construction can be surmised from one gigantic block of stone still lying in the ancient quarries half a mile from the town; it weighs a thousand tons. How this was hewn, and how it was intended to be moved, is still a matter for guesswork. The site has recently come to new life as the setting for an annual festival; one of the works presented was, appropriately enough, Monteverdi's *The Coronation of Poppaea*, for which the great terrace was once again filled with the richness of Roman ceremonial costume. UNESCO is developing a project for improving access to the site, and removing some of the humbler buildings surrounding it. There is nothing it can do to make it more monumental. But perhaps the most impressive sight of all is the contrast between the buildings and the tents still pitched on the fringes of the acropolis, with natives squatting beside their camels in the dust as they were doing when Nero began the work, or when Caracalla strutted through the temple: a perpetual reminder of the outlandish splendour that the Romans brought to the places they conquered.

THE BARBARIC FRINGE

A continent away from Baalbek lies an island which to most Romans was a black, legendary place. It had an evil reputation born of unfamiliarity; the early invasion forces almost mutinied rather than go there. Tacitus, writing of Britain after the conquest, and acknowledging many previous descriptions, is still making bizarre guesses about its geography. He describes an island rather like H. G. Wells's vision of the end of the world, where the sun never rises or sets but clings to the horizon; where the winds howl and the waves lick among the mountains, and the water, in an eery phrase, is 'viscous, giving rowers trouble with their oars'.[23]

Britain was the last major country to come under Roman influence. Although merchants hurried to trade in the new conquests of Gaul, there is no hint that they crossed the Channel, despite the fact that pre-Roman sailors had done business there. Many thought that it was, literally, the end of the world, the place where earth shelved off into boundless space. It was the Britons themselves who invited Roman interference, through their connections with Gaul and their internal disagreements. The country was divided into tribes, each under its own king or council of elders. The dissension between them was brought to the Roman attention, and held out an attractive possibility of conquest.

In 55 B.C. Julius Caesar made the first crossing, as an extension of his forays into Gaul. His reason, as offered to the Roman public, was a desire to prevent the Britons from assisting the Gallic rebellion. We may suspect more personal inducements. A consummate showman, Caesar must have been well aware of the publicity value of a campaign where no Roman had set foot before. His first landing was in no sense an invasion, but a reconnaissance in force, and less than successful. To redeem his *amour propre* he tried again, with better luck, the following year. Even then the results were not spectacular. Cassivellaunus, a king of the south-east, had surrendered; the Trinovantes of Essex accepted Roman protection; but the centre of the country was untouched, and the Romans had learned, the hard way, a new type of fighting from chariots.

Augustus, faithful to his policy of containing the Empire, failed to follow his predecessor's initiative. Caligula planned an invasion but abandoned it at the last minute, for reasons which must remain obscure. It was not until the reign of Claudius that the next attempt took place, with double Caesar's force. In A.D. 43 the Romans advanced up to the line of the Thames with little hindrance. The way was clear to Camulodunum, Colchester, and Claudius took personal command.

We may look at two monuments as illustrations of the varied Roman fortunes in Britain. The first is a camp, Segontium. It is in North Wales, a short distance from the medieval fortress of Caernarvon, that saw the proclamation of the first Prince of Wales. The trim shape of the Roman encampment, geared to efficiency and mobility, makes a provocative contrast to the grey, brooding hulk that their successors built. Close by are the Menai Straits and, over the water, the little island of Anglesey, Milton's 'craggy top of Mona high'. The reactions of the Roman legionaries on being transferred from the Mediterranean sunshine to the damp misery of the Welsh hills are unrecorded. In general, we hear little of the private soldiers; no Roman wrote a *Barlasch of the Guard*. Individuals are sometimes cited by historians for acts of bravery, but usually we see them collectively, as a magnificent fighting machine. This is the case in the Welsh conquests, over which the Romans spent thirty years. Suetonius Paulinus, rather patronizingly commended by Tacitus as a 'sound and thorough' commander, was appointed governor of Britain in 59. He pressed through North Wales, took his troops across the Menai Straits and invaded Anglesey. The crossing itself was not so formidable as the description makes it appear. Easily fordable, the Straits allowed a passage for stage-coaches round the mountains until the modern road tunnelled through. But the sight on the far bank was enough to daunt any Roman heart.

> There stood the opposing army, on the foreshore; a dense crowd, bristling with weapons, and their women running among them dressed as for a wake, like Furies, with their hair wild and blazing torches lighting up their faces. Around them stood the Druids, praying, cursing, holding up their hands to heaven. The troops had never seen anything like this. Petrified with astonishment, they made easy targets. Then came the voice of their commander urging them on, and they shouted at each other not to be frightened of an army of women and fanatics. Following the standards they cut a path through their opponents, and set them on fire with their own torches. The enemy was routed, a garrison established, and the grove where they had practised their barbaric rites cut down. Here stood the altars that waxed fat on the blood of their prisoners, where they had felt no compunction about taking the auspices with human entrails.[24]

The Druids presented the Romans with the most fanatical opposition that they ever had to contend with. They represented a tradition already old, and more powerful as the invaders moved further west: Caesar's remarks suggest that a Druid college may have existed in Britain, and extended its influence to Gaul. The Druids formed an order enjoying important privileges, including exemption from military service and taxation. Though guarding the mystery of their cult – so well that most of it is unknown to us – they were active in social and political life, with no monastic tendencies: Diviciacus, Druid of the Aedui, had a wife and family, and travelled on diplomatic missions to Rome. Despite certain unsavoury features – child-sacrifice is well-attested – the Druid teaching was of a high spiritual order. It included the doctrine of the immortality of the soul, and perhaps also of its transmigration, an old Pythagorean theory which may have derived from the Greeks of Massilia, Marseilles. Warriors who fought under such inspiration must have been particularly redoubtable enemies.

Though temporarily suppressed, the Celts continued to give the Romans trouble, and a projected invasion of Ireland was given up as a foredoomed cause. In a way, the Druids have triumphed; in their latterday, less ferocious revival they may still be seen marching through the streets of Caernarvon, while the Roman fort lies in ruins.

There may already have been a camp at Segontium in this early campaign, established by the legions marching out of Chester. If so, it can only have been a temporary wooden structure. It later became a permanent fixture, part of the interlocking system of defences stretching through North Wales. This would have been the form in which Agricola knew it. He had been singled out for a staff appointment under Suetonius Paulinus in 61, and after holding civil office in Rome returned to Britain first as commander of the Twentieth Legion, and later as governor. In the Roman system, public service admitted no division: the same man was required to be both soldier and civil administrator.

The excavations show what Agricola's camp looked like when he completed the conquest of Anglesey. Its form is the familiar one, the military version, and perhaps the exemplar, of the Roman town-pattern. It is built on the grid system with the principal street running down its length and intersected at right angles by others. In the centre stands the H.Q. with the commander's house and hospital adjacent; the commander kept the regimental chest. The granaries stand to one side, the barracks occupy the corners and a well makes the encampment self-sufficient. Leonard Cottrell compares such a structure to the layout of a small modern factory, neat, efficient and designed for the maximum utilization of space. Around the whole ran a wall and ditch, pierced by four gates. At larger bases the Roman soldier could expect more luxury, the equivalent of the U.S. Army rest and recreation centres; at Caerleon, for example, he had a race-course, a theatre and mains drainage; but even at Segontium he was housed reasonably comfortably, in trim stone buildings with tiled roofs, and could feel himself secure when the mists closed in and the wolves howled in the darkness.

The Romans in Britain behaved like the best and worst of the British Raj in India. Confronted with a hostile climate and an alien temperament, they constructed approximations of home on foreign soil, brought princelings back to the Roman equivalents of Eton and Harrow, filled the urban centres with symbols of their rule, exploited the natives and pampered the leaders who conformed. Against the excellent road and defence system we must set the examples of stupidity and brutality – the unsympathetic treatment of Suetonius Paulinus by Nero, and of Agricola by Domitian, both attributed by the historians to malice, seem to stem rather from the central administration's conviction that the governors were inadequate; against the occasional grandeur of Romano-British architecture, we must set the plethora of second-rate imitations of Italian design, far inferior to the original vigour of native craftsmanship. In New Delhi one may still dine from pseudo-Victorian furniture among the superficialities of a remote culture to the strains of the Indian orchestra playing tea-room music of the thirties. One has the same feeling at Fishbourne, in Sussex, where a British king built himself a palace and tried to make himself a Roman.

For, in the soft south, things were different from the rigours of the Welsh frontier. When Vespasian, with his bruiser's face – later to be carved in marble and stamped on coins as Emperor of Rome – led the Second Legion along the coast as part of Claudius's invasion force, he found ample local support. One king had already appealed to Rome for assistance, and others welcomed the troops when they came. In the territory of the Regenses, living round what is now Chichester, the Romans established a supply depot. The accidental discovery of this site by a workman digging for a water main in 1960 inspired one of the most exciting projects in contemporary archaeology.

The discovery took place at Fishbourne, a village not far from Chichester where the main Roman camp was. The site was a natural choice for a supply base. In Roman times the water came in further than it does now. Aerial infra-red photography, by distinguishing otherwise indetectable differences in soil and plant-life, has shown that boats could once sail almost up to the main Portsmouth road, now some distance inland. On this original coastline the earliest group of buildings was discovered. They were wooden storehouses, with the practical severity of all military architecture, raised on piles to keep the rats and ground-damp from the grain. Discovery and measurement of the post-holes made the reconstruction of the vanished buildings possible. Incidental finds hinted at the recreations of the soldiery off duty: spurs for fighting cocks, coins and counters for gambling. The military engineers laid down good metalled roads and a drainage system, improved and enlarged in the reign of Nero. They also built a harbour, which shows evidence of traffic with France and Spain.

But this simple site, abandoned when its military use was over, was later turned to a more magnificent purpose: a country house, or rather a palace, comparable to anything in contemporary Pompeii. Its builder, most probably, was the local king, referred to slightingly by Tacitus, who seems to have objected to quislings even when they served Roman ends: 'Certain territories were bestowed on King Cogidumnus, who has remained a staunch ally up to our time. This was in accordance with the long-established Roman tradition of turning even monarchs into instruments of slavery.'[25]

Cogidumnus – or Cogidubnus, to give him the local spelling – announces himself in a Chichester inscription as 'legate of the Emperor in Britain'. If the palace is indeed his, it shows the practical benefits of supporting Roman policies. It is in the form of four wings surrounding a central courtyard forty feet square. Only half has been recovered – the rest lies under modern houses and the main road – but its obvious symmetry makes conjectural restoration possible. Approaching from the harbour, the visitor passed under a pillared portico in the east wing to an entrance hall complete with fountain. To the right were small courtyards and a great aisled hall marking the corner, which still awaits excavation. To his left were the palaestra and bath-house. Coming once more into the light, he walked down the avenue dividing the central courtyard into two symmetrical gardens. As at Pompeii, the excavators have been able to trace the pattern of flowers and shrubbery from the original bedding trenches, and replant the lawns and hedges that surrounded them in an elegant formal pattern. Even the watering-system has been discovered.

Passing between two cypress trees, the visitor entered the audience chamber in the west wing. Here the floor has been excavated and re-covered for protection until money is available for roofing it. However, the north wing, fully excavated and enclosed, shows what the quality of the rooms must have been. Wooden runways allow visitors to study the elaborate mosaic floors; they are as impressed as the British of nineteen centuries ago must have been, at this exotic dwelling in so unlikely a place. Visitors from Rome probably objected to the climate, for at a later date central heating was added – this, in a country that still looks on such comfort as a sign of decadence. In one corner the hypocaust has been uncovered to show how hot air was driven down radiating channels from a central fire. There was marble on the walls, and painted decoration similar to that found at Stabiae. But the floors are the chief wonder; their designs, unparalleled outside the Mediterranean, suggest that they were laid by experts specially imported from Italy.

What the rest of the population thought of the palace as they scratched the soil in the fields outside is not recorded. There are signs that the palace fell on evil days. Subsequent mosaics were laid by local craftsmen, who botched them. Successive modifications suggest that the palace, like many English country houses since, was converted into apartments; new bathrooms were added, and perhaps a kitchen made out of a former courtyard. In the late third century the building was devastated by fire. We do not know who started it; perhaps the workmen who evacuated hastily, leaving their heaps of mortar with which they were refinishing a floor; perhaps pirates sailing into the harbour, for the barbarians were active in Gaul at this time, and raids on the British coast were frequent. But while it stood the palace was a Rome away from home, a testimony to the power of the conquerors to perpetuate their image on soil that could not have been more alien.

THE WORLD AS A VILLA

In the foregoing pages we have seen examples of the impact of Roman life and building on the provinces. For the reverse trend, we may look at the work of the Emperor Hadrian. When he came to the throne in 117, a Spaniard whose education had been predominantly Greek, it was as the successor to a man who had carried the bounds of the Empire further than ever before. Trajan had travelled to fight. Hadrian travelled too, but on peaceful missions, as a proprietor surveying his vast domains and making sure that everything was in order. He lived in a period when the world was in equipoise, when the Roman armies had gone as far as was practical, and the barbarians lay passive beyond the frontiers; a peacful time, when the impulse of conquest had been spent, and the necessity for defence had not yet begun.

Hadrian travelled everywhere – to Gaul, the Rhine, Spain, Greece, Asia Minor, Africa, Egypt – and bestowed buildings as an ordinary man might leave tips. In Britain he saw to the construction of the wall that bears his name, linking a system of forts that acted both as defence and customs barrier, policing the wild men from the North. The wall still stands, though perhaps not quite the same as Hadrian left it; a minor scandal was caused a few years ago when it was discovered that the Ministry of Works' labourers, rebuilding stretches of the monument, had been putting the stones back in the wrong order. To Nîmes he gave a temple. In Athens the arch erected in his honour gives a floodlit welcome to travellers driving in from the airport, while behind it lie the crumpled columns of the temple he dedicated to Olympian Zeus. In Rome he built too, reconstructing the Pantheon that Agrippa had dedicated, and giving it, apparently for the first time, its famous rotunda and dome, removing the Colossus of Nero (a project which, according to one account, took twenty-four elephants) to clear a site for his Temple of Venus and Rome, and designing the huge circular concrete tomb which served later emperors for a fortress, popes for a residence, and politicians for a prison.

Hadrian had a particular interest in building, for he was an architect himself – an original one, whose experiments with new shapes attracted unwise derision from the more orthodox. His most impressive feat was constructed for his private pleasure, in a fashionable resort eighteen miles from Rome. This was Tibur, the modern Tivoli, on the edge of the Sabine Hills and the banks of the River Anio, which makes a splendid waterfall there. In a hotel garden in the centre of town, a circular Roman temple, perhaps belonging to Vesta, perhaps to the local Sibyl, looks down on the river at its wildest. But as far as Tibur the Anio was navigable. This, coupled with an excellent road, the Via Tiburtina, which the modern highway closely follows, made the town easily accessible. Tibur sent Rome the travertine from its quarries, which may still be seen with an aqueduct nearby to supply power for the work. This became one of the favourite Roman building materials, being used for such diverse constructions as the Colosseum and St Peter's. In return Tibur received the rich and fashionable, who built their villas there.

Tibur, like the other hill-towns round Rome, had a long history. It was in this neighbourhood that Hercules fought the volcanic monster Cacus, and remained as a local deity. Tradition ascribed the foundation to a contemporary of the Evander who welcomed Aeneas; Virgil shows Tibur as fighting against the Trojan immigrants, and it preserved the dogged independence of its neighbours as late as the Gallic Wars, when it was still defying Rome. Once pacified, it quickly turned into a resort town. It was recommended for its winter climate. By the time of the Civil Wars it was already attracting the wealthy. Mark Antony had a villa there. Another great attraction was the baths of Aquae Albulae, four miles away, the modern Bagni Albule, one of the more beneficent by-products of the volcanic activity of the region.

The smell of sulphur is overpowering as you drive through. The nymph Albula, from whom the baths took their name, clearly took hers from the whitening of the sulphur deposits, which over the centuries have considerably diminished the two lakes from their Roman size. Nero had the water piped to his Golden House. It was generally believed that discoloured ivory would grow white again in Tibur. Martial records a Roman beauty who took her teeth there for the treatment, but came back with them as black as ever.

It was here that Hadrian chose to build. In Rome he had earned popularity by turning private land to public use, and taking part of the site of Nero's hated Golden House for his new temple. But his estate at Tibur was larger than even Nero could have dreamed of. It is known as Hadrian's Villa, but is really a one-man World Fair, where Hadrian collected buildings as Louis XVI did clocks, or George V stamps; it is the realized dream of the multi-millionaire tourist, an assembly, not of pictures, but of architectural reminiscences of the great places visited. If one seeks the appropriate moment, it is best, perhaps, to visit Tivoli in the early autumn, when the wind is already cooling, the leaves begin to fall, the first lick of rain comes over the hills, and the distant view of Rome is grey and melancholy. For it is an autumnal place. The melancholy does not come entirely from the fact that a place which was a Versailles before its time is now a shamble of ruins, or from the eighteenth-century cypresses which so appropriately shade the site. It is a built-in quality. Hadrian's Villa expresses a moment in time when the Romans had been everywhere, done and seen everything; when there was no longer a forward impulse; the beginning of a decadence which expressed itself in nostalgia for the past.

Hadrian revealed his complex personality in a Roman baroque which combined sophisticated technical accomplishment with an evocation of other times and places. The luxury of the time is seen in the *piazza d'oro*, an immense colonnaded courtyard surrounded by apartments where an intricate interplay of curving walls was surmounted by a dome with a central light, as in the

Emperor's Pantheon. The use of concrete made possible forms unknown to traditional Roman architecture. Where Augustus built four-square, Hadrian is fascinated by vault and apse; one room is shaped like a four-leafed clover, others are set on teasing diagonals, to lead the eye off into vistas mottled by shade and the play of water. Not far away is the so-called Teatro Marittimo, bespeaking the desire for privacy in an increasingly noisy world, now the privilege of the very rich. It is a circular island, approached by drawbridges, with rooms constructed on Hadrian's favourite curvilinear plan. There is a bathroom with access to the moat, so that the emperor could take his dip outside if the mood took him, a choice of alcoves for reading – he could move from one to another depending on the light – and an apsidal dining-room where he could receive his friends.

To delight his mind, there was a great library, and, to delight his eye, the series of buildings suggested by architectural master-pieces from abroad. Hadrian had his Lyceum and Academy, modelled after the most famous philosophical schools of Athens. In this, he was only following earlier precedent: Cicero had had a similar structure in the grounds of one of his country houses. But there was no precedent for the great rectangular colonnade named in honour of the *Stoa Poikile*, or painted stoa, where Zeno had first taught his philosophy. Its remains are the first to catch the visitor's eye. The columns have vanished, and only a broken wall remains. But the central basin is still flooded, for lonely swans to swim on. Further on is another watery extravagance, this time drawn from Egypt: an architectural fantasy reminiscent of Canopus, the district of Alexandria in which Antinous, Hadrian's boy-favourite, met his death. It is the best-preserved feature of the Villa now. One of the last structures to be completed, it shows how the emperor's originality had faded – perhaps because of his personal loss – to imitation. It is in the form of a long narrow pool, with arches framing statues of the deities at one end, and a shrine of the Egyptian Serapis at the other. There are sculptures of the rivers Tiber and Nile, and a stone crocodile peering out over the water; down one side are caryatids, painstakingly copied from those in the Erechtheum at Athens. Other statues from this setting stand in the adjacent museum.

The melancholic in Hadrian reveals itself in other monuments. Timon's Tower, named after the famous Greek misanthrope, stands among the olive trees down a side path. There is even an evocation of the Underworld. These things speak more personally of the builder than the more conventional theatres – there are three on the site – or the delightful Temple of Aphrodite, with the statue of the goddess, in a circle of columns, overlooking a landscape intended to recreate the Vale of Tempe in Greece, where the river Peneus flows between Olympus and Ossa. Modern houses have crept into the picture, and spoil Hadrian's view. The whole complex is designed to flatter the variable moods – and, some historians say, the sexual proclivities – of a ruler whose involved personality continues to excite interest. That such a work could come into existence at all shows the extent to which the character of the individual ruler had now become important. That it should take the shape it did shows the beginning of decadence, if we are to define that state as the expenditure of great technical resources on trivial objects. It is significant that Tivoli appealed greatly to Piranesi, who projected a reconstruction of the Villa; its combination of melancholia and architectural fantasy was close to his own tastes. In Roman history, it represents the last point at which an emperor can look out over the world and call it his own. Hadrian's successor, Antoninus Pius, seems never to have left Italy, and those who followed him were increasingly occupied with keeping others out.

NOTES TO CHAPTER EIGHT

1. Minutius Felix, *Octavius*, 2.
2. Pliny, *Letters*, II. 7.
3. The preliminary account of the salvaging of this wreck is given by Captain Ted Falcon-Barker, *Roman Galley Beneath the Sea*, Chilton Book, 1967.
4. Martial, *Epigrams*, I. 86. 1–2.
5. Ibid. I. 117. 7.

6. Seneca, *De Beneficiis* (*On Kindness*), VI. 15. 7.
7. Juvenal, *Satires*, III. 6–9, 268–75.
8. Frontinus, *De Aquis Urbis Romae* (*The Water Supply of Rome*), II. 75–6.
9. Tacitus, *Annals*, XV. 38.
10. Horace, *Odes*, I. 35. Appian, *Civil Wars*, I. 69; V. 24.
11. Martial, *Epigrams*, XI. 80.
12. Pliny, *Letters*, VI. 16, 20 (excerpted).
13. Statius, *Silvae*, V. 3. 207–8.
14. Martial, *Epigrams*, IV. 44.
15. Seneca, *Letters*, 56, 1, 2.
16. Apuleius, *Metamorphoses*, XI. 9–11 (excerpted).
17. Persius, *Satires*, II. 1–13.
18. Petronius, *Satyricon*, 75–6.
19. Tacitus, *Agricola*, 21.
20. Ibid.
21. Inscription from Lyons, *Corpus Inscriptionum Latinarum*, XIII. 1668.
22. Macrobius, *Satires*, I. 23, 12–13.
23. Tacitus, *Agricola*, 10.
24. Tacitus, *Annals*, XIV. 30.
25. Tacitus, *Agricola*, 14.

Chapter Nine

The Greater Change

To the long list of religions introduced to Rome we must now add two more, Mithraism and Christianity. They deserve to be considered together, for they have several features in common; and they stand apart from the rest in exercising a different kind of appeal, containing none of the sensational elements with which most Romans were by now familiar. They grew up side by side, and were seen by the thoughtful as rivals. It has been seriously suggested that, if Christianity had been stifled in its early development, the world would now be Mithraic. Certainly the Christians recognized the attractions of a cult which had so much in common with their own, and defended themselves by attacking Mithraism (as they also did with Buddhism) as a diabolical parody of the true faith.

Mithra was originally a Middle Eastern deity, the genius of divine light, associated with fire and the sun. Involved by the Persians in their own worship, he was surrounded by an elaborate sacerdotal apparatus. Represented sometimes on horseback, sometimes in the typical Persian long trousers, he was honoured with long liturgies and elaborate ceremonial, sometimes involving priests in animal disguises. At its lowest level the cult tended to amalgamate with orgiastic religions of the Cybele type. But on the whole it remained free of such manifestations, and was unusual among the Eastern beliefs in exercising a serious spiritual and intellectual appeal.

The Alexandrian conquests transmitted Mithraism, in a refined form, to Greece, though it made little impression there. It was left to the Romans to make the vital contact. This seems to have occurred, according to Plutarch, in the last years of the Republic, when Mithraism was introduced to Italy by Cilician pirates captured by Pompey. The number of devotees at this time must have been small, though the treasurer of the little town of Nersae refers, in A.D. 172, to a shrine of Mithra dilapidated from old age. Within a hundred years from its introduction, however, statues and inscriptions to the Persian god were numerous.

Mithraism was propagated by the oriental slaves who poured into Rome, and by the merchants who carried on their trade around the Mediterranean. But the principal mode of transmission was the army. Mithraism, with its emphasis on self-reliance, appealed to the soldiers; its devotees were encouraged to think of themselves as fighters for the faith, and the name *milites*, soldiers, was given to one grade of initiates. The average Roman serviceman did not share the fashionable agnosticism of the capital. He tended towards a simple, superstitious piety, easily influenced by any local beliefs with which he came into contact. Opportunities for such contact were many. When Rome began seriously to intervene in Eastern affairs three legions were posted to the Euphrates. This brought the troops into contact with the religion at its source. Subsequent tours of duty by soldiers and officials helped to popularize the faith, and transfers of militia enlarged its sphere of influence until it was known in every corner of the Roman world.

The Roman army was highly mobile, with legions shifted regularly to new trouble-spots. We may take as an example the picturesque history of Legion V, the Skylarks, which distinguished itself in Julius Caesar's African campaign in 47–46 B.C., and saw service the following year in Spain: after Caesar's assassination it was in Greece, fighting under Antony at Philippi and against Octavian at Actium. Transferred by Augustus to the German frontier it campaigned across the Rhine in A.D. 15–16; in 68, the Year of the Four Emperors, it followed its candidate, Vitellius, to Rome; from there it was sent to the Balkans. Individuals could see an even greater range of service. Under the customary system of promotion, every rise in rank was followed by a transfer. Tombstones commemorate Roman soldiers who died far away from home: Gaius Valerius Victor, standard-bearer of Legion II,

Augustus's Own, born at Lugdunum (Lyons), died at Caerleon in South Wales; Gaius Gavius Celer, centurion of Legion III, Augustus's Own, born at Clusium (Chiusi) in Etruscan country, buried in North Africa; Aurelius Alexander, standard-bearer of Legion II, Trajan's Own, born in Macedonia, buried in Alexandria. At Bath, one of the more luxurious Roman establishments in Britain, may be seen the epitaphs of soldiers from the Rhine and Moselle, the south of France and Spain. And on the journey to the grave these men might have served in half a dozen countries.

Thus the soldiers who had seen eastern service carried Mithraism with them. Legion XV, which had fought against the Parthians and later against the Jews, founded a centre of Mithraic worship on the Danube. Monuments and shrines have been discovered on the African coast, in Spain, in Armenia, along the Upper Rhine, possibly even in the Crimea, and in the north of England. One has been discovered in the Roman foundations of Colchester Castle, another in central London during excavations for a new office site near St Paul's. We have already noted the number of Mithraea in Ostia, which as a prominent sea-port would have had them early. The shrines have a standard shape. A small ante-chapel leads into the shrine itself, a long narrow, dark room intended to represent the cave where the god was born. Along each side run stone benches where the faithful knelt in prayer. At the far end stands an altar, originally backed by carved and painted representations of the mysteries of the cult. One shrine at Ostia has the unique feature of a black mosaic footprint inlaid into the white floor, in which the worshipper was presumably supposed to step for luck. Towards the altar end is another mosaic design, a serpent, the immemorial symbol of healing and fertility.

In the Roman world, Mithraism was originally a lower-class religion. This was inevitable from its mode of propagation. The earliest inscriptions are by freedmen, slaves and soldiers. But it gained status rapidly, and escaped the persecutions to which the other oriental religions were periodically subject. It had arrived too late for the worst of them. The authorities, now more complaisant, approved of a religion which adapted so well to the ruler-cult. The orientals had no scruples about identifying their deity with their king, and to many the Sun God and the Emperor were one.

But Mithraism had more honourable grounds for flourishing. In its transplanted form, it would have given even the Republic no reason for social concern. Its unsensational nature set it apart from the cults of Dionysus, Cybele or Isis, and no one could find its moral precepts offensive. The surviving evidence suggests that Mithraic doctrine saw the world in the Greek manner – and often with the use of names from Greek and Roman myth – as the product of successive generations. Time stood first in this cosmogony – sexless, dispassionate and portrayed on the monuments with a lion's head and a human body, around which was twined a serpent whose convolutions represented the passage of the sun. In his hands were a sceptre, thunderbolts and the keys of heaven, and on his body the signs of the zodiac. Time was seen as the creator and destroyer of all things, the lord and master of the elements. He was sometimes identified with destiny, sometimes with light and fire. The Stoics, who also believed in a primeval fire, found this sympathetic. The Romans *en masse*, who had long cultivated astrology, were attracted by the Persian emphasis on the power of the stars.

Time begot Heaven and Earth, who in turn produced the Ocean to complete the divine triad often identified with Graeco-Roman names. In the oriental, and quite un-Greek, manner, Mithraism conceived of a positive power of evil. Against the light was set the darkness, populated by devils who had carried out a vain assault on Heaven and were condemned to wander on the face of the earth spreading misery and plague.

In this system Mithra was the God of Light, airborne midway between Heaven and Hell. Like the Greek Heracles, he engaged in a series of epic adventures, including a fight with the sun, which ended happily in a pact of friendship and the bestowing on Mithra of a radiant and fiery crown. After this he fought a huge bull – a scene frequently illustrated on the monuments – mounted it, and was carried off. His long and arduous journey symbolizes the duration of human suffering. Life, for the followers of Mithra, was a battle in which victory could only come from the faithful observance of divine laws. The faithful should strive for perfect purity, symbolized in ritual by repeated washings, and in everyday concourse by abstinence from certain foods. After death there was promise of immortality: the soul travelled through a series of zones ridding itself one by one of the passions and faculties it had acquired during its stay on earth. Little could be said against such a doctrine. The most the satirists find to complain about is its foreignness: Lucian reproves Mithra because he cannot speak Greek.

Christianity, arriving later, originally found a similarly favourable environment. Judaea had been governed by Roman procurators since A.D. 6, and there were many Jews in Rome among whom the new creed could spread. In spite of considerable evidence of pagan anti-semitism – aimed rather at the exclusiveness of the people than at their religion – detailed studies have shown that in the capital at least, and under the early Empire, the Jews lived on equal terms with their neighbours, using the customary Roman names and active in all professions. The age of ghettos was not yet come. Julius Caesar and Augustus protected the Jews' individuality and their right to worship. Elsewhere in the Roman world Greek-speaking Jewish communities were established and respected.

By the reign of Claudius things had begun to change. We find that emperor disturbed by the quarrelsomeness of Jews in Alexandria, which some historians have attributed to the influence of Christian missionaries. Caligula, offended by the Jews' refusal to worship him, initiated the first persecutions, but until the reign of Titus they were fairly safe. In 66 Judaea revolted as a protest against the unjust Roman government. Four years later Jerusalem was destroyed. The Arch of Titus in the Roman Forum shows the army bearing home the temple treasures – the *menorah*, silver trumpets, and table for the show-bread. Kept at Rome for nearly four centuries, they were carried off in the Vandal conquest to Carthage, and from there to Constantinople, where the emperor, fearing that they brought bad luck, had them restored to Jerusalem. They finally disappeared from sight in the capture of the city by the Persians in 614.

The history of early Christianity runs, in part, parallel to that of Judaism in Rome. At first protected by the Roman religious tolerance, or indolence – for the authorities hardly recognized any difference between the Jewish and the Christian faiths – it was later subjected to persecution for political reasons. The first suspicion of this occurs in the case of Pomponia Graecina, wife of Aulus Plautius, the distinguished general who had led the invasion of Britain in 43 and remained as its first governor. In 57 his wife, a lachrymose woman, was charged with addiction to a foreign cult. Handed over to her husband for judgement, she was found innocent and spent the rest of her life in gloom. Christianity has hailed her as an early convert; but there is no mention of the faith to which she was addicted. Both Judaism and Isis-worship have been suggested, though at this time these were still legal. Another, and more picturesque, suggestion has been that Pomponia had become infected by Druidism during her stay in the new province; but these are mere speculations. For the Christian side, it may be said that Pomponia's complete withdrawal from social activities (though attributed by contemporary sources to sorrow at the death of a dear friend) may indicate a common manifestation of Christianity in Roman eyes, and that there certainly was a Pomponius Graecinus, possibly a relative, recorded as a Christian by an early inscription in the catacombs. But even if Pomponia was a Christian, it is evident from Nero's handling of the case that the charge was not yet sufficiently serious to warrant state action. It was still a domestic matter to be dealt with in the traditional way by the *paterfamilias*.

A more celebrated victim, again from the beginning of Nero's reign, was Paul himself, who, as a Roman citizen, had insisted on being tried in the capital. The charge was probably sedition, involving the introduction of gentiles into the temple and insulting the High Priest. Here, the Roman attitude was purely political. Judaea was a sensitive province, and at this time still friendly; the authorities were willing to sacrifice individuals to Jewish susceptibilities. The Romans always took great care to avoid offending local religious feelings, where these did not run counter to loyalty to Rome. In Egypt, for example, the killing of sacred animals was made a capital offence. Caligula's plan to erect his own statue in the temple at Jerusalem was a unique affront, re-garded by his subordinates as insanity and abandoned with a sigh of relief at his death. In this light, Paul was a political nuisance. His own religious beliefs were comparatively unimportant. According to Luke, he was allowed to live under guard in his own house, and to continue preaching the faith. The case was delayed and the verdict is uncertain. Paul had earlier voiced the desire to visit Spain, and a tradition, supported by the Pauline apocrypha, suggests that he may have done so, returning to perish in the persecutions that followed the great fire of 64.

It is in connection with this fire that we have our first mention of Christianity in Latin literature. It comes in Tacitus's account.

But no human efforts, no imperial largesse, no expiatory sacrifices could allay the slander that the fire had been started on Nero's orders. So, to quell the rumour, Nero found other scapegoats, and con-demned to the ultimate refinements of torture a group who already had a bad reputation for anti-social practices. Popularly known as Christians, they derived their name from the Christ executed under Pontius Pilate in Tiberius's reign. Suppressed for the time being, this malign superstition broke out with renewed force, not only in Judaea, the original seat of the infection, but in Rome itself, where all the scum of the world congregate. The first to be seized were those who confessed their sympathies voluntarily. Their evidence swiftly led to mass arrests; the offence was not so much arson as misanthropy. To add insult to mortal injury, they were wrapped in beast-skins and torn apart by dogs, or crucified, or set alight to illumine the night sky. Nero threw open his grounds for the spectacle, and turned it into a circus, mixing with the crowd in stable-clothes or driving his chariot. Guilty though they were and deserving of the extreme punishment, public sympathy was aroused; it was felt that they were being sacrificed not to the general well-being but to the whim of a sadist.[1]

Why were the Christians persecuted? For their faith, or for arson? The story of the fire is itself confused by the writer's desire to show Nero in as bad a light as possible. Tacitus passes on the rumour that the emperor's men were seen spreading the flames. There is an obvious, and innocent, explanation of this: they may simply have been trying to create a fire-break. But the rumour probably represents a substantial body of public opinion, aggravated by Nero's conduct after the fire in appropriating an enormous tract of land for his own building. If so, Nero may well have tried to take himself out of the public eye by diverting the blame onto a group already unpopular for other reasons. Tacitus is the only author who knows of any connection between the Christians and the fire, and even he implies that the charge of incendiarism was false: they were punished because they confessed to being Christians. Suetonius, writing later, states that they were persecuted for introducing 'a new and malevolent superstition'. The Christian writers unhesitatingly take the same view. Clement, third in succession to Peter as Bishop of Rome, writes in 96 that the Christians suffered torments similar to those of Hades because of their faith.

But Nero could have said, as Hitler did in similar circumstances about the Jews after the Reichstag fire, that if the Christians had not existed, it would have been necessary to invent them. If he really wished to distract the public attention, he could not have found more convenient scapegoats. How had the Christians made themselves unpopular? By Nero's time they were recognized as a body distinct from Judaism, and, while the Jews were still protected by law, Christians were not. There are suspicions that the Jews themselves initiated the persecution. Poppaea, Octavia's successor in Nero's favour, had flirted with Judaism, was on good terms with the Jewish historian Josephus, and used her influence to have certain Jewish prisoners in Rome released. It has been suggested that the Roman Jews worked through her to suppress what they now regarded as a dangerous heresy.

But we need not look for personal causes. It is difficult, after centuries of Christian bias, to understand that the Roman attitude was, in its time and place, normal. The authorities dealt with the Christians as with any subversive organization. For, in the eyes of the administration, the Christians formed an illegal society. They still had one thing in common with the Jews: both groups were unpopular because of their exclusiveness. The charge continues to be made long afterwards, and the Christians were doubly suspect because the most important part of their rites was performed in secret – as it still is in the Eastern Orthodox Church. Secrecy was frowned upon; the only politic course was to stamp them out.

The most famous martyr of the Neronian persecutions was, of course, Peter himself, the first Bishop of Rome. Legends have grown up about his last days – the *Quo Vadis* story, according to which he met Christ as he was fleeing the city, and was shamed into returning, and the tradition that he was crucified upside down. Another enduring story located his monument beneath the spot later to be occupied by the high altar of the basilica that bore his name. The same account unhesitatingly places Paul's tomb on the road to Ostia. In 1940 Pope Pius XII ordered excavations to search for corroborative evidence. The continuous remodelling of the altar complex had long ago uncovered monuments of great antiquity. Roman graves found in 1615, under Paul V, had been hailed as the tombs of the first popes, and further work under the altar eleven years later, to lay the foundations for Bernini's baldachin, had turned up pagan graves with coins dating back to the middle of the second century A.D.

It was thus already well known that the altar stood above a cemetery. The new excavations went deeper, not without some fears for the safety of the architectural mass above. One tradition was conclusively disproved. There was no trace of anything that might have been the wall of Nero's circus. But the excavators uncovered a street of tombs including one spot which seems to have been of particular sanctity. Subsequent building had been careful to avoid and enclose it, and one wall, identified by the excavators as the *muro rosso* from its colour, may have been the 'monument' of which Christian tradition speaks. If this was not Peter's tomb, it had at least been so regarded from early times.

The history of the Christians in Nero's reign and after has been highly coloured by their own apologists. In fact, there were reasonable grounds for friction. Christianity, like Mithraism, had its first converts among the lower classes. Educated Romans knew little of it, and disliked what they knew. From the defences, we hear some of the popular misconceptions: the eating of the Host distorted into stories of cannibal feasts; charges of infanticide and sexual orgies; and the prevalent slander, also spread about the Jews, that the Christians worshipped an idol with an ass's head. The last was less fantastic in Roman eyes than it is in ours: after all, the Egyptians worshipped animal-headed deities. A *graffito* on the Palatine shows such a figure hanging from a cross.

On a more rational level many found the Christian protestations disagreeable. The doctrine of the annunciation, crucifixion and resurrection was hard to swallow. Romans could not conceive why anyone would choose to worship a condemned criminal. Pliny calls the faith a disgusting superstition. Marcus Aurelius, most rational of men, finds the Christian view of death absurdly melodramatic when contrasted with the calm acceptance taught by his own Stoicism.

But what chiefly alienated the Romans was the Christian refusal to compromise. The mutual tolerance of the established religions was abhorrent to Christians; the slow process of absorption which had produced the cosmopolitan Roman pantheon had no place in their thought; and the Graeco-Roman gods were often regarded as demons. Mithraism was accepted by the Romans because it was tactfully syncretic. Christianity, by the laws of its nature, could never be.

This intolerance displayed itself on several levels. The Christians advertised their non-conformism with the hearty tactlessness familiar among new converts. Some took outlandish names – 'Thanksbetogod' or 'Whatgodwill' – foreshadowing the worst gaucheries of Puritanism. Tertullian, in his spluttering fury (he is one of the few Latin writers who needs exclamation marks to do him justice in translation) dismisses many harmless practices out of hand. Writing against idolatry, he condemns astrology, which is fair enough; but he goes on to include frankincense-merchants, sculptors and teachers of literature in the list of the proscribed. Writing on the public shows, Tertullian is on safer ground. Pagans before him had complained of their indignity. But as usual Tertullian goes too far:

> The other day I heard an original defence from one of these theatrical *aficionados*. The sun, he said – yes, even God himself! – can look down from heaven and not be contaminated. Yes, and by the same token the sun can cast his rays into a cesspool and be undefiled! If only God would turn a blind eye on all our offences! Then every man would escape judgement! But God looks down on looting and lying, on adultery and idolatry, on fraud and deceit – yes, and on the public shows as well.[2]

In his crusading zeal, he finds no manner of entertainment acceptable:

> The same man who will keep any foul language from his maiden daughter's ears will expose her to the same talk in the theatre, and gestures to match; the same man who stops street-brawlers from coming to blows, or at least cries shame on the combatants, will applaud more deadly fights in the stadium; the same man who shudders at the corpse of the departed, gone the way we all must go, will gaze down from his seat in the amphitheatre on bodies mangled, torn, and fouled with their own blood, and never blink an eye; yes, and the same man who attends the shows to signify his approval that murder must be punished will have a reluctant gladiator whipped and flogged into doing murder himself.[3]

He concludes with an apocalyptic vision of the entire personnel of the entertainment world writhing in the flames of Hell: 'And there you will hear the tragic actors in even better voice when the tragedy is their own; and you will watch the players, who have never danced so nimbly as in hell fire; and you will look upon the charioteer in his racing colours, red – from head to foot, in the heat of the flame.'[4]

In protesting against the slaughter, Tertullian and others succeeded where Seneca had failed. Gladiatorial games were discontinued at Rome in 404, though the wild-beast shows lingered over a century longer. But the blanket condemnation of all the theatrical arts set a dangerous precedent for later ages. Tertullian's spiritual progeny includes the Puritan divines, Jeremy Collier in the eighteenth century and any number of moralists in the nineteenth, who used his words as a text to preach against the theatre. Many of the early Christian writers, particularly in the East where the Greek tradition was still strong, were careful to distinguish between the plays of former days, which they found to have considerable moral dignity, and the barbaric atrocities of the arena. But there were also many like Tertullian. Even Plato, who raised strong moral objections to the theatre, would have found him heartless.

The Christians even objected to Roman table manners. Here is Clement of Alexandria reproving banqueters like a stern nanny at Trimalchio's feast:

> Is it not absurd to hang out from your couch till your face is practically in the dishes, like a bird perching on the edge of its nest, to get a nose full, as the saying goes, of the savoury aroma wafting through the air? Is it not senseless to keep poking your fingers into the sauces, or be forever grabbing at some dish or other, forgetting all decorum and propriety, as if you were not so much going to taste i: as commit assault and battery on it? Such gluttons are not fit to be called men. Swine and dogs would suit them better. In their haste to stuff themselves they cram both cheeks with food till their faces swell like balloons; the sweat pours off them in their efforts to fill the bottomless pit; they puff and pant with over-indulgence, and stow away food in their bellies with such incredible energy that you would think they were not so much eating as laying in supplies for the winter.[5]

More serious was the Christian indifference to social obligations. This was abhorrent to the authorities on political grounds and to the philosophers on moral grounds. Many objected to military service or civil office, though Paul had laid down that the powers that be were part of God's design. Though not revolutionaries, the Christians could not escape the taint of disaffection. The practice arose of making the worship of the emperor a loyalty test. As evidence of the problems this created, we have the correspondence between Pliny and Trajan, a conscientious administrator trying to restore order to a trouble-ridden province and a humane emperor provoked against his will into severity:

Imperial Majesty:

It has always been my custom to seek your advice in time of doubt. Who, after all, could better guide my irresolution, or enlighten my ignorance? I have never served on an inquisition of Christians, and so am ignorant of the nature and extent of the customary penalties and inquiries. I have been not a little perplexed as to how far age is a factor, and whether those of tender years should be treated any differently from mature offenders; whether repentance guarantees pardon, or whether once a Christian, always a Christian, with all that this entails: whether the name alone is a punishable offence, though the defendant's record is otherwise clean, or only illegal activity connected with the name. I have provisionally taken the following action against those accused of Christianity. I asked them if they were Christians. If the answer was affirmative, I put the question a second and a third time, warning them of the penalties. I had the stubborn cases taken into custody, having no doubt in my own mind that, whatever it was they were admitting to, such obstinacy and wilful persistence deserved to be punished. There were others, victims of a similar lunacy, whose cases I docketed for trial at Rome, as being Roman citizens. As usual, bringing the matter into the public domain increased the number of offences. An anonymous pamphlet was brought to my attention, containing a whole list of names. Those who denied that they were, or ever had been, Christians, I let go when they had repeated a prayer at my dictation, offered wine and incense to your statue, which I had brought into court for this purpose together with the images of the gods, and blasphemed against Christ. Confirmed Christians, I understand, will do none of these things.[6]

Pliny admits that he finds nothing but a 'perverse and excessive superstition', and that even under torture the Christians admitted to nothing worse than holding watch-night services and keeping the Commandments. Nevertheless, he sees the faith as a contagion that must be stamped out, and congratulates himself on the fact that under his administration the temples are beginning to fill again. Trajan replies:

My dear Secundus:

Your investigation of the accused Christians has been quite proper. It is impossible to establish a mode of procedure equally valid in every case. Witch-hunts are to be avoided. If they are accused and convicted, the law must take its course. However, recantation supported by positive evidence – namely, an act of worship to our gods – implies that the offender has seen the error of his ways, and should carry remission of punishment, whatever suspicions he may have incurred in the past. Anonymous pamphlets are not admissible as evidence. This would set a disastrous precedent, contrary to current policy.[7]

Finally, there was a strong element of cultural prejudice. The educated Roman valued style and beauty in speaking and composition. Brought up on Cicero and Virgil, he found Christian literature, at least in Latin, considerably inferior to their standards. Several of the major Christian writers – Tertullian, Arnobius, Lactantius, Augustine – were Africans, coming from a part of the world where a renascent Carthage was the chief seat of learning, where Greek, the prestige language of the cultivated classes, had never secured a foothold, and where Punic had been directly superseded by a new style of Latin, that made up in vigour what it lacked in elegance. Of course, the Christians brought a new literature with them, but few Romans were equipped to appreciate Hebrew. The pre-Vulgate translations of the Bible were primarily concerned with meaning, and made no pretensions to style. Even the Christians admitted this deficiency. Augustine and Jerome were pained to read the writings of their own kind. Lactantius, writing in the fourth century, claims that the scriptures lack appeal because they are so undistinguished as literature.

These prejudices, some not in themselves unreasonable, were exaggerated by the Christian apologists, fierce fighters for the cause, into tales of systematic persecution, productive of martyrs. A case in point is the reign of Domitian. He was unpopular among the pagan historians, who level at him the now familar charges of cowardice, extravagance and terrorization. Of these the second at least seems to have been exaggerated. Domitian inherited the debts of his predecessors, but held firm against an inflationary policy: in his reign, the silver content of the denarius actually increased. The third charge, though it had some basis in fact, was similarly distorted. Domitian was accused of a number of deaths, the most famous being that of the general Agricola. Tacitus, the dead man's son-in-law, mentions the suspicion that he was poisoned on the emperor's orders. But there is no foundation for a charge which even Tacitus voices hesitatingly. The records show a sharp rise in the death-rate at this time, due to nothing more sinister than unusually inclement weather. But the Christian writers, particularly Tertullian and Eusebius, seized the opportunity to present Domitian as a second Nero, with a particular fondness for slaughtering Christians.

We are told of the Christian martyrdom of Flavius Clemens, the emperor's cousin, and his wife Domitilla. But the story is much confused. One source describes Domitilla as Clemens' niece: there may be two ladies in question here. No pagan source refers to the offence of Christianity, though Suetonius's description of Clemens as a man who lived 'a disgustingly indolent life' may refer to the withdrawal from public activity for which the Christians were notorious. Cassius Dio associates the pair with others who had 'drifted into'Jewish ways'; he may, of course, be committing the still common error of lumping Christianity and Judaism together. A Domitilla – not necessarily the same one – owned property on the Via Ardentina, which housed the later Christian cemetery identified with her name. On such slender grounds was the Christian legend built.

The case of Acilius Glabrio is similarly doubtful. Consul in 91, he was ordered by Domitian, for reasons unknown, to fight a lion in the amphitheatre. Contrary to established procedure, he won, and attempted to escape further persecution by going into voluntary exile. But Domitian's resentment pursued him, and he was eventually killed. Some of his descendants at least were Christians, and the family crypt was eventually developed into a larger complex, part of which was a Christian cemetery known by the name of Priscilla. There were several women of this name among the Acilians. Christian legend, hunting for distinguished victims, has thus seized on Acilius Glabrio as an early supporter of the faith, condemned to a martyrdom of a familiar type. But there is no historical support for the tradition at all.

That there was persecution is undeniable. The emperors could not tolerate an allegiance that ran counter to their own. Yet the more gory stories are unfounded. In spite of the fact that the major pogroms did not come till later, legend and accumulated propaganda have presented the early Christian life as necessarily furtive, conducted in the shadows, under the constant fear of intimidation. The effects of this romanticizing are still very much with us. A word-square discovered in the palaestra at Pompeii (another copy has turned up in England), though it continues to baffle scholars, has been claimed as a cryptic Christian device, and interpreted either as an acrostic of the opening words of the *paternoster* or a sentence of vaguely Christian application. It is pointed out that if one frames the central row of letters vertically and horizontally, the sign of the cross is revealed. But this would be true of any five-letter-word square, Christian or otherwise. In Herculaneum a cruciform mark in the upper room of a house near the forum has been identified as the remains of a Christian cross hanging over a small *prie-dieu*. In this case the attribution is more plausible, and if it is in fact Christian it is early archaeological evidence for such worship in Italy. But the more picturesquely minded historians have seen it as evidence that Christianity was even then a hidden rite, carefully secreted from the official eye in a remote corner of the house. Confused etymology produced other legends. The Latin *macellum*, 'market', became the Italian *macello*, 'slaughterhouse', and folklore was not slow to identify the Roman buildings as places devoted to the butchery of Christians.

A whole spurious tradition, fostered by popular novels and films, has arisen about the Roman catacombs. These winding subterranean passages, filled with relics of the Christian dead, were already attracting tourists in the Middle Ages. Graffiti record these pioneer visits. An inscription of 1321 exhorts visitors to 'gather together in these caverns, read the holy books; sing hymns in honour of the saints and martyrs who, having died in the Lord, now lie buried here'. About the same time, a bishop of Pisa was in the catacombs; six German priests record their visit in 1397; some forty years later, members of the Roman Academy inscribed their names. But for all practical purposes the catacombs were forgotten until their accidental rediscovery in 1578, when Gregory XIII was in the Vatican. Labourers digging in a vineyard on the Via Salaria found what turned out to be the catacombs of St Priscilla, neglected for seven hundred years. They were promptly explored by ecclesiastical historians. The most determined investigator was a Maltese, Antonio Bosio, who published his account of thirty-six years of mole-like explorations under the title of *Roma Sotteranea, Underground Rome.*

Christian tradition saw these tunnels as the hiding-places of the believers, forced below ground to conduct their worship while their savage persecutors sought for them above. In fact, most of the graves and inscriptions date from after Constantine's Edict of Toleration. The catacombs are exactly what they seem to be – burial places, and nothing more.

We may not be able to forgive the Roman attitude to Christianity but we can surely understand it. A minority group which is deliberately nonconformist, and which derides the values of the establishment; which arms itself with slogans too easily misinterpreted; which professes a higher allegiance than to the forces of law and order; which holds a creed that few outside the group can begin to understand: the phenomenon is familiar enough in our own time, and so is the official attitude which condemns it. But the Christians, in spite of all the obstacles placed in their way, had to establish themselves in Rome. It was the chief city of the world. Anything of importance had to happen here.

The Christians had some things in their favour, which eventually spread the appeal of their faith into the upper reaches of the class-structure. They had a superb organization, which took strength from opposition. They had writers who, though not polished stylists, were intelligent and forceful, and could triumphantly refute the absurd slanders uttered against them. They had a sense of mission unusual in a complacent age. And, most important, Christianity, once its outlines were understood, was seen to fit into a familiar ancient pattern. In its promise of immortality to initiates who bound themselves by its laws, it resembled the great mystery religions of the Graeco-Roman world – for example, the Eleusinian cult, of great antiquity, which held out just such a promise of individual survival, and into whose ranks Augustus, among others, had been proud to be admitted as a member.

By 120, Christianity had established a firm doctrinal basis. Fifty years later, its adherents were already beginning to claim the direct intervention of their deity in Roman affairs. The Emperor Marcus Aurelius was engaged in a war against the northern barbarians – a defensive war, for the tide of conquest was turning, and the Roman frontiers were feeling the harassment of the peoples who would eventually overthrow them. The campaign had not been going well, and in an action in Moravia, probably in 172, the Romans were suffering from lack of water. They were saved by a sudden rainstorm, which brought them welcome relief and discomposed the enemy. The scene is graphically depicted on the triumphal column of Marcus Aurelius erected near the Pantheon, and still to be seen in Rome: the streaming rain spirit hovers over the combatants, with on one side the Romans gratefully catching the water in their shields, and on the other the barbarians swept away by the deluge. Another panel shows a further instance of celestial favour: an enemy siege-engine being struck by lightning. Pagan chroniclers attributed this assistance to the traditional sources: to the prayers of Arnuphis, an Egyptian magician who invoked the aid of Hermes, or of Marcus Aurelius himself, who was to represent himself on his coins as Jupiter hurling thunderbolts against the Germans. The Christians had another story.

> But the soldiers of the legion named after Melitene, in the faith that has sustained them from that time to this against their enemies, knelt on the ground in our customary attitude of prayer and made their entreaties to God. The enemy had never seen anything like it before. But, according to the story, something stranger still was in store for them. At the same instant lightning struck, driving them into chaotic retreat, and a shower fell on the army that had prayed to God, refreshing them when they were about to die of thirst.[8]

For this reason, it was argued, the Melitene legion received the nickname *Fulminata*, 'The Thunderers'. From pagan sources and inscriptions it would appear that it had already been known by this name at the latest under Nero, and possibly even in the time of Augustus. But the Christians were not going to waste a good story.

Marcus Aurelius, for all his philosophical condemnation of Christianity, was on the whole tolerant. We possess his instructions to the governor of Lyons in 177, which have the same tone as Trajan's letter to Pliny. This was the pattern of the times. Emperors were prepared to sacrifice their personal convictions to their desire for harmony. It was feared that public proceedings against the Christians might cause more trouble than they were worth. In the second century, the persecutions have the same character as the history of European Jew-baiting in the early years of Nazi influence: prosecutions were more likely to stem from private animosity or greed than from official sources. In the years that followed, a Christian's life was not easy, but could be reasonably safe, if he were discreet. In some reigns Christianity was accepted simply as one new faith among many: statues of Christ stood beside those of Buddha and the pagan deities. In others, the rulers had no time for internal religious squabbles. We are now in the period of the soldier-emperors, who took power by force and campaigned vigorously to keep their opponents down and the armies too busy to support a rival.

In the third century the picture changed. The state now took an active part, attacking not merely individuals, but the Christian Church as an entity. Decius, who began his brief reign in 249, conducted the first of the general persecutions. Commissions were set up, a census conducted, and compliance with the traditional forms of worship insisted upon. Each individual was compelled by law to appear before the tribunal and make a sacrifice. Those who complied were issued with certificates, as detailed as a modern passport, several of which survive. Anyone not holding such a certificate by a fixed date was automatically declared a Christian, and liable to the penalties. Trajan's stipulation that there be no witch-hunts was still in theory observed, for the regulations applied to the entire population, but in practice the Christians were forced to identify themselves. Many were frightened into compliance, to the mockery of the pagans for whom the law had no terrors. Some, acknowledging a time-honoured feature of Italian bureaucracy, found that a bribe would secure the necessary document. Others obtained general certi-fication for their whole families from officials only too eager to expedite the paper-work. It is clear that the persecution failed, both from the comments of the Christians themselves and from the fact that Valerian, who became emperor in 253, was forced to reinstitute it.

His methods were somewhat different. He attacked not life but property, banishing the bishops, closing Christian homes to worship and cemeteries to burial, and endeavouring to shatter the tightly knit Christian organization. This too failed, and in 258, following a second and more vicious edict, Christian lives were again in danger. The persecution ended only with Valerian's capture in battle. His successor, more tolerant, permitted the return of some Church property. In 303, under Diocletian, the hostilities broke out with renewed force. A wave of executions was accompanied by a hitherto unprecedented type of harassment, the seizure of ecclesiastical documents and archives. Again, as in the Nazi persecution of the Jews – the parallel forcibly reintroduces itself – some areas escaped more lightly than others. Diocletian acceded to an empire with administrative problems so complex that he was forced to quadruplicate his office, naming two Augusti, of which he was one, and two Caesars, thus making imminent the great schism between East and West. Constantius Chlorus, Caesar of the West with responsibility for Britain and Gaul, was sufficiently well disposed towards the Christians to dis-regard the orders emanating from the capital. In Rome itself, as in Africa, the blood flowed freely.

In the confused period following Diocletian's death, Maxentius, another persecutor, usurped the throne. He was opposed by Constantine, the son of Chlorus, and defeated in a battle fought, according to the Christians, under the eye of God. The last great building of the Roman Forum shows the transition of power. It is the basilica at the north-east end, designed to fulfil the same functions as the Aemilian and Julian structures near the Capitol, but no longer in the same form. The Romans had devised more fluid ways of enclosing large spaces. A system of vaults, looking forward to the Renaissance, shaped the largest hall in the ancient world. Maxentius planned it and began the construction; in 313 Constantine reoriented it, moved the judges' tribunal and filled the vacant apse with a colossal statue of himself, ten times life size. The surviving fragments – head, feet, left knee and right hand – were discovered at the end of the fifteenth century and moved to the Capitol, where the head glowers down and the fractured hand points admonishingly to heaven, providing a constant delight to photographers. Enough survived of the basilica itself, in spite of the enthusiasm with which later Romans hacked at it, to provide Michelangelo, it is said, with inspiration for the building of St Peter's.

In his statue, perhaps, Constantine paid tribute to his Christian inspiration. As Lactantius tells the story, a vision granted to him on the eve of battle instructed him to place the Christian symbol on his soldiers' shields. He did so, and Maxentius was defeated. Eusebius, copying the statue's inscription, notes that it bore 'the symbol of salvation'. Was this the Christian sign, or something more non-committal? Constantine may have preferred to leave it vague. There is certainly much ambiguity about the triumphal arch erected about the same time between the Forum and the Colosseum, around which the traffic now swirls menacingly – an ambiguity appropriate to a monarch whose reign saw a confluence of contradictory traditions. It is a patchwork of new sculpture and second-hand pieces. Some reliefs are reworked from the period of Marcus Aurelius. Art historians have found in it a combination of traditional Roman techniques and others revealing a powerful Eastern influence. The emperor is shown among pagan deities, Mithra, Mars and personified Rome, while the inscription attributes his triumph to *instinctu divinitatis*, 'divine

Inspiration', with the precise source of the inspiration, perhaps deliberately, left unclear.

But in other ways Constantine showed his bent more decisively. In 311, by proclaiming the Edict of Toleration, he allowed the Christians to breathe in peace at last. A silver medal of 313 shows the emperor wearing the Christian monogram. In the same year, he induced his eastern colleague to grant the Christians full legal standing. By 323, the tetrarchy established by Diocletian had vanished, and Constantine reigned as autocrat over the entire Roman world. He sought a united Church, as well as a united Empire, and, in addition to reconciling the pagan and Christian factions, attempted to heal the doctrinal disputes within the Church itself. Seeking a fresh start in a new Christian capital in the East, he chose Byzantium, a city favourably situated on important trade-routes, and first colonized by the Greeks in 657 B.C. Recently brought into new prominence as the scene of a naval victory over Constantine's enemies, it was a natural choice. The work of building began in 324, and took six years. Called New Rome; or, more familiarly, Constantinople, the new foundation imitated many features of the old. It had its duplicate senate, influential families were induced to migrate, and the administrative system devised by the hater of Christians, Domitian, became the basis for the world-wide church. Constantine did more than he intended. At one stroke he cast the old capital adrift and, by diminishing its importance, exposed it to its enemies; he created a dichotomy of language, for the Eastern Empire, now honoured by the presence of the supreme ruler, gave new prestige to the Greek tongue which it had always spoken; and he established conditions under which theological quarrels were almost inevitable. It would not be long before the Pope in Rome and the Patriarch in Constantinople divided their flock.

We began this history with one émigré, Aeneas. We end it with another, who takes the reverse journey to a place not far from Troy. The withdrawal to Constantinople spelled the end of the Western Empire, though its demise was a slow and not wholly unpleasant one. The voices that rise from the Roman cities after

Constantine has left their capital show the confusion of a culture no longer certain where it stands. In the fourth century, with paganism increasingly under a cloud, age-old rites are still practised, and writers cling pathetically to the values of the past. Decius Magnus Ausonius lives the life of a cultivated country gentleman in a completely Romanized Gaul. Professor of rhetoric, tutor to princes, holder of high office – a latter-day Seneca, in fact, in a less neurotic age – he retires to his birthplace in Bordeaux, good wine-growing country then as now, already notable for its *grands crus*. A grower himself, he participated in the new pattern of trade in which luxury goods were shipped to Rome instead of being received as exports. According to a venerable tradition, the present Château Ausone, a prestigious name among oenophiles, is built on the site of his villa at Lucaniae, the ancient name of St-Émilion. At least a nominal Christian, Ausonius is still responsive to pagan sentiments, and to life's sensual pleasures. He can write a description of a journey down the Moselle in the form of a hymn to the river-nymph, painting a charming picture of a countryside that shows the best effects of Roman rule, and whose features have hardly changed:

> *And as I gazed, there leapt into my mind*
> *A vision of my country of Bordeaux:*
> *The same well-husbanded and smiling fields,*
> *The roofs of country houses, perching high*
> *Above the overhanging riverbanks;*
> *The hillsides green with vines, and in the valley*
> *The murmurous delights of the Moselle.*[9]

He can also write a comfortable account of the rich provincial's daily round, and a dramatic sketch, in effect a pagan morality play, based on the Seven Sages of the ancient world. And, thumbing his nose at 'the moralists, armoured in propriety', he publishes a dry piece of academic pornography, defending himself on the grounds that it is made up of tags from Virgil.

Other aspects of contemporary life Ausonius finds less pleasant. He keeps up a long and largely one-sided correspondence with his fellow-countryman and former pupil Paulinus, whose religious fervour alarms him. He maintains a running fire of questions. Why have you abandoned the delights of literature? Why have you chosen the monastic life? And, above all, why don't you write? Paulinus censoriously replies:

> God has forbidden us to waste
> Our time, at work or play,
> In foolishness or fairytales.
> His laws we must obey
> If we would see that greater Light
> That poets' cunning lies
> And rhetoric, and sophistry,
> Have hidden from our eyes.[10]

There are other voices, some not touched by Christianity at all. Claudian, born in Alexandria and come to Rome to serve the Western Emperor Honorius (for the rule was now divided again), writes of new matters in old ways: Juvenalian satires on corrupt ministers of the Eastern court; panegyrics on the mercenary Stilicho, in whom he saw the only hope of Roman unity; poetic accounts of the Gothic Wars; and a *Rape of Persephone*, the most traditional of classical subjects, perhaps inspired in this instance by current attempts to alleviate the corn shortage. An unrepentant pagan in an officially Christian world, Claudian's work became one of the classics of the Middle Ages.

But the voice heard loudest over the centuries is that of Augustine, militant against Rome's vices, but shocked by her fall. 'The news is horrifying. Bloodshed, fire, rape, murder, atrocities. It is all true.'[11] The disaster to which he refers, the capture of Rome in 410 by Alaric and his Goths, inspired Augustine to write his twenty-two volumes on a more substantial kingdom, that of God. The Goths were appeased with land, and the city returned to apparent normality, but this invasion was only the first of many.

The Rome of Constantine was already learning the role it plays in the modern world. A city that was a colossal museum piece;

cursed with an excess population, an inefficient administration and a traffic problem; redolent with a titillating odour half of sanctity, half of moral decay; housing its citizens in niches carved from crumbling antiquity or teeming tenements described as 'the cities which Rome carries on its back'; the picture is a familiar one. The guide-books were already being written, listing the sights in order of importance and impressed, as guide-books tend to be, by quantity: one of them records 28 libraries, 6 obelisks, 8 bridges, 11 fora, 10 basilicas, 11 public baths, 19 aqueducts, 2 circuses, 2 amphitheatres, 3 theatres, 80 statues of the gods in gold and 74 in ivory, 46,602 apartment blocks, 144 public lavatories and 46 brothels. The Emperor Constantius II, visiting Rome as a tourist from Constantinople, was provoked to reactions not dissimilar to those drawn from visitors today. But as the tourists arrived many were leaving, drawn in Constantine's wake.

One of those who departed was Rutilius Claudius Namatianus. Born in Gaul, he had held important offices in Rome – most of the administrators, in these late days, were foreigners – and had been prefect of the city after the Gothic invasion of 410. In 417 he returned home to his war-ravaged estates. We know him by the poem he has left. He shows himself as a man still keeping simple faith with the pagan past, Roman in his suspicion of the Christians, medieval in his dislike of the Jews. At the moment of his departure he offers tribute to the city he has come to love:

> *Queen of your world, and beauty's paragon,*
> *Rome, whose place is set among the stars.*
> *Mother of men and gods, to you I cry.*
> *In your temples we come near to heaven.*
> *We sing your praises, and if fate allows,*
> *Shall sing for ever. In the minds of men*
> *You live eternally. We could sooner hide*
> *The sun in criminal oblivion*
> *Than let your glory vanish from our hearts.*
> *You spread your blessings as the sun his rays,*
> *To the waters at the world's end. Very Phoebus,*

> *Who holds all in his compass, turns for you*
> *And beds his horses in you, where they rose.*[12]

He leaves by sea; the land passage has been unsafe since the invasion. Sailing from a Tiber already closing itself to traffic, he hears the echo of past happiness ringing in his ears:

> *So to the ship. And where the Tiber parts*
> *I took the channel on the starboard side,*
> *For sand has choked the other. There is no way.*
> *Aeneas landed here. Nothing remains*
> *But memory of glory. . . .*
> *A shout rose from the Circus. Others followed.*
> *We heard, and wondered, as the cheering swelled*
> *To a crescendo, telling of the crowd*
> *That packed the stands. The old, familiar noise*
> *Came bouncing from the heavens. Was it real,*
> *Or had fond memory played tricks on us?*[13]

Crawling north along the Tuscan coast, he passes places changed out of all knowledge since their first inhabitants settled them, beaches given over to great lonely, luxury villas, 'great mansions now, where once small townships stood', or the husks of vanished cities:

> *Next the scattered rooftops of Graviscae*
> *Hove into sight. In summertime, the smell*
> *Of marsh hangs over them. But trees still grow*
> *Green all around. Pines crowd along the shore*
> *To cast their bobbing shadows. There we saw*
> *Some ancient ruins, no one left to guard them,*
> *And the walls of Cosa, long untenanted*
> *And tumbled down. The cause of their decline*
> *May seem too frivolous in a sober tale,*
> *But laughter has its place. The people*
> *Were forced to leave, because a plague of rats*
> *Had made their houses uninhabitable.*[14]

So to the former stronghold of the Etruscans, now almost inaccessible by sea:

> And then to Volaterrae, properly
> Called Vada. Unfamiliar with the channel
> I held to deeper water, while the pilot,
> On look-out on the prow, controlled the rudder
> And told us where to head. The harbour mouth
> Is hard to find, between a pair of trees.[15]

And then past a barren outpost tenanted only by those practising the Christian eccentricity of self-abnegation:

> And in the middle of the water rises
> The isle of Gorgon, with the Pisan coast
> On one side, that of Cyrnos on the other.
> And opposite, a rock that held for me
> A memory of lately suffered loss:
> A man of my own city, buried here
> Alive; a youth of noble ancestors
> And matching them in marriage and estate.
> At least, he was. A madness came upon him
> To leave the lands and company of men
> And go to exile and ignominy
> Among the shades. Poor, superstitious fool,
> To think uncleanliness is godliness
> And bring more savage torments on himself
> Than heaven in its anger could devise.[16]

Rutilius's journey takes him only from the former capital to Gaul, by a much travelled route from one part of the vast Roman world to another. Yet his verse logbook, the last classical poem, shows an awareness of a greater journey. He sails from one age to another, and the hazards of the Dark Ages begin to close upon his ship. The old order vanishes, and rats begin to creep among the ruins; the music blown across the water is no longer the invitation of the Sirens that haunted the first visitors who sailed along these shores, but the droning of monks. He steers towards the centre of a new civilization, which takes most of what it knows from Rome, and inspires this heritage with a new impulse and new ideals, and towards men whose distant descendants are to look back hungrily on a world whose glories they only dimly perceive:

> There were giants once. This was the wonder
> They fashioned out of stone. Now it has fallen
> To rack and ruin. Fate rode over it.
> Its towers are tumbled, and its roofs torn down,
> And there are holes where gates stood, frost
> Has crept between the bricks, the wind and rain
> Have rent the shelter open. Time
> Burrows like a mole. Where are the builders now?
> Gone, all gone, held in the clasp of earth
> That clings fast to its own. These lichened walls
> Have seen a hundred generations come and go;
> These russet stones have seen great kingdoms rise
> And fall again, while storms broke over them.
> And now the soaring arch is reft in two.
>
>
> Swift and sure, invention worked its will.
> Fashioning miracles of metal, binding
> The foundations fast together, hooping stone
> With bands of iron. The halls were gold
> Beneath proud pinnacles. There were pools to bathe in,
> And the rattle of armed men marching, drinking together,
> Sharing their laughter. Fate was too strong for them.
> There came a change, a pestilence;
> They died where they fell, in street and field.
> Death took them all. All the brave men.
> The bulwarks were broken. Desolation walked
> On the shambles of the city. And the men
> Who might restore them, they were gone too, with the warriors
> Under the earth. The halls were empty. Gaps appeared
> Among the red tiles on the vaulted roof

And walls tumbled down. Among these ruins
Strode warriors with laughing faces, clad
In pride.of shining armour, flushed with wine,
And where they looked were rich stuffs, gems and silver,
Lands and good living, all the broad domains
Of a splendid city. In this stone embrace
There was a bubbling of springs, a surge of waters,
Warm to bathe in, heated by the fire
Deep in its heart.

It was a good life, then.[17]

NOTES TO CHAPTER NINE

1. Tacitus, *Annals*, xv. 44.
2. Tertullian, *De Spectaculis* (*On Spectacles*), 20.
3. Ibid. 21.
4. Ibid. 30.
5. Clement of Alexandria, *Paedagogus*, II. I. II.
6. Pliny, *Letters*, x. 96.
7. Ibid. x. 97.
8. Eusebius, *Ecclesiastical History*, v. 5.
9. Ausonius, *Moselle*, 18–22.
10. Ausonius, *Epistles*, 21. 33–8.
11. Augustine, *De Excidio Urbis* (*The Fall of the City*), 2. 3.
12. Rutilius Namatianus, *De Reditu Suo* (*The Return*), I. 47–58.
13. Ibid. 179–82, 201–4.
14. Ibid. 281–90.
15. Ibid. 453–7.
16. Ibid. 515–24.
17. Anonymous Old English poem, *The Ruin*, probably describing the ruins of Bath, the Roman Aquae Sulis.

Index

An Introduction to the Greek World

PETER ARNOTT

The unique distinction of Peter Arnott's book, is that he
brings to life, in the scope of a single volume, the entire span
of Greek history and civilisation.

In chronological sequence, each chapter spotlights a
different aspect of the Greek character and achievement:
the geography of Greece and the national character of its
peoples: an historical outline from the Cretan Empire to
that of Alexander the Great; the Greek pantheon of Gods
and the cults they inspired; the great epics of Homer and the
world they reflected; the social and political achievements of
the City State; Greek theatre and philosophy; and the
aftermath to Alexander's conquests.

A Sphere Library Book   75p

All Sphere Books are available at your bookshop or
newsagent, or can be ordered from the following address:

Sphere Books, Cash Sales Department,
P.O. Box 11, Falmouth, Cornwall.

Please send cheque or postal order (no currency), and allow
7p per book to cover the cost of postage and packing
in U.K., 7p per copy overseas.